GEORGE SEDDON

GEORGE SEDDON

Selected Writings

Edited by
Andrea Gaynor

LA TROBE
UNIVERSITY PRESS

IN CONJUNCTION WITH BLACK INC.

Published by La Trobe University Press in conjunction with Black Inc.
Level 1, 221 Drummond Street
Carlton VIC 3053, Australia
enquiries@blackincbooks.com
www.blackincbooks.com
www.latrobeuniversitypress.com.au

La Trobe University plays an integral role in Australia's public intellectual life, and is recognised globally for its research excellence and commitment to ideas and debate. La Trobe University Press publishes books of high intellectual quality, aimed at general readers. Titles range across the humanities and sciences, and are written by distinguished and innovative scholars. La Trobe University Press books are produced in conjunction with Black Inc., an independent Australian publishing house. The members of the LTUP Editorial Board are Vice-Chancellor's Fellows Emeritus Professor Robert Manne and Dr Elizabeth Finkel, and Morry Schwartz and Chris Feik of Black Inc.

9781760641627 (paperback)
9781743821169 (ebook)

 A catalogue record for this book is available from the National Library of Australia

Cover design by Akiko Chan
Text design by Peter Long and typesetting by Marilyn de Castro
Cover photograph of George Seddon courtesy of
The University of Western Australia archives

CONTENTS

Classics

Gardens in Context

The Art of Advising

PREFACE

Andrea Gaynor

Georg Seddon had many titles in his time, but 'Fremantle's Renaissance Man', captures both the breadth of his expertise, and his intense engagement with locality.[1] While traversing a wide range of subjects, Seddon's writing is characterised by an enduring attention to both landscape and environment, and a bringing together of knowledge from the arts and sciences. As we hurtle headlong into climate breakdown and the sixth mass extinction, the need for boundary-crossing knowledge is ever more clear. Seddon did not grapple with the emerging climate crisis, nor the imperative of Indigenous reconciliation, but his writing provides both provocation and inspiration that may yet be useful for our times.

Seddon promoted a pragmatic yet sophisticated approach to the fashioning of landscapes that could sustain both non-human nature and human lifeworlds, including the manifold psychological and social benefits of amenity, or 'pleasantness'. He was unashamedly anthropocentric. While Seddon's sights might at first seem too firmly trained on aesthetics at the expense of deeper environmental concerns, his interest in landscape is not elitist; he views the landscape as a collective endeavour, an investment by both public and private entities in everyone's quality of life. Decades of neoliberalism have eroded hopes that we might yet inhabit landscapes that are both functional and beautiful; Seddon provides us with a vision of how it might be otherwise.

While attuned to the aesthetic possibilities of cultural landscapes, he remained a vocal advocate for retention and preservation of urban bushland, for water-sensitive cities, and for environmental education. The everyday, actual conditions of life were an abiding interest, and he had little time for the abstract and impractical. He did not resile, though, from big questions: 'Why has the world become so complicated? Has it really become more complex, or is it merely that we are now better at perceiving its complexity?' Can a conserver society only be achieved through a totalitarian state? Why do we anthropomorphise? What do we mean by 'Nature'?[2] Seddon also delighted in challenging environmental orthodoxies. For example, well before American environmental historian William Cronon's landmark critique of the concept,[3] Seddon believed that adulation of 'wilderness' was counterproductive. In a 1972 essay on 'The Rhetoric and Ethics of the Environmental Protest Movement' (pp. 29–49), Seddon wrote:

> the pantheism urged by rich North Americans is largely make-believe, often self-indulgent. The 'wilderness cult' is full of it: the return to simplicity – by canoeing down the Colorado, for example – is for three weeks, and based on a logistic that is anything but simple. And it all diverts attention from 'the relation of man to man', the moral arena in which terrible things are done daily. Black militants in the USA were quick to point out that the 'ecology jag' has diverted attention from racial injustice.[4]

The first part of this book, 'Classics', contains a selection of Seddon's essays treating aspects of landscape and environment, especially the manifold ways in which settlers come to terms with place – or fail to do so. These pieces were written at different career stages, from 1972 to 2001, and in different places (mainly Perth and Melbourne), though discernible within them to varying degrees are Seddon's enduring interests in language and geology, in plants and people, in deep and historical time. Many of them also reflect the language of the day, around 'man and environment' and 'Aborigines', for example. This terminology, while outdated, has been retained for faithfulness to the past; that it now appears jarring is testament to the work of Aboriginal scholars and feminists in changing language and, along with it, habits of thought.

A particular subset of Seddon's broader environmental writing arises from his enduring interest in gardens. A selection of these essays forms the second part of this book, 'Gardens in Context'. Seddon himself was an enthusiastic and self-reflexive gardener across a range of locations, but he also understood that it was in these often intimate spaces that we can gain the most candid insights into human relations with the wider living world. Also, as he points out in 'The Garden as Paradise' (pp. 214–229), gardeners are 'one of the most important groups of land managers in this country, since between us we manage more than 50 per cent of all urban land in Australia, that is, the land that carries 80 per cent of the population'.[5] Seddon interrogates both grand public gardens and modest private spaces with the same wit and wisdom. He cuts to the heart of the ways in which we interpret gardens through language and inherited cultural frameworks, without losing sight of their particular materialities and ecologies. Gardens are not 'just' gardens, but sites of both meaning-making and environmental transformation. They are firmly located in particular geological and ecological contexts. They are linked to diverse networks, including water infrastructure, as well as the movement of people, ideas and materials. Seddon led the way in regarding gardens – including vernacular gardens and backyards – as important sites for sustained and serious environmental and social analysis.

Seddon was in no way interested in preaching to the converted. And so, he was a model public intellectual who boldly sought out the appropriate audiences and avenues for his ideas. He wrote in both literary journals and the magazine of the Local Government Engineers' Association of Victoria. Whether in *Meanjin* or *Memo*, he assumed he was writing for an intelligent and engaged readership amenable to persuasion and activation. A pragmatic orientation and attention to what can be done now was no impediment to invoking William Blake and Charles Dickens.

He was appointed founding Director of the Centre for Environmental Studies at the University of Melbourne in 1974, and the consultancies conducted in that role are salutary examples of the potential for scholarly thinking to directly inform policy and institutional practice. In an age in which so many reports to government provide uninspired advice in bland and technical language, Seddon's robust assessments are breathtaking in their combination of imagination and deep knowledge. He also assumes that public authorities and utilities will go beyond the minimal services we have now come to expect from privatised or corporatised providers. In his landscape assessment for the Loy Yang coal field project in the Latrobe Valley (pp. 265–269), for example, he argues that the State Electricity Commission of Victoria should provide not only power but also amenity – for workers and tourists alike. Extracts from Seddon's landscape assessments and interventions tucked away in industry journals and grey literature form the third part of this book, 'The Art of Advising', as a study in possibilities for intellectual, humanistic intervention in public environmental cultures.

As well as his abiding attention to landscape and environment, and his commitment to public engagement, Seddon's work is characterised by wit: sometimes acerbic, always sharp. It is not difficult to imagine Seddon explaining to the Venetians that 'we are much better at solving the problems of incompetent agriculture in Australia because we have been practising it longer, while they took it up only after the last war' (p. 141). The problems we face today are deadly serious, as Seddon well knew, but perhaps such wit enables us to face them more squarely.

Notes

1   Ron Davidson, *Fremantle Impressions*, Fremantle Arts Centre Press, Fremantle, 2007, p. 209.

2   George Seddon, 'Managing a Resources Boom, or In Praise of Country Boys', in Stephen Murray-Smith (ed.), *Melbourne Studies in Education*, Melbourne University Press, Melbourne, 1982, pp. 35–48; '*Cuddlepie* and Other Surrogates', *Westerly*, vol. 33, no. 2, June 1988, pp. 143–155; 'The Nature of Nature', *Westerly*, vol. 36, no. 4, December 1991, pp. 7–14.

3   William Cronon, 'The Trouble with Wilderness: Or, Getting Back to the Wrong Nature', *Environmental History*, vol. 1, no. 1, 1996, pp. 7–28.

4   Seddon, 'The Rhetoric and Ethics of the Environmental Protest Movement', *Meanjin*, vol. 31, no. 4, December 1972, p. 436.

5   Seddon, 'The Garden as Paradise', in *Landprints: Reflections on Place and Landscape*, Cambridge University Press, Cambridge, 1998, p. 183.

INTRODUCTION

Tom Griffiths

GEORGE SEDDON (1927–2007) WAS SOMETIMES called 'the Professor of Everything'.[1] He did indeed hold appointments as a professor of Geology, a professor of History and Philosophy of Science and a professor of Environmental Science, and he also taught in departments of English and Philosophy. But there was something very *un*academic about Seddon. Although he respected the scholarly literature, he also prized his organic originality. 'I arrived at it in my own way' he might say of an intellectual insight, pleased to have formed a position without the guidance of academic authorities. There was a cheeky pride in his native wit, in his ability to improvise and invent, to trip lightly over difficult terrain. This was the Man from Snowy River speaking.

These two images of Seddon – 'the Professor of Everything' and 'the Man from Snowy River' – are not as contradictory as they may at first seem. Professors are generally *of* something quite specific – even of Accounting these days – and they preside over scholarly disciplines and social systems that discourage movement across them. To be a professor of everything is to be undisciplined. It is to be a maverick and a show-off; it is to elevate ideas over method, reality over abstraction, wit over earnestness. These are Australian bush virtues.

Seddon considered himself an intellectual more than a scholar. Being undisciplined, or temporarily disciplined, was his preferred state. In some senses he didn't want to steep himself for too long in any one academic discourse, because his aspiration was not so much to master it as to reconnoitre (or even pre-empt) it. He enjoyed coming at things obliquely. That was the source of his originality. And it was perhaps an awareness of this that kept him moving, geographically and academically. Seddon was lured by the challenge of new fields in which to apply his adaptable intellect, and propelled by an uneasiness about becoming mainstream. The more one knows, or is expected to know, the harder it is to be cheeky. In the spaces and tensions between scholarly disciplines lies the freedom to be original. But one can't dwell there, you have to keep moving.

Seddon's family kept him moving from the moment he was born. His father was a bank manager and took jobs in various country towns in north-western and central Victoria: Berriwillock, Romsey, Heathcote, Mildura, Nhill, Horsham. His adult life maintained the pattern on a larger canvas: Melbourne, England, Portugal, Canada, Perth, the United States, Sydney, Melbourne, Venice, Perth. His academic behaviour, as we have seen, was just as nomadic: English, Geology, Philosophy, History, Environmental Science, Australian Literature. The first kind of mobility is common in academia, the second almost unheard of.

Academia – a wonderful word that concatenates arcadia, dementia and media – is international in orientation. In Australia at least, publishing or presenting overseas still has more clout than performing locally, and many Australian academics know Europe better than their own state. Seddon was an unusual academic in that he always knew where he was. 'I'm a catchment boy', he said, 'I like to know where the rivers run.' Bushwalking was his favourite recreation. He fell between two stereotypes (or perhaps he straddled them). One is the intellect that is organic – that is emotionally and physically attached to one place and derives insights and meaning from that place. The other is the mind that develops through restlessness and, in becoming international, becomes almost placeless. Seddon presented a rare combination of the two: he was able to move easily in an international scene and say things of relevance to many places – he acquired Portuguese, Spanish, French, German and Italian, and in English he spoke with what he hoped was a 'placeless accent' – yet he regularly invested creative energy in one place, and wanted to get to know it, physically and intellectually, from the inside.

This paradox was resolved, or at least accommodated, in his passion for gardening. Wherever he went, Seddon cultivated the soil and, quite literally, put down roots. The gardens he created have the same mixture of influences he carried himself: historical traditions that have to be respected, a dash of international style and a commitment to intimate native associations. He was determined to foster gardening habits that were frugal, ecological and local. His intensive local and regional studies – of Perth (with David Ravine), the Swan River, the Snowy River, and his own suburb of Fremantle – were his gardening writ large. They were the big backyards of his urban existence. In the 1970s, when Seddon was founding director of the Centre for Environmental Studies at the University of Melbourne, he became a key player in Premier Rupert Hamer's reconfiguration of Victoria as 'The Garden State'.[2] His instinctively comparative mind was fascinated by contrasts of scale: he wrote in *Sense of Place* that 'the world is now our toxic oyster' and he characterised the global village and the rebirth of regionalism as the tension between 'jet-set and parish pump'.[3] Seddon challenged the comfortable wisdom of 'the tyranny of distance' and suggested we think of Australia as 'a small country with big distances'.[4] His work made strong connections between garden-ing and environmental history, putting the backyard into the national narrative, observing for example that 'domestic lawn is one of the major irrigated crops in Australia'.[5] An enthusiastic review of his 1997 collection of essays, *Landprints*, in the *Sydney Morning Herald* was even entitled 'Backyard solutions to save the world'.[6]

It would be easy to suggest that Seddon's gardens and his regional studies were his response to city living and to a life of mobility, a sort of displacement therapy with its origins in a peripatetic child-hood. (Even his birth certificate is dislocated. It says that he was born in Sea Lake, whereas it should have paid tribute to the nearby and otherwise little-celebrated Mallee township of Berriwillock.) Perhaps Seddon's habit of attaching himself to place – and such a conscious, intellectual form of attachment – was his way of com-pensating for the social disorientation he experienced. He talked often of 'orienting' himself – or, like the good naturalised Western Australian that he became, of 'occidenting'. His strongest childhood memories were of landscape – the giant red gums of the Murray River and the damp volcanic undulations of Ballarat, where he went for secondary schooling – and he recalled the social stratification of country towns, where a bank manager's family drifted somewhere in the middle tier of the professional hierarchy, with the doctor and lawyer above, the clergy and headmaster below. He experienced the marginality of boarding at a distant private school and of doing a compressed university degree at the end of the war. He then left Aus-tralia at the age of twenty-one to explore and work in Britain, Europe and America, to become a kind of occidental tourist. 'I did all my youth very young', he recalled.

Arriving in Europe was a revelation. Reflecting on his passage to England through the Mediterranean, he wrote: 'This was the world of my schooling, yet I was experiencing it for the first time; the world where I was born and have lived most of my life, I have had to learn for myself.'[7] He discovered that his education was upside down and that he had allegiances to both Europe and Australia. In Europe he encountered the sources of the concepts of harmony, proportion and composition that were deeply embedded in his aesthetic training, and he began to explore what was both enabling and disabling for an Australian working in these inherited cultural traditions. Much of Seddon's thinking and writing was to grow out of this dialogue across hemispheres, this self-consciousness as an 'antipodean', as Peter Beilharz has observed.[8] Seddon's intellectual fellow travellers included Bernard Smith, the author of *European Vision and the South Pacific* (1960), Keith Hancock, the Commonwealth historian who was famously in love with 'two soils', and Joe Powell, a British-born Australian historical geographer who studied the fate of European images in the New World.

Seddon had two consuming passions: landscape and language. He was expert at reading landscapes and weeding the garden of words, and he believed in the practical insights that language offers to landscape design. His book *Landprints* united earth and paper in its title and was illustrated with inscriptions of nature and culture: concentric and radial sheep tracks, the feeding patterns of small crustaceans, the lines of middle-class Melbourne suburbia oriented to the compass. Seddon sought to master the grammar of landscape. He was interested in the history of words and loved playing with them. And words opened doors for him. He recalled his two years as an English Master at Winchester College, England, in the early 1950s, as 'one of the most intense periods of my life'.[9] In this setting, where 'trained minds' were acquired by studying Latin and Greek, he felt 'more alive than I have ever been before or since'. He found the college community to be 'inclusive, deeply humane and deeply serious, committed to human decency, scholarship and ideas'. 'But it was also exuberant, exhilarating, full of fun … I have never since been in a community of people who so loved their language … who delighted in its every inflection and richness and absurdity, and played with it, tossed it back and forth, as a precious toy.' He wrote to a fellow teacher there: 'I saw myself [at Winchester] as socially disadvantaged in some ways – I didn't have an upper middle class or aristocratic background – but the one entry to that society was verbal dexterity, wit. I could make people laugh and they could make me laugh.'[10]

Seddon had an impish sense of humour, light and occasionally savage, as scathing as it could be self-deprecating. At Winchester he came under the spell of Walter Oakeshott, headmaster of the College from 1946 to 1954 and a notable scholar of medieval literature.[11] Seddon had access to the college's collection of medieval manuscripts, including the famous Winchester manuscript of Sir Thomas Malory's *Le Morte d'Arthur* discovered by Oakeshott. He also relished the opportunity to work with the headmaster on a notebook of Sir Walter Raleigh's that contained preparatory material for his *History of the World*.[12] All Seddon's early mentors – Jack Dart, headmaster of Ballarat Grammar School, 'the first person I met for whom intellectual inquiry was a passion', Nonie Gibson (later Dame Leonie Kramer) and Ian Maxwell at the University of Melbourne, and Oakeshott at Winchester – were ardent teachers and scholars of literature.[13]

Seddon described himself as having 'a literary intelligence', one that finds exceptions to the rule, argues from the particular to the general and is philosophical rather than theoretical, speculative rather than abstract. His linguistic bias made him interested in metaphors, especially in the language of science. To strengthen his understanding, he enrolled part-time in undergraduate Biological and Earth Sciences while lecturing in English at the University of Western Australia. With the help of study leave, he completed an MSc and PhD in geology at the University of Minnesota in 1964–1966. This lover of poetics found himself studying geology right at the time that it was embracing plate tectonics, a dramatic paradigm shift for the discipline. He found that geology shared with English 'the taste for particularity, the delight in the infinitely varied living earth'.[14] Geology deepened his sense of time – Fernand Braudel, master of *la longue durée*, thus became his favourite historian – and strengthened both his empiricism and pragmatism. Seddon's geological imagination enabled him to suggest that, from an agricultural point of view, a useful question to ask a continent was 'Did you have a good Pleistocene?'[15] It was a question that Australia failed.

I can't help but see George Seddon as part of a masculine tradition of nature and landscape writing in Australia that goes back to the nineteenth century, one that celebrates country childhoods and explores tensions between the city and the bush, the field and the academy, and the amateur and the professional. Writers such as Donald Macdonald, Charles Barrett, R.H. Croll, Alec Chisholm and Crosbie Morrison promoted Australian nature and landscape to the general public through newspapers, books and, later, radio. They identified an informal bush education as the source of special moral and physical virtues, and advocated a combination of indoor and outdoor learning, of intellect and feeling, science and romance.[16] Seddon once wrote an essay entitled 'In Praise of Country Boys', exploring the practical and political benefits of a country upbringing (see pp. 76–87).[17] He was more scholarly than any of these predecessors, but he shared their combination of vernacular and learned wisdom, their fascination with the determinism of place, their love of the essay and occasionally their scepticism about 'armchair theorists'. He was eager, for instance, to assess the likelihood of ancient Aboriginal occupation of parts of the Snowy River gorge by drawing on his own experience of camping there, his intimate canoeist's knowledge of where the sun falls and the wind blows.[18]

He was himself very much a country *boy*. 'Boyish' is one of the words I would choose to describe Seddon. It is a term now out of vogue, but in the early traditions of Australian nature writing, there could be no more positive an adjective. Macdonald, Barrett and Chisholm wrote 'Notes for Boys' as well as 'Nature Notes' in early twentieth-century Australian newspapers. 'Boys' was, for them, expressive of a sort of freedom and emotional irresponsibility that they hankered after for life. In 'Notes for Boys' they passed on bush lore, martial instruction and the sense of a sacred male camaraderie that thrived in the open air of Australia. 'Boyhood', and a country boyhood at that, was the ideal of this masculinist culture.

Although Seddon did his youth very young, it stayed with him. Perhaps it was the benefit of having a long-lived mother. Seddon in his seventies still had a spring in his step and a youthful air, and he loved being cocky and cheeky, at once infuriating and lovable. He refused to be politically correct. His prose was manly, his metaphors often masculine. Robyn Williams wrote of Seddon's 'intellectual physicality' and Sam Pickering of his 'muscular' prose. This was partly Seddon the field scientist coming through, his commitment to a vigorous outdoor inquiry, but it is also the 'boy' testing himself and revelling in his sensuous engagement with nature.

But if Seddon in this sense brought echoes of an early twentieth-century culture unfashionably into the beginning of the twenty-first, he was also, in many ways, ahead of his time. Seddon was a connoisseur of landscape, of its surface forms, the arrangement of its features, its felicitous routes of passage, yet he was able also to plumb its depths and mysteries, to analyse it formally and technically. Whereas his approach may have been received initially as a novel contribution to environmental planning, historical geography or landscape architecture, it came to be celebrated as a forerunner of environmental history. By subtitling his 1994 book on the Snowy River 'An Environmental

History', Seddon recognised this shift in his concerns and invoked a lineage he admired, one that embraced Keith Hancock's *Discovering Monaro* (1972) and Eric Rolls' *A Million Wild Acres* (1981). *Searching for the Snowy* was like them in its scholarly devotion to, and creation of, a region, and in its integration of scientific, literary and anecdotal sources. Also like them, it featured the author in the landscape and offered a subplot of discovery, of *searching*, setting a modern, personal exploration alongside the earlier ones recounted. As Seddon put it: 'The basic form of the river, perhaps appropriately, is that of a giant question mark'.[19] And so was his book. It began with the confession that writing about the Snowy was 'hard going', largely because of the challenges posed by environmental history, a mode of inquiry demanding a new kind of literary and scientific integration. As with Hancock and the Monaro and Rolls and the Pilliga, it is the relationship between Seddon and the Snowy, between person and place, that is so intriguing. The three authors explore ways of knowing a tract of earth, ways of coming to possess it, materially, economically, intellectually and emotionally. They want to own it, not in the sense of dominating it but of belonging to it, of learning to identify and live with it. Instead of the illusion of Australia's apparent 'empty spaces', Seddon yearned for the 'fine detail of our land [that] was celebrated by those who came before us'.[20]

'Sense of place' had long been an everyday phrase with Romantic origins, but Seddon gave it Australian substance and academic currency. He acknowledged that *Sense of Place* (1972) was his best-known book in Western Australia and described it later as 'an old-fashioned regional geography'.[21] But what made it distinct and prophetic was its concern not just with physical patterns, but with the imaginative apprehension of the land, and the fact that both perspectives appear in the one book. It is subtitled 'A Response to an Environment', and this was a further novelty, for the book was an emotional as well as scientific document, a personal search for identity and belonging through the use of observation and research, through science and history.

Seddon's self-revelatory foreword to that book (see pp. 23–28) explains how, upon his return to Perth after six years away from Australia, he felt cheated: 'The country was all wrong … This wasn't what I had come back for; where were the ferntree gullies, the high plains, the trout? All the plants scratched your legs … you couldn't take a running stream for granted. It was slowly borne in upon me that I wasn't an Australian at all, but a Victorian.'

In Seddon's later years, the study of place – how it's constructed and understood, and what connects people to it – returned as a primary concern of social scientists. And in the same period, local history assumed new significance as a means of decentring orthodox and national histories.[22] The homogenising effects of international mobility and global commerce renewed questions about what constitutes local distinctiveness, and elicited a new curiosity about the resilience and power of place.[23] 'Place' also came to have particular significance in postcolonial societies where it denotes territories that are often still contested, where settlers are still coming to terms with a land that is theirs but not theirs, that is neither the Old World nor a sanctioned indigenous inheritance.[24] In an Australian polity percolating with contested native title politics and green sensibilities, local history acquired a new moral and environmental edge. In the decades after the appearance of Seddon's book, 'sense of place' became a fashionable term that sharpened into political questions of 'belonging'.[25] As he himself observed in 1995, the phrase had come to invite the question: *whose* place?[26]

Seddon the antipodean turned Australian histories upside down, thus righting and reorienting them. He helped to generate the new environmental narratives that emerged in late-twentieth-century

Australia in place of the imported, imperial accounts of origins, those views from outside that looked longingly to distant shores. The discovery of deep time – biological and human – entailed a journey into the continent itself, an 'inside' view that demanded a truly indigenous history; it meant abandoning the narrative of the nation as a footnote to empire. Plate tectonics literally undermined Australia's history of original isolation. It revealed that the island continent only became a separate entity in the recent geological past and that most of the country's fossil history is cosmopolitan. It focused the attention of Australians on a geological genesis in the southern hemisphere, followed by a relatively brief, formative journey north. From the 1960s, archaeological research took Australia's human history back into the Pleistocene, bringing geological time and storytelling into an exciting and unexpected convergence.[27] George Seddon, that ebullient offspring of English and Geology, delighted in articulating and elaborating this revolution.

The ability to move between those two worlds, and to connect them meaningfully, remains impressive and invigorating to an academia that is often adrift. He happily combined poetry and practice, William Blake and Loy Yang.[28] Seddon's work inhabited these exhilarating imaginative spaces, yet it was always, at heart, deeply practical. He was an active consultant for government and business, including the mining industry, and served on many committees concerned with environmental design, gardens and landscape evaluation, particularly in Victoria and Western Australia. He took part in route selection for nearly every 500-kilovolt power line in Victoria for nearly two decades, with some involvement also in Western Australia, South Australia, Queensland and the Northern Territory. '[B]y force of circumstance', he reflected, 'I became the "power line man" in landscape planning.'[29] He aimed to unite 'good science, good planning, good design, and good communication'. His consultancy prose was like everything else he wrote: clear, fluent and witty. Much of it was hidden from the general public yet it had a sustained, practical impact. If his scholarship anticipated the ecological subversiveness of Tim Flannery's *The Future Eaters* (1994), his planning aesthetic built on the critical analysis of Robin Boyd's *The Australian Ugliness* (1960).[30]

This 'applied conservation', as he called it, locked him into a certain politics. He described it as 'a controlled idealism': 'What I tried to do is to understand the genuine constraints, gauge the intentions of the clients, and pitch the recommendations two notches higher than they had thought they were prepared to go, but not higher to the point of rejection …'[31] In his private life he sometimes manned the conservation barricades, but he was also an early and perceptive critical commentator on the rhetoric of the environmental protest movement (see pp. 29–49).[32] More often he was engaged in debate at the dinner table and in the boardroom. Critics of Seddon were suspicious of this collaboration. In the 'powerline man' they discerned someone 'middle-class to the marrow'. In a phrase such as 'gardeners are the key land managers' they heard a voice emanating from under 'a verdant bourgeois canopy' and detected the 'politics of an urban kulak shaking the secateurs from those tree-lined streets on the right side of the river'. 'A radical praxis will not grow from under Seddon's hedgerow', wrote Robert Hodder in his 1998 review of *Landprints* for the journal *Overland*.[33]

I think Seddon *did* enact a radical praxis, but it was one committed to hope. He was a savage critic of irrigation, sheep farming, the failures of Australian agriculture and the history of land use, but his inclination was to be constructive. As he wrote of environmental protest movements in 1972:

Rhetoric that induces despair and hence inaction will not help
us. Contempt for and alienation from Western society may be

productive to the extent that it produces critical self-awareness but many go beyond that. Western society has, historically, been self-reforming in a degree unmatched by any other, and it is not dead yet. It is counter-productive to destroy the faith of the young in their own society.[34]

In his review of *Landprints* in *Thesis Eleven*, Peter Beilharz aptly characterised Seddon's rationale: 'He respects nature, but his commitment is to humanity and therefore to the ethic of custodianship. Anthropocentrism is a problem, but antihumanism is no solution.'[35] Seddon's clear-eyed but cheerful public consultancies, his steady, courteous curation of environmental perception and taste for the benefit of all, reveal his faith in his fellow citizens and in evolutionary cultural change. He came to consider this advocacy his most important work.

I will finish by returning to the Man from Snowy River. A fine example of Seddon's reports to government was his 1998 submission to the Snowy Water Inquiry, which emerged from a decision by the Commonwealth, Victorian and New South Wales governments to corporatise the Snowy Mountains Hydro-electric Scheme.[36] The inquiry was intended to define the environmental operating conditions of the new business.[37] The result was that the federal and two state governments agreed to work together towards a restoration of some of the original flow down the Snowy, water that had been diverted inland by the Snowy Mountains Scheme thirty years before. Seddon's submission was a superb piece of writing, pitched to take the authorities those 'two notches higher' than they thought they were prepared to go. He addressed the members of the inquiry as if they were human beings rather than faceless bureaucratic automatons. He spoke to them directly, with respect and forthright opinion, in prose as clear and fresh and fast as the waters of the Snowy once were.

His recommendation began with these words: 'This submission … is unashamed advocacy. The Snowy needs a voice, struggling to be heard above the clamorous irrigators and the employees of the government agencies dependent on them.' Seddon energetically grasped the opportunity 'to review the irrigation culture' and 'to recognise a great environmental wrong'. But he was not unduly condemnatory. '[I]t is hard to change direction', he acknowledged, hard 'to admit that much current land use is unsustainable'. 'Our experience of this continent', he reminded the inquiry, 'is so brief that land use practices must be seen as experimental.' His submission did not in any way question the utility of hydro-electric power generation, and he also recognised the high quality of the Snowy Scheme's engineering achievement (in his book on the Snowy he had admired the elegance of 'a beautifully flexible engineering system').[38] He knew very well that the Snowy is doubly iconic: there is the poem, but there is also the Scheme. Both have wielded immense psychic power for Australians; rugged individualist pastoralism and melting-pot nationalist engineering. The Scheme has always had a capital S; Robert Menzies declared that it was 'teaching us … to think in a big way … to be proud of big enterprises and … to be thankful for big men'.[39] And one has to be particularly big to admit a mistake.

In advocating an increase to the flow of the Snowy, Seddon marshalled utilitarian, ecological and social evidence with equal seriousness. He told the inquiry that 'three of the natural wonders of Australia' adorn the river – the Stone Bridge, Currowong Falls and the Snowy (or Jimenbeuan) Falls – and he described them, yes, with boyish enthusiasm. The committee must understand what makes for good canoeing – additional releases, he explained, 'would be very helpful', for several of his own canoe trips on the river had needed to be aborted due to inadequate water. Extra water would also ensure clearer sandbanks for canoeing campsites. Seddon could provide personal testimony of the unfortunate progress of blackberries. And willows are not only ecologically obnoxious, he said – and of a bright green colour that is un-Australian – they are also 'dangerous to canoeists, who have been trapped and drowned by underwater limbs'. And then the inquiry members were urged to marvel at the fact that:

> there are little water dragons dropping into the river as you paddle by, and the lace monitor, shinning up a tree when disturbed, and the fishing eagles and fruit pigeons, and the stories, the wildflowers, the complex geology; the Snowy River Volcanics, the granites, the columnar basalt at New Guinea Bend. Everything else at New Guinea Bend: the Buchan Limestone, the grass trees in the upper cliff, the caves, with their evidence of Aboriginal occupation during the Pleistocene (when the woolly mammoth was roaming the icy wastes of Europe).

The professor-poet stirred his audience into a state of wonder about the river, a wonder with economic potential, too, because of the undeveloped opportunities for ecotourism that he went on to illustrate with international parallels. And, of course, an augmented Snowy would have other benefits: it would give heart to local communities, it would reward sensible planning and it would strengthen awareness of the catchment as a natural unit.

In his submission to the Snowy inquiry, Seddon presented a seamless blend of evidence and advocacy, of history, science and common sense, a holistic humanism combined with a genuine respect for and understanding of nature on its own terms. The result was environmental wisdom that was both highly intellectual and extremely practical.

Judith Brett has argued that academics rarely write convincing prose because the bureaucratic organisation of their working lives and the institutionalisation of knowledge into disciplines makes it very difficult for them to take writing seriously. It is, she suggested in 1991, often against the grain of their jobs to communicate with people outside their discipline or with a wider public.[40] That Seddon was such an elegant writer is another *un*academic thing about him. It was Brett who, as editor of *Meanjin* in 1986, published his first thoughts on the Snowy, the essay that brought his work forcefully to my attention (see pp. 88–109). Seddon's restlessness, as we've seen, freed him of some of the shackles identified by Brett. It's why his natural medium was the essay, which after all is an *essai*, an attempt, a trial. The essay is a prose form that enables movement, subjectivity, a lightness of touch, a brave synthesis, and sometimes sacrifices substance for stimulation; Seddon mischievously called the essay 'sub-academic'. It's a form that allowed him to find heaven in a grain of sand, range across traditional boundaries of knowledge and parade his cleverness in an entertaining way. Seddon was Australia's most distinguished landscape essayist, our equivalent of Britain's W.G. Hoskins and America's J.B. Jackson.

Among the many fruits of academic restlessness is that no-one really owns you – but nor do they necessarily celebrate you. That's why this selection of Seddon's writings is so welcome. Seddon's vision has enduring significance today: he made life better, planners more thoughtful and landscapes more beautiful; he helped us see our country from the inside. He was a maverick, an original. He was steeped in the classics and planted in the earth; literature and place were combined creatively in his chemistry. In his boyish way he encouraged us to 'wag school' from time to time, to climb fences, to play, and to challenge what we read with what we feel, hear and see.

NOTES

1   This introduction is a revised version of essays published in *Southerly*, vol. 58, no. 1, 1998, pp. 116–122, and *Thesis Eleven*, no. 74, August 2003, pp. 7–20. Quotations from George Seddon, unless otherwise referenced, are drawn from an interview I conducted with him in Melbourne on 8 March 1994. Additional biographical details can be found in David Oldroyd, 'George Seddon (1927–2007), Australian Academy of the Humanities, *Proceedings*, no. 32, 2007, pp. 55–58; Trevor Hogan, 'Introduction to George Seddon', *Thesis Eleven*, 65, 2001, pp. 65–68 and 'Obituary: George Seddon, 23 April 1927 – 9 May 2007', *Thesis Eleven*, no. 91, 2007, pp. 107–109. Robyn Williams called Seddon 'the Professor of Everything' in *The Uncertainty Principle*, ABC, Sydney, 1991, pp. 297–307, as did Tim Flannery in 'Last Works by the Professor of Everything', *Meanjin*, vol. 55, no. 2, 1996, pp. 216–220.

2   On Seddon's characterisation of his relationship with Hamer (he lunched regularly with the premier), see Robyn Williams and George Seddon, *In Conversation*, ABC Radio National, 3 November 2005, transcript available at https://www.abc.net.au/radionational/programs/archived/inconversation/ george-seddon/3364912#transcript. I am grateful to Sharon Willoughby for her perceptive analysis of Seddon's 1970s vision of Cranbourne Gardens 'as a subset of the larger landscape' in 'Gardening the Australian Landscape: An Environmental History of the Royal Botanic Gardens Cranbourne', PhD thesis, Australian National University, forthcoming.

3   George Seddon, *Sense of Place: A Response to an Environment, the Swan Coastal Plain Western Australia*, facsimile ed., Bloomings Books, Melbourne, 2004 [1972], p. 262; Seddon, *Landprints: Reflections on Place and Landscape*, Cambridge University Press, Melbourne, 1997, Chapter 14.

4   Seddon, *Landprints*, p. 222.

5   Seddon introduced two books by Australian gardeners: T.R. Garnett, *From the Country: An Anthology*, (ed. and introduced by George Seddon, illustrations by J.S. Turner), Bloomings Books, Melbourne, 2001; and Diana Snape, *The Australian Garden: Designing with Australian Plants*, Bloomings Books, Melbourne, 2002. His book *The Old Country: Australian Landscapes, Plants and People*, Cambridge University Press, Melbourne, 2005, brought together much of his gardening wisdom.

6   Peter Pierce, review of *Landprints*, *Sydney Morning Herald*, 13 September, 1997, Spectrum, p. 10.

7   Seddon, *Landprints*, p. 247.

8   Peter Beilharz, review of *Landprints*, *Thesis Eleven*, no. 53, 1998, pp. 136–138.

9   Correspondence between George Seddon, John Dancy and John Gammell (with the author) about their days at Winchester in the early 1950s, copies in the author's possession.

10   Seddon, letter to John and Angela Dancy, 26 August 2002.

11   John Dancy, *Walter Oakeshott: A Diversity of Gifts*, Michael Russell, Norwich, 1995.

12   Seddon referred to his work with Oakeshott in his February 1957 application for the position of lecturer in English at the University of Western Australia (he had been appointed temporary lecturer there in 1956). My thanks to Andrea Gaynor for consulting these files in the UWA Archives.

13   Seddon, 'George Seddon', in Hume Dow (ed.), *More Memories of Melbourne University: Undergraduate Life in the Years Since 1919*, Hutchinson, Melbourne, 1985, pp. 73–88.

14   Seddon, *Swansong: Reflections on Perth and Western Australia, 1956–1995*, Centre for Studies in Australian Literature, University of Western Australia, Perth, 1995, p. 9.

15   Seddon, *Landprints*, p. 224.

16   Tom Griffiths, *Hunters and Collectors: The Antiquarian Imagination in Australia*, Cambridge University Press, Melbourne, 1996, Chapter 6.

17   Seddon, 'Managing a Resources Boom, or In Praise of Country Boys', in Stephen Murray-Smith (ed.), *Melbourne Studies in Education 1982*, Melbourne University Press, Melbourne, 1983, pp. 42–48.

18   Seddon, *Searching for the Snowy: An Environmental History*, Allen & Unwin, Sydney, 1994, pp. 117–118.

19   Seddon, *Searching for the Snowy*, p. 7.

20   Seddon, 'Formative Years', draft autobiographical essay in possession of the author.

21   Seddon, *Sense of Place*, p. 262.

22   Felix Driver and Raphael Samuel, 'Rethinking the Idea of Place', *History Workshop Journal*, vol. 39, 1995, pp. v–vii; David S. Livingstone, 'The Spaces of Knowledge: Contributions Towards a Historical Geography of Science', *Environment and Planning D: Society and Space*, vol. 13, 1995, pp. 5–34.

23   Seddon, *Swansong*, p. 211.

24   David McCooey, *Artful Histories: Modern Australian Autobiography*, Cambridge University Press, Melbourne, 1996, p. 137.

25   Peter Read, *Belonging: Australians, Place and Aboriginal Ownership*, Cambridge University Press, Melbourne, 2000; Mark McKenna, *Looking for Blackfella's Point: An Australian History of Place*, UNSW Press, Sydney, 2002.

26   Seddon, *Swansong*, p. 14, 211.

27   Billy Griffiths, *Deep Time Dreaming: Uncovering Ancient Australia*, Black Inc., Melbourne, 2018.

28   George Seddon and John Turner, *Loy Yang Project Landscape Assessment: A Report Prepared for the State Electricity Commission of Victoria*, Centre for Environmental Studies, University of Melbourne, Melbourne, 1975, p. 1.

29   Seddon, *Landprints*, p. xvi.

30   I am grateful to Andrea Gaynor for suggesting this pairing.

31   Seddon, *Landprints*, p. xvi.

32   Seddon, 'The Rhetoric and Ethics of the Environmental Protest Movement', *Meanjin*, vol. 31, no. 4, 1972, pp. 427–438.

33   Robert Hodder, 'A Word on Landscapes', *Overland*, no. 151, 1998, pp. 102–103.

34   Seddon 'The Rhetoric and Ethics of the Environmental Protest Movement'.

35   Beilharz, review of *Landprints*.

36   Seddon, Submission to the Snowy Water Inquiry (copy made available to the author), later published as 'Saving the Throwaway River', *Australian Geographical Studies*, vol. 37, no. 3, 1998, pp. 314–321.

37   S.J. Gale, 'The Snowy Water Inquiry: Food, Power, Politics and the Environment', *Australian Geographical Studies*, vol. 37, no. 3, 1999, pp. 301–313.

38   Seddon, *Searching for the Snowy*, pp. 19–20.

39   Seddon, *Searching for the Snowy*, p. 36.

40   Judith Brett, 'The Bureaucratisation of Writing: Why So Few Academics Are Public Intellectuals', *Meanjin*, vol. 50, no. 4, 1991, pp. 513–522.

CLASSICS

1

——

SENSE OF PLACE

1972

I GREW UP IN COUNTRY TOWNS IN VICTORIA. FROM Mildura, a compact irrigation settlement along the Murray River, we could ride a bicycle for a few hours and camp the night in empty country, or so it seemed then, with nothing but crows and river gums, and the broad Murray for fishing and swimming. Later, we moved to the Wimmera. I went to school in Ballarat, on the edge of town, where the fields began. They were fields, too, rather than paddocks; not very big, often with gorse around them, unwisely brought by early settlers, and double rows of pines as windbreaks in that windy place. It was a formed landscape, with landmarks made by man and nature, and a landscape with a past. The natural landmarks were two worn-out volcanic hills, Mount Buninyong and Mount Warrenheip, both with clear outlines that changed as you saw them from different directions, but always distinctive on the skyline.

Behind the school there was a mullock heap, an abandoned pile of mining refuse. Ballarat had made its money from gold in the roaring days eighty years before I got there; what was left after the gold had gone was a solid, well-built town of stone, set on a low remnant of the Great Dividing Range in good farming country. There were also a lot of dead Chinamen in the cemetery, Irish names on the pubs, and mullock heaps. The word 'mullock' was a dialect word in England 150 years ago for rubbish or dust, ultimately from the Teutonic root *mul*, meaning 'to grind', but the word survives now only in Australia and New Zealand. Behind the mullock heap was Dead Horse Creek, a gentle stream despite its name, with a white-railed wooden bridge, and beyond that, a good gravel road with hawthorn hedges along the side of it in places; it went to Mount Rowan, a rounded hill a few hundred feet high and well grassed. I once rode a bicycle from Ballarat home to Horsham through Ararat and Stawell, and another time I rode down to the coast at Portland. One way and another, I got pretty much all over Victoria, but hardly ever out of it, except for hitchhiking up the Coast Highway to Sydney once, and for a summer walking through the Tasmanian highlands and strawberry picking in the Huon Valley. When I was at the University of Melbourne I went walking through the Victorian part of the Australian Alps two or three times a year, and got to know them well. This was before the Snowy scheme; there were no roads, and you carried your food for up to two weeks. It was a stiff climb up the valleys onto the dissected plateau that makes up most of these highlands, but when you got up on top it was like a golf course without any golfers. I don't recollect ever running into another party when we were up there.

When I was twenty-two I went to England, and later to Portugal and Canada. I was away for over six years, and I had a good time, but I was often homesick for Australia, for the smell of the bush, and the trout straight out of the Howqua onto the pan, and the springy turf and great skies of the Bogong High Plains. My last view of Australia had been of Perth, the only time I had seen it, on a cloudless day, and I remembered Kings Park and the river below. At the University of Toronto I heard of a job at the University of Western Australia, so I applied for it and got it. I had been away from Australia for long enough, so I married a girl in Canada and we set sail. We landed in Sydney, drove across the Nullarbor and got to Perth. I was home in Australia.

I hated it. Partly this was the malaise of the returning traveller, partly cultural snobbery, partly genuine regret for the more cultivated society I had left behind. This story has been told often. But I had a more specific grievance: I just didn't like Western Australia. The country was all wrong, and I felt cheated. This wasn't what I had come back for; where were the ferntree gullies, the high plains, the trout? All the plants scratched your legs. The jarrah was a grotesque parody of a tree, gaunt, misshapen, usually with a few dead limbs, fire-blackened trunk, and barely enough leaves to shade a small ant. If you went camping in the summer, you carried water – you couldn't take a running stream for granted. It was slowly borne in on me that I wasn't an Australian at all, but a Victorian. Here I was stuck on the edge of a continent I knew next to nothing about, and didn't like. But I liked the city of Perth itself, and the people, and the job, so we stayed. Slowly I came to understand the land better.

I was ill-prepared for Western Australia, and I think this must be a common experience. Even the Western Australians whose families have been here for three and four generations are ill-prepared in some basic ways, because our primarily British background is still apparent in our attitudes towards the way we use the environment; and in nothing so much as our attitude to water. Centuries of water-riches makes it hard to grasp our water-poverty and its implications, although these are better understood in Western Australia than they are in the coastal cities of eastern Australia. In Perth (and Adelaide) the aridity of this most arid of the continents is a part of one's consciousness. The south-west of Western Australia is an island, with sea to the south and west, desert to the north and east, and one cannot leave it north or east without crossing mile after mile of desert.

But it wasn't the desert I disliked, it was the country within a hundred miles of Perth. The coastal plain is flat: the Darling Ranges are nothing more than a 1000-foot step-up to the flat plateau. The vegetation seemed monotonous, the soils little more than sterile sand. And apart from the upper Swan Valley with its vineyards, there was no landscape.

> An environment becomes a landscape only when it is so regarded by … people, and especially when they take action to shape it in accord with their taste and needs. Nature can produce the raw material of scenery unaided … To transform it into landscape demands the magic powers of the seeing human eye and the loving human hand.[1]

In much of the country around Perth, the hand of man has been heavy, and my eyes were not able to see the subtleties of the natural landscape.

So my first job was to understand this land. I was lucky in the people I met, and I began to learn. Much of this learning is called 'science', but I would rather forget that word for the time being. For me, it was learning to see. Like so many others, I began with the plants. The wildflowers are easy to like. Then I became interested in the way different plants make a living, and how they have come to be as they are; and so I was off into evolutionary history. In time I came to find this an absorbing place, full of questions and rewards. I must have acquired a new range of landscape images, from the painters, although I have no memory of the transition. Sir Arthur Streeton's hazy landscapes, and others of the Heidelberg School, were supplanted in my mind's eye by the gaunt, clear images of Sidney Nolan, one of whose best paintings hung in my study at the university for years. But I also learned to change focus. Much of the interest of the landscape around Perth comes from very small things rather than from 'scenery' as conventionally understood, and this change in the scale of attention is also one of the moves of science. Finally, I became interested in the structure of these landscapes, the evolution of the landforms and of the coastline, of the creeks, rivers, swamps and off-shore islands – and of the way in which man has used them.

[...]

The word 'conservation' has some negative uses, especially when it is used to mean the same as 'preservation'. To some people, all country-side that has been touched by man is spoiled, and so an unspoiled environment is an empty one. This may be true in particular cases, and it is often necessary to fight for a specific area against the improv-ers. In a report by the Swan River Conservation Board, an exemplary body in many ways, we are told that the Board 'is still developing the Upper Reaches of the Swan River'.[2] The development consists mostly in dredging, desnagging, filling the low-lying areas and plant-ing couch grass. Later we are told that six riverside acres have been bought in Middle Swan by the Swan Shire and will be developed as a picnic spot. *'Even in its natural state* it provides a very attractive ren-dezvous for a river excursion. Temporary toilets have been erected.'[3] One thinks of the eighteenth century: 'I hope I may die before you', said one of Capability Brown's contemporaries, 'so that I may see Heaven before you improve it.'

But it is not possible to deep-freeze the ecology of a whole area, or go back to the Swan estuary as it was before the first Kleenex was dropped. The most enchanting dream that has ever consoled mankind is the myth of a Golden Age, in which man lived on the fruits of the earth peacefully, piously, and with primitive simplicity. But the com-plex problems of today's world are hardly to be solved by our all going camping, or sitting around taking in each other's wishing. The view that an unspoiled environment is one untouched by man can hardly be pushed to its logical conclusion, and in any case it is misleading, first because it sets Man against Nature, where it is more illuminating to see man as a part of nature; and secondly, because man is not always a despoiler. He can also be creative. Some of the world's finest landscapes are man-made: much of Europe, for example, or the terraced hillsides of the Philippines, and Machu Picchu in the Andes. These are all examples that were moulded before the technological revolution of the last hundred years, but one could add to the list the graceful concrete rail bridges of Switzerland, each of which is a work of art that ties together the elements of a fine natural landscape. The Narrows Bridge in Perth is both functional and beautiful, and it enhances the landscape of which it is a part. The concrete mixer and the bulldozer can make landscapes as well as mar them, and the emphasis in conservation, especially in urban areas, should be on intelligent land use and on environmental design as well as on preservation, although there is also much that should be preserved. The first step in design is recognition, the ability to see what there is. Only then can we ask whether a given structure is appropriate to its setting, or whether a proposed land use is appropriate in a given environment.

Notes

1   M. Nicholson, *The Environmental Revolution*, Hodder and Stoughton, London, 1970.

2   Swan River Conservation Board, *Up-river to Middle Swan* (a pamphlet guide), Perth, 1970.

3   Swan River Conservation Board.

2

───

THE RHETORIC AND ETHICS OF THE ENVIRONMENTAL PROTEST MOVEMENT

1972

THE ENVIRONMENTAL PROTEST MOVEMENT HAS occasioned much cheap rhetoric, and I propose here to look at some of its characteristic modes. In doing so I must first clear myself of potential misunderstanding. I do not for a moment intend to suggest that there are not grave environmental problems ahead of us. There are. Nor do I want to suggest that we should somehow disinfect all discussion about them from emotion. We can't. One sometimes hears senior scientists in universities and government employ say that 'we must get rid of all this emotionalism.' People will continue to feel strongly about matters that concern them so deeply, and such scientists merely show themselves unfit to comment on the human environment if they so patently misunderstand people.

Fear, guilt, self-righteousness and hate are the emotions most commonly exploited by cheap rhetoric, although there are others, from greed, despair and self-disgust to the noblest idealism, which is not, however, given an effective outlet in action, and is thus frustrated. The rhetoric of the environmental movement has at least three distinctive modes, all with a long ancestry. For ease of reference I shall call them the Jacquard, the Revivalist, the Bucolic.

1. The Jacquards

The Revivalists are by far the most common, but the Jacquards are more interesting. They are named for Jacques, from Shakespeare's *As You Like It*, and they are the jakesmen, poised forever above a cesspool.[1] The melancholics are especially well defined in late Elizabethan and Jacobean drama, and their defining character is disgust – a generalised disgust rather than specific disgust with specific abuses, which is healthy and may lead to corrective action. The times themselves are out of joint: 'Fie, 'tis an unweeded garden'. The early seventeenth century and the latter half of the twentieth seem to have been the great ages of the melancholics. They are intelligent, hypersensitive, civilised and aristocratic, but not in the direct succession to power, and thus privileged but dispossessed.

The melancholia can often be seen to be a projection of personal despair onto the cosmic screen, and its moral danger is that it so often leads to paralysis of the will. Melancholics are often charming and witty people, but the melancholia is a form of neurotic self-indulgence. They are not prophets: the prophets may foretell terrible things, but this is a conditional doom, because the emphasis with the true prophet is not on future events, but present behaviour, and 'Lest ye repent' is the heart of his cry. Paul Ehrlich[2] has the true prophetic ring, in that the doom he predicts is seen to follow only from the neglect of certain specified courses of action. Whether or not he is always right, he always gives an argument, backed by a wealth of detailed information, and his passionate polemic is not cheap rhetoric.

The melancholic is often a manic depressive, and in his manic phase is Utopian, with a great belief in, to take a twentieth-century example, town planning as a cure for all ills. Sometimes the despair comes of asking too much, in the manic phase, of human behaviour and human institutions. The rhetorical style of the Jacquards is 'Galgenhumor'. Here are a few samples, collected over a period of a year in the USA:

> I am an urban planner – that is to say, it is my job to rearrange the chairs on the decks of the *Titanic*.

> Those who think the world is coming to an end are guilty of wishful thinking.

> My fear is not that we will fail to adapt to the changes in our environment, but that we will succeed.

A cosier, small-town version is offered by Ogden Nash: 'The trouble with the present is that the future's not what it used to be', an epigram that charts the decline of optimism in America. That optimism was sometimes shallow, but there is no advance in replacing it with a shallow pessimism.

Gallows-humour shows high courage when the doom is certain, and it offers a release we all may need at times; but it is not good for the conduct of our daily affairs, in which we need, in Aneurin Bevan's words, 'to achieve passion in the pursuit of qualified objectives', for qualified objectives are the only ones we are likely to realise, whereas the whole point of gallows-humour is that we are absolved by the circumstances from further action. When a whole society becomes addicted to this mode it may lose its will to survive, and our only defence against it as individuals is patience and the courage of perseverance. The individual's contribution to global problems must always seem trivial compared with the size of the problems, but he must not be discouraged from making it. He has some choice in what he buys, and he can buy the articles with a lower environmental cost, he can live more frugally, he can exert himself in political protest against specific abuses.[3] These efforts are all so petty that he can easily lose heart, especially if he is periodically frightened out of his wits by the Jacquards, who tell him that these efforts are irrelevant 'in the face of the global problems'. But it is this all-or-nothing logic that is at fault.

Categorisation such as that attempted here is always itself an oversimplification and one can easily work the analogy between the Jacobean and Neo-Elizabethan melancholics too hard. It is perhaps worth insisting on dispossession as a common feature, in the case of the Jacobeans tied to the rise of the class of courtiers, who were generally educated, privileged and able, but with little power and thus inadequate outlet for their abilities. The present case is also related to a restriction of upper-class privilege, a 'restriction' that follows from an extension of privilege in an affluent society. The outrage of dispossession comes out very clearly in the common claim most common in crowded Europe – that a certain place is 'spoiled'. The implication is not that *no-one* should be allowed to go to this place, but that no-one other than one's self and a small group of like-minded people should go there. It is always others who spoil a place. This claim is often a just one, because the small group that went there before 'the invasion' usually came from a privileged class with an educated respect for landscape, and their impact was small because the group was small. Until very recently, mobility was a high and rare luxury. Today I and my family can decide at 10 o'clock on a Sunday morning to leave our home near the centre of a city of three million people, for a magnificent national park some thirty miles away – and be there within an hour. The price we pay for this privilege is that others have it, too. Places that are to remain 'unspoiled' must continue to be hard to get to, and the Forest of Arden out of reach by car. (A place may be 'spoiled' by bad design as much as by crowds. But the 'bad design' usually turns out to consist in service stations, motels and other such plebian structures indicating mass use.)

11. The Revivalists

The Revivalists are far more common than the Jacquards, and they too have a long ancestry. There have always been men who have made use of catastrophes to induce guilt, and to show that their enemies are allied with the forces of darkness, themselves with the children of light. Earthquakes or plagues were held by some to be a Divine visitation upon our sins. Now that we know the natural causes of earthquakes and plagues, the environmental crisis is an opportunity to revive a dichotomy of the saved and the damned. To suggest that we have a range of specific practical problems before us, which we must work at with skill, patience and resolution, is as little relevant in Revivalist eyes today as it would have been 300 years ago to suggest to their precursors that we should investigate the natural causes of plague rather than cover ourselves with ashes. But the unacknowledged goal of Revivalist rhetoric is the self-gratification of the Preacher. It is relatively easy, if you have the knack, to induce guilt, fear and terror in your audience, and a gratifying exercise of power.

It is easy to find examples of Revivalist rhetoric among the environmental protesters. Ian McHarg has shown himself the Billy Graham of the environmental scene in his address to the Royal Institute of Architects in Sydney in 1971. This talk from a distinguished (and rather expensive) overseas guest was received with acclaim. It has been printed in several prestigious journals. It was a very bad talk and would not be worth analysis if it had not met with such an enthusiastic reception.[4]

Professor McHarg's paper threatened hell-fire, offered salvation, and presented an aggressively puritanical world view. It was anti-science, anti-rationalist, anti-education. To support these charges it is necessary to quote at length. The paper, bearing the lurid title

'Is Man a Planetary Disease?' began as follows (my italics):

> I am about to discuss *two values*, and because I am not objec-
> tive, I will excoriate the one I do not like and laud the one I like.
> The two values are, first, that one which we have absorbed with
> our mother's milk, in kindergarten, high school, through theol-
> ogy, and so on: *the western view* of the relation of man to nature,
> also called *anthropocentrism*. The other is *salvation*: the ecologi-
> cal view of the world.
>
> The first thing I have to say about the view which is abso-
> lutely implicit in *the whole of western culture* is that it has no
> correspondence to *reality* and is the best guarantee of extinction.[5]

This piece of rhetoric is so empty that there is no arguing with it, but we note the two-valued logic, the promise of salvation, and the absurd oversimplifications in identifying the enemy, especially when we remember that the speaker flew by jet from America to give the talk in a centrally heated, electrically lit auditorium with sophisti-cated acoustic devices.

There is no single 'western view' of the relation of man to nature. We think of the Great Chain of Being which lay behind much medi-eval thinking, and later of the Argument from Design; we think of Saint Francis of Assisi and Rousseau and Gilbert White and William Wordsworth and Charles Darwin as well as the ignorant whalers who clubbed the Galapagos turtles to the point of extinction. We remember that the sciences of biology and ecology are western achievements, and that although Europeans hunted the whale, it is largely through their intervention that Africa still has a fair sample of its magnificent fauna. As for anthropocentrism, there is no intelli-gible alternative. Man can regard the world only from his own point of view. He may take a long view of his own interest, or a short one, but he cannot take an insect's view, nor that of a plant pathogen, and it would be plain silly to try.

The enemy then stand up to be counted. They turn out to be the Generals, the Mad Scientists, and the Captains of Industry:

> The men who constitute the very quintessence of the planetary disease are the heads of the Defence Department, the General Overkills … They are the absolute incarnate planetary disease: they are pus, they threaten the survival of all mankind, and they must be chained.
>
> To the Generals Overkill must be added the maniac Dr Strangeloves, men who begin life pulling the wings from flies and gravitate to bombs and high explosives and atomic weapons. In the US they can make explosions legally underground and illegally above ground, attacking the genetic inheritance of the world.[6]

How convenient that they should bear the guilt, not ourselves. These figures are bogeymen, got up to frighten the children in the dark. Not all biologists begin their career by pulling the wings off flies, although I take it (perhaps wrongly, but who knows when the rhetoric is so wild) that this sadistic image is intended to indicate a violence that is inherent in the scientist's analytical approach to nature, whereby he takes things apart. It is easy to arouse feelings that are hostile to science and technology today, but this Luddite revival is dangerous and misconceived. For example, it requires sophisticated technology to measure mercury or DDT levels, and indeed most environmental monitoring is highly complex. It would solve nothing to smash the machines. This is not to deny that we urgently need *changes* in present technological practice, including widespread recycling of resources. Such changes are beginning to be made now. They are the outcome of arduous research programs, needing the support which the anti-science movement denies them.

Next, we find McHarg adopting a Jacquard world view (my rhetorical modes are not mutually exclusive):

> The world body is covered with lesions ... The very heartland of the planetary disease is the US ... We all share the view which is implicit in all western cultures and always has been. It is very difficult to find the origins of this attitude of man to nature but it is verified in *Genesis*. (Being a Presbyterian, I can never escape from theological questions.)[7]

A good Presbyterian takes theological questions a little more seriously than this, but the oversimplification goes on at a great rate:

> The basis of our attitude to nature, whether we are Jews, Christians, agnostics, or atheists, is quite explicit in three lines. The first one is that man is made in the image of God. No atoms; no micro-organisms; no animals, save one. The implications are clear: the world consists of a dialogue between man and God and atoms are unable to speak to God because of his interminable dialogue with man. If you covet your neighbour's wife, the church, the priest and society will rap you across the knuckles, but if you want to kill every single whale, or fell forests of redwoods, or destroy or rape or poison any part of the natural world, you may do so, if not with the church's blessing, at least with its consent. *There is only one moral arena: the relation of man to man.* If you so examine our cultural history, you will see that this is so. There are no defined duties or rights for beasts and thing. Only man has rights ... The intent of the text is that man is given exclusive divinity, man is given dominion, and man is enjoined to multiply

and subdue the earth. This one text explains all the despoliation that western man has accomplished in Asia, in Europe, and in North America. *It is the only text you have to know.*[8]

The 'only text you have to know', which offers salvation in three gospel lines, is the authentic note of the revivalist; but I prefer the Book of Genesis, a myth of such richness and complexity that it has been subject to a multitude of interpretations, although it is generally agreed that Man and Beast lived in harmony in the Garden of Eden. Much, of course, follows from the Fall, when man was enjoined to earn his bread by the sweat of his brow. This has been inescapable, but it led to the good husbandry of the old Spanish missions in California as well as to the felling of redwoods. Doubtless the Church has much to answer for, and the sharp distinction between Man, unique in having a soul, and the other animals, all soulless, is one of the least attractive aspects of Christianity. But it is too simple to lay all the blame at the door of one text. The Romans had most of the qualities McHarg objects to before they became Christian. The role of the Church in Western Man's attitude to Nature has been complex: a number of advances in agriculture and husbandry were made within the walls of monastery gardens, among them Gregor Mendel's genetic discoveries, which have fed so many hungry mouths.

In the next few paragraphs McHarg's global view continues, and a 'planetary doctor' is brought on stage to announce that 'the brain is not the apex of biological evolution but a spinal tumour'. The anti-rationalism then comes thick and fast: 'I want to go into a tirade against education, which is a device for producing functional cripples. It manages to avoid teaching all the most important things.'[9] One might wonder in passing what non-functional cripples would be like, but this kind of query is relevant only when words are used with care for their meaning. We then proceed to fantasy. General Overkill, the mad scientists and all the other baddies are shot off into space in a non-returnable rocket, and lo! we are saved: 'After they had left the Earth, if you listened very, very closely, after the reverberations, you would begin to hear the sound of healthy tissue growing, the Aeolian hum of regeneration.'[10] This is the organic metaphor run mad. Nature is not benign,[11] and that Aeolian hum might well turn out to be a new and massive plague of locusts hatching in Abyssinia – to be fought with sticks, since the mad scientists presumably took their aerial sprays with them into space.

After this nothing need surprise us, not even to learn that 'Algae know about creativity, but man does not'.[12] My own preference is for Mozart and Einstein, but perhaps I have not met the right algae. Finally, we have to learn a prayer, and this is where we find the eagerly awaited extension of the moral arena, hitherto unreasonably restricted to the man–man relation: 'It is simply a plain prayer addressed to the world at large, revealing an understanding of the way the world works. It is addressed to the elements, to hydrogen, helium and so on. "Matter, exist for the benefit of the universe."'[13] No matter how desperate the environmental crisis, I will not say prayers to helium, and I find 'the benefit of the universe' unintelligible. Ethics is to be replaced by pantheism. As this suggestion has been argued more carefully by others, I shall leave it until later.

III. The Bucolics

My third, last, and least well-defined rhetorical mode is the bucolic, annihilating all that's made to a green thought in a green intellect. It reached its nadir in Charles Reich's *The Greening of America* which offers the following:

The extraordinary thing about this new consciousness is that it has emerged out of the wasteland of the Corporate Slate, like flowers pushing up through the concrete pavement. Whatever it touches it beautifies and renews: a freeway entrance is festooned with happy hitchhikers, the sidewalk is decorated with street people, the humourless steps of an official building are given warmth by a group of musicians. Every barrier falls before it.

The new consciousness is sweeping the high schools, it is seen in the smiles on the streets. It has begun to transform and humanize the landscape. When, in the fall of 1969, the courtyard of Yale Law School, that Gothic citadel of the elite, became for a few weeks the site of a commune, with tents, sleeping bags and outdoor cooking, who could any longer doubt the clearing wind was coming?[14]

The image of the flowers pushing up through the pavement is sinister in a way hardly intended by Reich. It happened in London after the Blitz and it marked the destruction of a city, with all the suffering that entailed. As for the sleeping bags outside the Yale Law School, it would be well if our troubles could be solved by going camping (even high camping). This rhetoric has in common with that of the revivalists the offer of simple solutions for complex problems. The language and logic are so childish that Henry Fairlie, in a brilliant review of *The Greening of America*, coined a word for it: *Babyspeak*, by analogy with George Orwell's *Newspeak*.[15]

The pastoral idyll is a recurrent literary mode, usually a by-product of urban malfunction. Many writers have recoiled from the political and social instability of the city to the good husbandry of the countryside, or the purity of the wilderness. But Reich wants more than this: the city must *be* the country. This odd theme is presented visually in many public lectures on 'The Environmental Crisis'.

In the USA a common rhetorical device is to project side-by-side a breathtaking colour-slide of, say, the High Sierras, and a freeway interchange or gas-station and parking lot in Los Angeles. These are presented, often without comment, but as if they were alternatives, which of course they are not. One cannot buy gas in the High Sierras, and it is foolish to go rope-climbing or backpacking in downtown Los Angeles. It may come as a shock to some to learn that the Sierras and Los Angeles are in a high degree complementary. The prime reason that so much of the Sierra Nevada is still near-virgin country is that the city jealously guards its water-catchment. Without Los Angeles, the Sierras would probably by now be mined and logged and ranched to death.

The agrarian myth has been potent in the USA, as in Australia.[16] Perhaps American society might have been happier had it remained an agrarian society; but whatever might have been, it is now urban and industrial. The major environmental problems, both in America and Australia, are in the cities; but in neither country is there a full emotional grasp of this reality, and the conservation issues that inflame the passions still tend to be the despoliation of the countryside, the threatened extinction of the red kangaroo or the bald eagle, dam-building at Hetch Hetchy or Lake Pedder. These are proper concerns, fought in major part by city people, but in the meantime they turn their back on the city, which is one reason why American and Australian cities lack the civility of their European counterparts. The contrast in attitudes comes out nicely in cigarette advertising: Australian and American cigarettes are smoked by lean horsemen, eyes slitted against the glare and dust – but Benson and Hedges are a love-offering to a girl in a city restaurant.

iv. Conclusion

The rhetoric of the Marlboro countrymen or Madison Avenue bucolics is usually tinged with animism, which is also the creed of some of the revivalists. It was expounded at length in 1967 by Lynn White, a Professor of History at the University of California, Los Angeles, in a paper entitled 'The Historical Roots of our Ecologic Crisis'.[17] This much-admired paper is on the reading list for all those proliferating courses on the environment in the USA. It set the fashion, followed by McHarg and many scientists who are short on history, of blaming all our problems on 'Judeo-Christian teleology', because 'God planned all of this explicitly for man's benefit and rule: no item in the physical creation had any purpose save to serve man's purposes'.[18] This is not the view of the psalmists:

> Praise ye him, sun and moon: …
> Mountains, and all hills; fruitful
> trees and all cedars:
> Beasts, and all cattle; creeping
> things, and flying fowl;
> Kings of the earth, and all people; …
> (Psalm 148)

Even the first chapter of *Genesis*, to which Professor White's knowledge of the Judeo-Christian tradition seems to be restricted, gives the lie to so simple a view: 'God created great whales … and every winged fowl after his kind: and God saw that it was good' (*Genesis* 1:21). It was good before man, they were good after their own kind, and although all this was for man's use, this was never their only 'purpose'.

Next we learn that 'by destroying pagan animism, Christianity made it possible to exploit nature in a mood of indifference to the feelings of natural Objects',[19] and that, 'To a Christian a tree can be no more than a physical fact. The whole concept of the sacred grove is alien to Christianity and to the ethos of the West'. '"When you've seen one redwood tree, you've seen them all"'. 'For nearly 2 millennia Christian missionaries have been chopping down sacred groves which are idolatrous because they assume spirit in nature'. This is so confused it is hard to know where to begin. The 'concept of the sacred grove' as White conceives it owes at least as much to the Greeks and their dryads, a part of western cultural history, and to Wordsworth and Naturphilosophie[20] of the nineteenth century as it does to New Guinea tribesmen who think that trees must be placated. As for trees as 'no more than a physical fact' – I suppose if we want to make such statements, they are a biological rather than physical fact, but what then? What more can they be? And it certainly does not follow from such a view that 'when you've seen one redwood tree, you've seen them all'. I can, I suppose, concede that a tree is no more than a biological fact – although I find it hard to think of circumstances under which I should want to make such a remark – but this does not stop me from liking trees, nor from admiring a redwood grove more than a single freestanding redwood, nor from trying to stop people from cutting trees down unnecessarily, and I doubt that any of these attitudes would be reinforced if I thought there were spooks in trees. Incidentally, nearly all of the major re-afforestation programs around the world, in the Middle East, around the Mediterranean, in Africa and elsewhere, have been the work of Europeans; and the Jews have done wonders in Israel.

Lynn White doesn't really think there are spooks in trees either, but he wants us to pretend there are. 'More science and more technology are not going to get us out of the present ecologic crisis until we find a new religion, or rethink our old one.'[21] Saint Francis of Assisi is to be our guide, and we should recognise Brother Ant and Sister Fire, praising the Creator in their own ways as Brother Man does in his. This is hardly novel; it is the view of the psalmists. But what then? A fable. 'The land around Giubbio in the Apennines was being ravaged by a fierce wolf. Saint Francis, says the legend, talked to the wolf and persuaded him of the. error of his ways. The wolf repented, died in the odor of sanctity, and was buried in consecrated ground.'[22] Well, bully for Saint Francis; but most of us are not much good at talking to wolves or exhorting the birds, as White later acknowledges. Thus this fable can have no real application, and although White proposes Francis as a patron saint for ecologists, the new religion will not help us. Brother Ant, perhaps. Brother Streptococcus?

It is now in fashion to think ill of our own species. I read in a recent book that 'If I were God I might well prefer swallows, squirrels and butterflies to man.'[23] I suppose this to mean that in some moods the author prefers them, and the rest is anthropomorphic extension of a perverse variety. If this is a new religion, it would be a very odd one for a member of our species. But I do not think we need a 'new religion', least of all if it turns out to be a romantic, nineteenth-century animism. There is, perhaps, a case for the extension of our ethical consciousness. McHarg complained of the view that 'there is only one moral arena: the relation of man to man'. This plaint goes back to Aldo Leopold, who argued the case carefully more than twenty years ago.[24] Leopold discusses the extension of ethical criteria through history to new fields of conduct, 'with corresponding shrinkages in those judged by expediency only'. Odysseus, for example, applied ethical standards to his relations with his wife but not to his slaves. They were property. To quote Leopold:

This extension of ethics, so far studied only by philosophers, is actually a process in ecological evolution. Its sequences may be described in ecological as well as in philosophical terms. An ethic, ecologically, is a limitation on freedom of action in the struggle for existence. An ethic, philosophically, is a differentiation of social from anti-social conduct. These are two definitions of one thing. The thing has its origin in the tendency of inter-dependent individuals or groups to evolve modes of co-operation. The ecologist calls these symbioses. Politics and economics are advanced symbioses in which the original free-for-all competition has been replaced, in part, by co-operative mechanisms with an ethical content.

The complexity of co-operative mechanisms has increased with population density, and with the efficiency of tools. It was simpler, for example, to define the anti-social uses of sticks and stones in the days of the mastodons than of bullets and billboards in the age of motors.

The first ethics dealt with the relation between individuals; the Mosaic Decalogue is an example. Later accretions dealt with the relation between the individual and society. The Golden Rule tries to integrate the individual to society; democracy to integrate social organization to the individual.

There is as yet no ethic dealing with man's relation to land and to the animals and plants which grow upon it. Land, like Odysseus' slave-girls, is still property. The land-relation is still strictly economic, entailing privileges but not obligations.

The extension of ethics to this third element in human environment is, if I read the evidence correctly, an evolutionary possibility and an ecological necessity. It is the third step in a sequence. The first two have already been taken. Individual thinkers since the days of Ezekiel and Isiah have asserted that the despoliation of land is not only inexpedient but wrong. Society, however, has not yet affirmed their belief. I regard the present conservation movement as the embryo of such an affirmation.[25]

I would agree that the despoliation of land is wrong, and Leopold goes no further than this. But why is it wrong? Surely because it is an infringement of the rights of later generations, and not because the land has some mystical rights of its own. We must take the custodial view. From time to time we are told that we should learn to respect wild things 'for themselves', and not merely as potential items of use. With this, too, I can agree. Anyone who regards a redwood as no more than so much merchantable timber is an impoverished soul. But I can respect redwoods 'for themselves' and readily concede that they have a life of their own that is different from mine without supposing that they have feelings. It is *my* feelings that matter, and if they are mean, it is I, or my grandchildren, who suffer.

Our relations with animals are more complex. A society that supports a Society for the Prevention of Cruelty to Animals and upholds it in the law courts clearly supposes that animals feel. Moral obligations to animals are generally recognised, I think, and more so in western than in most non-western cultures. For example, it seems to me a moral commonplace of our society that it is wrong to keep a dog and not exercise it properly. There is also a feeling, deeper than this, that we degrade animals by making them pets, and even more by locking them up in zoos. There is a general recognition of the beauty and power of animal lives other than our own, and that it is best displayed when the animals live their own lives untouched by man (*Born Free* was a best-seller, Professor White). Many individuals are cruel to animals, or needlessly destructive, but the mere use of the word 'cruel' in this context shows that society does take an ethical view of the relation, although it does too little to reinforce it. But no matter how much we respect the feelings of animals we are still going to eat them and/ or the plants, and this paradox is much older than Judeo-Christianity.

The superb Palaeolithic paintings of bison and other animals at Lascaux and Altamira show a great knowledge of and sympathy for the animals depicted. But this sympathy is not sentimental pantheism. Palaeolithic man imitated his prey in painting and in ritual dances. All primitive hunters know a tremendous amount about the animals they hunt, and they respect their cunning and skill – indeed to be a successful hunter you have to learn to think like your prey. The fruit-eating primates, from which the hunting apes diverged in the course of evolution, did not kill other species for food, but it is unlikely that they held them in reverence either. Presumably they knew very little about them. Our reverence for life derives, in this sense, from our being the killer apes. But this is a far cry from romantic pantheism. If I seem to labour the point it is because the pantheism urged by rich North Americans is largely make-believe, often self-indulgent. The 'wilderness cult' is full of it: the return to simplicity – by canoe-ing down the Colorado, for example – is for three weeks, and based on a logistic that is anything but simple. And it all diverts attention from 'the relation of man to man', the moral arena in which terrible things are done daily. Black militants in the USA were quick to point out that the 'ecology jag' has diverted attention from racial injustice.

The custodial view of nature has long been inherent in good agricultural practices. The agrarian resources of Europe have been conserved for centuries. The custodial view is weakest in newly set-tled lands, and needs all the encouragement we can give it through legal and tax support, but it is not new. What *is* new is the extension of the custodial view to our industrial activities, to make sure that renewable resources are renewed and that non-renewable resources are kept in cycle. This view is now accepted in principle by all think-ing people, and the formidable problem for the future is to put it into practice. The state of Oregon has just passed a law that all drinks be sold in returnable containers. Minneapolis recycles its garbage. It is dull stuff compared with religious conversions, but it points to the way ahead.

There is perhaps one other novel element in the expansion of the custodial view: we are becoming a great deal more conscious of the unintended consequences of intentional actions.[26] Any act has physical consequences, only part of which stem from the intention. These may be trivial; they may not. The men who invented DDT did not intend to weaken the eggshell of the American eagle any more than Professor McHarg intended to contribute to atmospheric pollution by flying from Philadelphia to Sydney. But both things happened. Our managerial responsibilities now extend to care for the atmosphere, to oceans, the biosphere – and thus our custodial role is on a new scale. This is directly contrary to the view of White and McHarg and Reich that all our troubles arise from man's pretensions to dominion over nature. We were expelled from Eden, and the gates are guarded with a flaming sword. Or to put the point plainly and without rhetorical flourish, it is rare to find simple solutions to complex problems, and we are not likely to do so in the present case. Rhetoric that induces despair and hence inaction will not help us. Contempt for and alienation from western society may be productive to the extent that it produces critical self-awareness, but many go beyond that. Western society has, historically, been self-reforming to a degree unmatched by any other, and it is not dead yet. It is counterproductive to destroy the faith of the young in their own society. Extreme rhetoric is socially divisive, and it is sure to provoke ecologic backlash. It debases the quality of public debate. For all these reasons, it should be eschewed.

Notes

1   'Jakes' was Victorian slang for privy. The jakesman was someone employed to keep the privy pits clean. [A.G.]

2   Paul R. Ehrlich and Anne H. Ehrlich, *Population, Resources, Environment*, W. H. Freeman and Co., San Francisco, 1970.

3   There is a good list in *What Can I Do?* (guidelines for citizen action on environmental problems) put out by the Society for Social Responsibility in Science (Canberra). Environmental cost-benefit analysis of our machines is a necessary exercise. Some answers are obvious, some not. No-one needs a power-mower, and those who can afford them are usually those desk-workers who would be better off pushing a hand-mower. But the refrigerator is a boon in Australia.

4   Printed in the *Journal of the Royal British Institute of Architects* in July 1970; reprinted in *The Architect*, WA, Chapter of the RAIA, in September 1971, pp. 39–44. Page references are from this journal. I must say here that I greatly admire Professor McHarg, and regard this talk as the aberration of a busy and over-generous public speaker. I admire both his School of Landscape Architecture at the University of Pennsylvania and his *Design with Nature* 1969. To be fair one should also admit that there is an element of self-parody in this paper. McHarg knew it was a hell-fire sermon, and he would doubtless argue that the end – arousal – justifies the means. I think he was indulging himself.

5   McHarg, *The Architect*, WA, September 1971, p. 39.

6   McHarg, p. 39.

7   McHarg, p. 40.

8   McHarg, p. 40.

9   McHarg, p. 41.

10   McHarg, p. 41.

11   Nor malign, but that is now a rare assumption, whereas the assumption of benignity is common. It is often said that man is guilty of 'upsetting the balance of nature' and it is true that, as with every organism, he has an impact on the environment – in his case a very great one. But there are no discernible grounds for the blithe assumption that the 'balance of nature', left to her own devices, would be favourable to man. Both the logic of the metaphor itself and the common experience of any home gardener are enough to deny it – and further, some of the 'natural' checks, on over-population, for example, are plague and famine, to which we should not submit ourselves by choice.

12   McHarg, p. 42.

13 McHarg, p. 42. The rest of the prayer is rather good: "'Sun, shine that we may live, Earth is home and the ocean is ancient home. Clouds, rivers, and rain, replenish us from the sea, we erstwhile sea creatures. Atmosphere and all the oxygen therein and the exhalations of all planets, protect and sustain us." The plants we should address with inordinate reverence. "Live, breathe, and grow, that we may live, eat and breathe. Fungi and worms, honourable and dishonoured creatures, reconstitute the wastes of life in life and the substances of life after death in order that life may endure."' This, however, puts precisely the sensible, anthropocentric view that McHarg elsewhere claims to attack. 'Sun, shine that we may live.' Amen, to that.

14 Charles Reich, *The Greening of America*, Random House, New York, 1970; Allen Lane, The Penguin Press, London, 1971.

15 'The Practice of Puffers', *Encounter*, vol. 37, no. 2, August 1971, pp. 3–13.

16 There is a good account of its workings in that remarkable book by Leo Marx, *The Machine in the Garden: Technology and the Pastoral Ideal in America*, publisher, New York, 1964.

17 Lynn White Jr., 'The Historical Roots of our Ecologic Crisis', *Science*, vol. 155, no. 3767, 10 March 1967, pp. 1203–1207.

18 White, p. 1205.

19 White, p. 1205.

20 *The Golden Bough* surely takes its place in the romantic literary tradition, and is in any case itself a part of the cultural history of the west. In fairness to Professor White, however, I admit that his target is specific, Judeo-Christian teleology – it is Professor McHarg who locates the view he attacks as 'implicit in all of Western cultures'. This is demonstrably untrue, whereas White's central thesis is substantially true, in that much of the Church for much of its history has held that 'no item in the physical creation had any purpose save to serve man's purposes'. Thus McHarg's thesis is false, White's merely overstated.

21 White, p. 1206.

22 White, p. 1207.

23 Bruce Allsop, *Ecological Morality*, Frederick Muller, London, 1972.

24 Aldo Leopold, *A Sand County Almanac*, Oxford University Press, London, 1949. This remarkable book has had a great and deserved 'revival' in the USA in the past few years, and it has become one of the holy texts of the hippies.

25 Leopold, pp. 202–203.

26 I owe this and some other points to the suggestion of Julius Kovesi, Department of Philosophy, University of Western Australia.

3

———

THE EVOLUTION OF PERCEPTUAL ATTITUDES

1976

This essay appeared in a collection of papers, edited by Seddon and Mari Davis, from a symposium entitled 'Man and Landscape in Australia', held at the Australian Academy of Science in 1974. The symposium was part of the Unesco Programme on Man and the Biosphere and addressed Project 13, on the perception of environmental quality.

THE COMMON AIM OF THESE PAPERS IS TO SHOW the evolution of the perceptual attitudes of Australians to their land. Some are descriptive: that is, they attempt to show how Australians have in fact perceived their environment through time (and for this reason, much of the book is historical). Some are also prescriptive, suggesting ways in which our environmental perceptions might be heightened and more finely attuned to the needs of the land that is now home. The Programme on Man and the Biosphere which occasioned this book is biologically oriented, and the subtitle, 'Towards an Ecological Vision of Australia', derives from that orientation. All contributors to the book would agree with the general proposition that Australians should become

50

more sensitive to the special needs of their unique landscapes, but agreement probably ends there. We have different prescriptions, and different diagnoses of the past.

It is not surprising that there are differences of opinion. It cannot be assumed that we know a great deal either about what Australians 'see' or about the forces that have shaped their perceptual worlds. Further, there is no such thing as 'the Australian environment': Balmain is not much like Eucla. Thirteen million different people see a great variety of different places, in different ways, at different times, and any one person sees the same place in many different ways in the course of a day. For example, in 1971 Melbourne had 108,000 people of Greek origin, most of them living in and around South Melbourne, and thus a city within a city. There have been a few studies of this Greek community from specific points of view (e.g. housing), but none of their perceptual responses to their environment. Contemporary perceptual studies of any kind are few.[1] We have been a little better served by historical studies, especially by Bernard Smith's subtle and provocative *European Vision and the South Pacific*[2], Geoffrey Blainey's *The Tyranny of Distance*[3] and studies such as R.L. Heathcote's *Drought in Australia: A Problem of Perception*.[4] Sir Keith Hancock's history of land use, *Discovering Monaro*,[5] may mark a new beginning among professional historians, who have generally ignored the land.

Part of the difficulty with such studies is that it is not always clear what should count as evidence. The only perceptions we know directly are our own. We guess at the perception of others from what they say they perceived, what they record, what they omit, how they behave. Poetry, painting, old films, advertisements and newspapers are all records, but they all need interpretation – early pictorial artists drew the indigenous flora and fauna, topography and Aboriginals in certain ways, partly because of current traditions of draftsmanship, and because of the function of their work (e.g. to serve as scientific illustration rather than decorative wall hangings), partly because of individual idiosyncrasy, or limitations of skill with the pen, partly because of cultural preconditioning (which led, for example, to the portrayal of Aboriginals first as Noble Savages, and a few years later, in reaction, as comic scarecrows) – and partly as a genuine visual response to the object before them. This last comment, the only one which some would call the genuinely perceptual component, is not in fact separable from the cultural and biological predisposition to see in certain ways.

If it is hard to interpret individual perceptions, it is harder to make useful statements about those of a community. From the outset, individual responses varied widely as the following early descriptions of the site of Sydney show well enough:

The first is from Major Robert Ross:

I do not scruple to pronounce that in the whole world there is not a worse country than what we have yet seen of this. All that is contiguous to us is so very barren and forbidding that it may with truth be said here that Nature is reversed; and if not so, she is nearly worn out ...

The second is from Lieutenant Ralph Clark:

This is the poorest country in the world – overrun with large trees, not one acre of clear ground to be seen ...

The third is from Captain Watkin Tench:

The general face of the country is certainly pleasing, being diversified with gentle ascents, and little winding vallies, covered for the most part with large spreading trees, which afford a succession of leaves in all seasons. In those places where trees are scarce, a variety of flowering shrubs abound, most of them entirely new to a European, and surpassing in beauty, fragrance and number, all I ever saw in an uncultivated state: among these, a tall shrub, bearing an elegant white flower, which smells like English May, is particularly delightful, and perfumes the air to a great distance.

The fourth is from Mrs Elizabeth Macarthur:

> The greater part of the country is like an English park, and the trees give it the appearance of a wilderness or shrubbery, commonly attached to the habitations of people of fortune, filled with a variety of native plants, placed in a wild, irregular manner.

The fifth is from Surgeon Bowes:

> To describe the beautiful and novel appearance of the different coves and islands as we sailed up is a task I shall not undertake, as I am conscious I cannot do justice to the subject. Suffice it to say that the finest terras's, lawns, and grottos, with distinct plantations of the tallest and most stately trees l ever saw in any nobleman's grounds in England, cannot excel in beauty those which nature now presented to our view.[6]

Yet despite the apparent range of responses expressed here, they are easily sorted and a much wider sample would fall under much the same headings. The two unfavourable responses are utilitarian ('not one acre of clear ground'); two of the three favourable respond to the scene as 'picturesque', and this division has persisted to the present day, with one group taking the picturesque view ('superb and unique tract of *E. camaldulensis* riverine woodland') while the utilitarian has a bleaker response ('a muddy paddock with a few scruffy old gum-trees'). It is a misfortune that these two responses are so sharply distinct in Australia – many of the finest landscapes of Europe are man-made, productive and yet harmonious with the natural environment. The Australian landscape, by contrast, was not as a rule immediately hospitable to human needs, so that utility and natural beauty have become sharply defined alternative categories. The heart of our environmental design problem, in my view, is to fuse those categories.

Other elements in the responses quoted above that recur again and again are the reason given for liking the landscape by Mrs Macarthur and Surgeon Bowes, that it is 'park-like'; the rather open woodlands have an imported value attached to them, in that they suggest a noble estate. The comments that 'Nature is reversed' and 'worn out' by Major Ross are also much repeated. This is the Antipodes, where all things are topsy-turvy. It is also tired, the last of lands (see Alec Hope's 'Australia'). This latter view is another potent myth, although it is a biological and geological absurdity, not so much 'wrong' as meaningless. In the sense that Australia probably broke off from the Antarctic land-mass in the Eocene, only fifty million years ago,[7] it is one of the youngest continents. It has large exposures of ancient Precambrian rocks, but so do Europe and North America. The soils are old, and some of the landforms are old. The flora has been evolving continuously to the present; it is certainly not 'ancient' in any sense, and since it is predominantly angiosperm, with fewer gymnosperms than any other continent, it is at least in that sense a 'young' flora. Its mammals are marsupials rather than placental, and thus represent an ancient lineage, but they are not, of course, Cretaceous mammals, or even Pleistocene ones (the Pleistocene fauna was quite different): they are the outcome of quite recent evolutionary events – as, of course, are the gymnosperms of the other continents.

When they called it old or tired, they meant that it was strange, harsh, rugged – unlike the green and gentle, temperate homeland. If Australia had been settled by Spaniards, for example, the responses and behaviour might have been very different. Spanish agricultural experience, respect for water, styles of architecture and of shaping towns might have led to a society more in harmony with the Australian environment, although it would probably have lacked the Anglo-Saxon virtues – for example, the talent for political stability – which also characterise our society. But whatever might have been, it was the Anglo-Saxons (and Irish) who came, thus generating the central paradox, that of a people whose cultural traditions and aspirations derive from a fundamentally different physical environment.

Of course the strangeness can be exaggerated; some visitors to Sydney in the 1820s remarked on the familiarity of the vegetation in its natural setting, because they knew the flowers already from English gardens. Visiting botanists generally had a good knowledge of the flora before they set foot in Australia, and flowers from all over the continent were illustrated in works such as Robert Sweet's *Flora Australasica: or a Selection of Handsome and Curious Plants, natives of New Holland, and the South Sea Islands – most proper for the Conservatory or Greenhouse* (1827–28),[8] drawn from flowering specimens in English gardens before Perth, Adelaide or Melbourne were settled. Thus the strangeness obviously depended on the experience of the observer.

The strength of the Anglo-Saxon cultural tradition can also be exaggerated. In some ways, behaviour was modified rather quickly to suit local conditions – for example, the evolution of dry-farming techniques – yet the Anglo-Saxon conditioning was, and is, strong. The shortness of our pre-industrial history is also significant. By the end of the nineteenth century, Australians were beginning to accommodate themselves emotionally to their new setting; and physically, as illustrated by country towns like Beechworth, Clare, York, Bathurst. But evolving local tradition did not have long enough to establish itself firmly before it was overwhelmed by the homogenising technology of this century; in which so many forces are at work to over-ride regional differentiation. Americans had stronger resources; for example, the landscape tradition established by Olmsted persisted into the twentieth century, and has been a base from which schools of landscape design have been able to tackle the new problems of a new century. Guilfoyle's work in Australia in the nineteenth century was as good as Olmsted's, but the skills died with him, and we have almost had to start all over again in the last decades.

Some of the dissonance between expressed perception of the environment in Australia and environmental behaviour is due to the speed of urban and industrial growth, so that the way we see ourselves and our setting is often at odds with the way we behave. The Man from Snowy River still rides through the advertisements of the tobacco companies, although he is rarely met in Pitt Street. The bronzed Anzac, the lifesaver, the Great Australian athlete, the skilled bushman, lurks within us all, although by generally accepted health standards, Australians are among the least healthy groups living in 'developed' societies.[9] We are aware of these inconsistencies, and many of our perceptions of the environment have undergone rapid evolution in the last few years: for example, the 1972 election, which brought Labor to power, marked the effective political recognition that most Australians lived in cities, and this recognition, if belated, will never again be neglected politically. Our perception of our cities themselves has also undergone rapid changes – within a period of ten years, Paddington, for example, passed from an official slum, 'totally substandard' suitable only for demolition, to the most expensive real estate in Sydney.

Our capacity to adapt and evolve new responses is real, but we are still in trouble, I think. There are basic incompatibilities in our responses which we are reluctant to face. For instance, most Australians are perfectly sincere in saying they 'love the bush', including its fauna. Of British stock, they also love cats and dogs. To live in the bush without destroying its native animals, for example at the Bend of Islands outside Melbourne, residential co-operatives find it essential to ban cats and dogs. This has met with passionate resentment: it is hard to accept the stark incompatibility. Ecologists have been saying that the Australian environment is fragile for so long that 'fragile' is now a part of the popular vocabulary, but it does not seem to control basic thinking about our future in any significant way (for instance, population policy is still not a major political issue). No other western, highly urbanised and industrial country is as ecologically vulnerable as Australia. Advanced technology makes massive demands on natural systems. Flushing of pollutants, for example, depends on natural rainfall, yet the sum of the run-off from all Australian streams at their outlets is less than that of any one of the world's major rivers, for example the Mississippi. Our large cities are all in exceptionally favoured corners of the continent, but even in those corners flood, fire and drought are recurrent realities, although we seem to be taken by surprise with every renewal. Both city and country life in Australia are dependent on massive power consumption, much of it currently drawn from non-renewable sources, as is the fertiliser on which Australian agriculture depends so heavily.

The cities are in many ways insulated by technology from environmental realities, and thus generate a world in which myths can grow and flourish, the most pernicious of which is the myth that Australia is a big country, whereas in terms of permanent life-supporting systems it is a relatively small one, with about the same amount of arable land as France, much of it of inferior quality, with a high variability in rainfall. (Although Australia could undoubtedly increase both her total cereal production and her yield per hectare if it were profitable to do so, present yields are very low by world standards, yet the average Australian is incredulous on being told that in 1972, for example, the United Kingdom grew one and a half times as much cereal as Australia, on one third the area.)[10] It is a large country only as a communication system – the tyranny of distance still rules, to use Blainey's phrase. Australia is a small country with long journeys. Much of our wealth, the wealth that has directly and indirectly supported our massive urban growth, has come from mineral resources, from gold in Victoria, silver-lead at Broken Hill, gold again at Kalgoorlie, through to the present boom. Geoffrey Blainey called his book on mineral exploitation in Australia *The Rush that Never Ended*[11], but there could be a postscript, and I can imagine a complacent and well-fed New Zealand economic historian two hundred years hence writing an epitaph for Australia, as for Nauru: 'She was cursed with great riches in non-renewable mineral wealth'.

Although the riches are great, they are not inexhaustible, a fact to which our ghost towns bear witness. This is no argument against using them, but it would be unwise to base estimates of the permanent carrying capacity of the continent on current rate of resource consumption. Mineral wealth seems to engender a recklessly expansive view of the future, while the evidence that Australia is *not* a big country is disregarded, even though it dominates our lives. We are, in fact, already short of land, and absurd though this may seem at first sight, we read about it in every newspaper (but with a different set of perceptions, not our 'Big Country' perceptions, but our 'Urban Problems' perceptions). When the newspapers report a shortage of land, we know that not enough building blocks are coming onto the market around the capital cities. We may then urge the government to make more land available. The outward expansion of the cities can be speeded up in various ways, but no government can make more land – except, perhaps, the Dutch. All, or almost all, the habitable land in Australia is already under competing pressures (for housing, for farming, for mining, for roads, for recreation); a fact starkly illustrated by the cost of land of any kind for any purpose within 80 kilometres of the major cities. An even clearer example of the shortage of land for specific purposes is the difficulty of finding an acceptable new site for almost any substantial enterprise in Australia – an airport for Sydney, a container terminal, a new power station in Melbourne. Every new freeway site, major housing subdivision, sewerage works, dam site, quarry application, is bitterly contested, usually with good reason, namely that the site already has valid uses, and the new uses would conflict with the old. The curious feature of this situation is that an acute community awareness of all these specific problems has not yet become a national perception that Australia is already short of land for some of its needs, which are primarily urban. Because of its geology and latitude, Australia is short of water and good soils. These observations are commonplace. (Because of her latitude, Australia was exempt from the extensive glaciations of the Pleistocene that so profoundly modified the lands of the northern hemisphere, in ways that contribute greatly to their capacity to sustain large populations.) It is less well known that, compared with the other continents, Australia is poorly supplied with natural harbours, estuaries and wetlands. The limited supply of estuaries and wetlands presents us with acute problems in land use, because they have a special biological function (as nurseries) that is incompatible with the demands that technological man makes of them. This conflict is to be found in all industrial countries, but it is exceptionally acute in Australia.

These are all essentially problems of urban and industrial land use. Meanwhile, down on the farm things may be worse. Sir Keith Hancock has said of his own childhood:

In *Country and Calling* I commented as follows on the privileges
and deprivations of my boyhood in Gippsland: 'As a healthy
young barbarian I found vivid joy with the Australian outdoors;
but might not my joy have been deeper if somebody had taught
me to read the story which time had written upon Australian
earth?' (p. 53). My teachers could not help me to use my eyes,
because nobody had helped them to use their eyes. I wonder
whether things are different today in Gippsland?[12]

A country boy may now be lucky enough to find people who
know something of the land he lives in, but it is still likely to be an
impoverished environment. One of the most telling comments for
me in Donald Horne's *The Education of Young Donald* is his account
of his upbringing in Muswellbrook, in the heart of the country, but
cut off from nature.[13] Horne learned about nature in the city, on his
trips to Sydney, where he could walk the beaches and explore the
Royal National Park and Port Hacking, much richer than the paddocks of the upper Hunter.

In a book published in 1966, a few years before its time and
therefore without the impact it should have had (*The Great Extermination*, edited by A.J. Marshall), there is a chapter with the title
'The Decline of the Plants' by John Turner.[14] Writing of the basaltic
grasslands of western Victoria, he remarks that 'the native flora was
virtually exterminated over hundreds of square miles'. He quotes an
estimate of 2200 native plant species for Victoria, with 550 aliens –
'about five new weed species established themselves every year
between 1870–1930. This is an index of the progressive deterioration
of the natural plant communities, for these are rarely invaded when
in the natural state.' In fact, of the native plants, some 277 species
are either extinct or survive only in isolated pockets. But the loss of
individual species is less serious than the loss of whole communities:

'throughout the better watered pastoral belt' of Australia 'the original vegetation was a mosaic of many different plant communities, dominated by different species of *Eucalyptus* (White Box, White Ironbark, Yellow Box, etc.). Each had its characteristic topography, soil, climate, flora and fauna. With pasture improvement all these diverse communities are losing their individuality and are converging to one more or less uniform pasture, carrying a few exotic species of grass and clover – the surviving trees themselves are rarely allowed to regenerate; they are a diminishing asset.'

Some Australians who 'love the bush' have in mind such cleared pastures with a few stands of remnant eucalypts. Many have no idea of what an undisturbed environment is like. I have heard of a tattered few acres that has been logged, cleared and burned three times in a hundred years, and is now tertiary regrowth eucalyptus woodland choked with blackberry and watsonia, described and ardently defended as 'natural bushland'. I have been shown degenerate rainforest (a so-called national park) from which all of the valuable timber was removed over a century ago, beginning with the cedar-cutters, so that little remains today other than lawyer vines and the Giant Stinging Nettle Tree (*Laportea*), a weed species. This sorry relic was presented as pristine rainforest.

Many Australians know no better, because they have had little opportunity to learn. To be sure, they would have had no opportunity at all if we had never settled this continent, thus preserving the pristine environment in its entirety. Given settlement, of course the land had to be cleared, the trees felled, the native grasses ousted. Yet in Europe, the fields have been tilled for centuries without obliterating the indigenous flora. In England, and China or Japan, and equally in much of North America, the native flowers and grasses and shrubs and trees survive in meadow and hedgerows, and along the roadsides, as well as in woodlands and natural reserves. The difference lies in the isolation of the Australian flora, which rarely survives competition with introduced species in disturbed areas – that is, in most of agricultural and pastoral Australia – whereas the native flora of the temperate lands of the northern hemisphere can often co-exist with the species of agriculture, themselves plants of the northern hemisphere, with relatives among the natural communities of the regions in which they are cultivated. In Australia, the original communities are wiped out directly by clearing and indirectly by competition along the roads and elsewhere; where the original communities were rich and diverse, the flora that replaces them is very poor in species, consisting of a few agricultural species, together with their attendant introduced weed species, and it is in this sense that the environment is impoverished. Of course, much depends on the region. The young Keith Hancock had riches on his doorstep in east Gippsland, and his deprivation was the lack of a natural history tradition in his upbringing. But Donald Horne had neither the riches nor the natural history at Muswellbrook; and my own experience was closer to Horne's than Hancock's.

I spent a part of my youth in the Wimmera. I do not believe that I had a deprived childhood – it was a happy one for the most part – but it was deprived in three significant and inter-related ways. First, it was socially deprived. Like most country towns in Australia, ours was quite rigidly socially stratified. As I and a very few others went away to boarding school, I was not on holidays at the same time as the children who went to the local state school, and I hardly even knew them. This spelt alienation of one kind. I also had Sir Keith Hancock's problem of environmental education. Although I must have had a latent interest in natural history when I was young, there was no-one to foster it, no-one to tell me about the birds or the plants or the geology, or even the history of settlement of my own countryside. (We were familiar with names like Muller and Dahlenberg in the district, but knew nothing of the cultural history of the German settlers in the Wimmera, nor of their traditions of land use, other than that they were respected as 'good farmers'.)

Finally, much of the Wimmera was and is an impoverished countryside. I do not recollect ever seeing a marsupial (except the possum) in its natural setting while I was young, and the natural vegetation had nearly all gone, replaced by exotics that certainly serve man's economic purposes better, but are very few in number of species, so that a complex ecosystem has been replaced by a monotonous and simple one. There was no Walden Pond at Horsham or Nhill, and could have been no Thoreau or Gilbert White, or even Huck Finn. Most English and American country children enjoy much greater natural history resources than most Australian country children, except perhaps in part of the American Midwest, although there at least the corn is indigenous. If I seem to labour this point, it is because it is contrary to the popular view. Many English children have seen, sometimes even studied, rabbits and foxes, weasels, stoats, squirrels, water-rats, badgers perhaps, occasionally even otters. At least fifteen native mammals are to be found today within the confines of metropolitan London, and some of them, including the fox, mole, vole, shrew and hedgehog – together with the non-native grey squirrel – are common.[15] Many children know at least the popular names of the wayside flowers, and many of the birds, including those of the wetlands and the migratory species. This is partly the tradition of a culture biased to country pursuits, partly opportunity.

I grew up among paddocks of wheat, planted sugar-gums from South Australia, weeds, a few surviving eucalypts, and the limited range of exotics common to country-town parks and gardens. The only animals with which I was familiar were dogs, cats, rabbits, horses, sheep and cows. There were birds, but I knew little of them, other than the magpie, and around the houses, sparrows, starlings and mynah. None of this is to deny that the resources *potentially* available to me were richer than those of my English counterparts. I *could* have explored near-pristine bushland in the Grampians, and we did sometimes 'go for a drive' or even a picnic in country such as this, but it was not my day-to-day environment. I was obscurely drawn at this time of my life to a swamp down behind the town (Nhill, in this case) and to the Little Desert, long before it became a *cause célèbre*, but I did not know why, and never learned much about it.[16] Almost the only other places where indigenous grasses and herbs were to be found in the area were the graveyards, but I did not know that either. I did not begin to learn until years later, and then at first out of books. I had to learn to begin to see Australia. Alec Hope's account of us as 'Second-hand Europeans, pullulating on alien shores'[17] has been quoted too much, but it sums up much of our history to date. I think my experience is typical, and it is not therefore surprising that we have among the lowest standards of environmental design in the world. Australians are still learning to see where it is they live. The imaginative apprehension of a continent is as much a pioneering enterprise as breaking the clod.

Notes

1   D.J. Walmsley and R.A. Day, *Perception and Man–Environment Interaction: A Bibliography and Guide to the Literature*, Geographical Society of New South Wales, New England Branch, Armidale, Occasional Papers in Geography, no. 2, 1972.

2   B. Smith, *European Vision and the South Pacific 1768–1850: A Study in the History of Art and Ideas*, Clarendon Press, Oxford, 1960.

3   G. Blainey, *The Tyranny of Distance: How Distance Shaped Australia's History*, Sun Books, Melbourne, 1966.

4   R.L. Heathcote, 'Drought in Australia: A Problem of Perception', *Geographical Review*, no. 59, 1969, pp. 175–194.

5   Sir W.K. Hancock, *Discovering Monaro: A Study of Man's Impact on His Environment*, Cambridge University Press, Cambridge, 1972.

6   See Lionel Gilbert, 'Botanical Investigation of Eastern Seaboard Australia 1788–1810', BA Honours thesis, University of New England, 1962.

7   See, for example, J.J. Veevers, 'Phanerozoic History of Western Australia Related to Continental Drift', *Journal of the Geological Society of Australia*, vol. 18, no. 2, 1971, pp. 89–96.

8   Robert Sweet, *Flora Australasica*, James Ridgeway, London, 1827–28.

9   Basil Hetzel, *Health and Australian Society*, Penguin, Harmondsworth, 1974.

10 *Australian Yearbook, 1972*, AGPS, Canberra, 1973, and FAO, *Production Yearbook*, 1972, vol. 26, FAO, Rome, 1973.

11 G. Blainey, *The Rush that Never Ended: A History of Australian Mining*, Melbourne University Press, Melbourne, 1963.

12 Sir W.K. Hancock, review of G. Seddon, 'Sense of Place: A Response to an Environment', *Canberra Historical Journal*, February 1974, p. 72.

13 D. Horne, *The Education of Young Donald*, Angus and Robertson, Sydney, 1967.

14 A.J. Marshall (ed.), *The Great Extermination: A Guide to Anglo-Australian Cupidity, Wickedness and Waste*, Heinemann, London, 1966.

15 Don Gill and Penelope Bonnett, *Nature in the Urban Landscape: A Study of City Ecosystems*, York Press, Baltimore, 1973.

16 The Little Desert was the subject of a high-profile environmental conflict following the Victorian government's 1968 proposal to subdivide the area for agriculture. See Libby Robin, *Defending the Little Desert: The Rise of Ecological Consciousness in Australia*, Melbourne, Melbourne University Press, 1998.

17 A.D. Hope, *Selected Poems*, Angus and Robertson, Sydney, 1973.

4

———

THE *GENIUS LOCI* AND AUSTRALIAN LANDSCAPE

1979

THERE IS A LATTER-DAY PROVERB THAT ANYTHING xeroxed begins to lose its value. This is the Age of Easy Copying. I have a similar maxim of my own, that any place that you can get to by jet is unlikely to be very different from the place you just left. International technology and easy communications have a homogenising effect all over the global supermarket (whatever else, it is no village), and thus work to reduce regional diversity in urban form, architecture, food, dress, and even vegetation. For example, as little as twenty years ago, most cities in the humid tropics were distinctive at least in their trees. Now there is a very limited and small vocabulary of street trees from Cairns to Chiang Mai: *Delonix regia*, the Royal Poinciana; several species of *Cassia*; *Spathodea campanulata*, the African Tulip Tree; a few palms; *Terminalia catappa*, the Tropical Almond; *Dillenia indica*; and the ubiquitous Rain Tree. These are all magnificent trees, extravagantly beautiful in flower, but it is extraordinary that a part of the world remarkable for the diversity of its tree species should so quickly be reduced to uniformity in its towns.

Does it matter? I believe that it matters a great deal, for a variety of rather different reasons, ranging from ecological through aesthetic

66

to psychological. Some of them will be illustrated later. The psychological dependence on regional and local identity is marked in all technologically 'primitive' societies – in much of Papua New Guinea, for example, there is a wealth of local knowledge about particular places, their physical characteristics, their special uses, and the kind of behaviour that is necessary to maintain both, encoded in a series of taboos, negative and positive constraints on behaviour that westerners have sometimes described as superstition. The early Greeks had very similar beliefs and practices, and a legion of tutelary deities – the spirits of place – to guard each stream or grove or mountain. That body of legend embroiders the cloth of our western tradition, but it now has no functional place in it, only a decorative one.

We make sense of experience by generalising, and could not function without so doing. Every noun in our language takes meaning from a perceived likeness between different objects, and every verb, from a perceived likeness between different events or actions. Yet experience itself is of the specific, and each of us is an individual with a need to see ourselves in a unique set of relations, as well as in general ones. This need is not fully met in a homogenising world, and many features of our life, including much of the fashion industry and the bizarre featurism still characteristic of domestic architecture and suburban gardens, are evidence of unfulfilled cravings for personal identity set in a distinctive environment.

Those who are responsible for the care of landscape in this country can do much to resist the effects of homogenising technology, to individuate by understanding and clarifying the locally distinctive – in short, by respecting the *genius loci*. What follows are some suggestions as to how this might be done, and some possible reasons for doing so. The suggestions are all commonplace, but they are nevertheless regularly disregarded:

1. Understand the geology, and display it where you can.

Road and rail cuttings often reveal the geology of an area in a satisfying way. If the rock is not strong enough to stand as a cutting, then it may be necessary to face it, or to use crib walling or reduce the slope and cover it with turf. But it is not uncommon for the natural rock face to be covered over for reasons that are primarily aesthetic. In Melbourne, for example, one of the most significant internal boundaries is that between the Tertiary basalts of the western third of the metropolis, and the Silurian mudstones and sandstones of the eastern two-thirds. This boundary coincides in part with the Yarra, although it is not the river that makes the significant boundary, but the geology, as Ivanhoe and Heidelberg show clearly (both 'eastern' suburbs, west of the Yarra, but east of the basalt). It is very fashionable in the eastern suburbs of Melbourne to use large basaltic boulders to make gardens in imitation of the Ellis Stones gardens.[1] Basalt does not belong in these areas, and anyone who uses it should be very clear in his own mind just why it is being introduced. Fantasy gardens which create their own environment are legitimate in special circumstances, especially if they are self-contained and not continuous with a larger, semi-natural environment, but they should be exceptional.

The gold of Hawkesbury Sandstone is part of the riches of Sydney, and it is everywhere, in cliffs, cuttings and buildings. Rock and stone are as a rule used well in Sydney, because the natural example is omnipresent, yet even Sydney has some very inept stonework. Toodyay Stone, a hard flaggy quartzite, is often used thus in Perth and Fremantle, with deplorable results. The outcropping calcarenite and limestone of coastal south-western Australia has a distinctive beauty that seems not yet to be adequately valued, since outcrops are often vandalised by developers and public authorities.

2. Study the landform, and build in sympathy with it, if possible.
The handling of landform is particularly clumsy and insensitive in
Australia, although many farm houses of the last century were beautifully sited. *Camden Park House*, built by John Macarthur's sons,
is a striking example, facing west down a long gentle incline to the
Nepean, rising again to a low hill, where, a little off-centre, stands the
tall tower and spire of Camden's Church of St John, built by the Mac-
arthurs to the Glory of God and to improve their views; behind it in
the distance, the backdrop of the Blue Mountains with the peaks of
Mount Victoria and Mount Wilson accenting the skyline. This view
is a combination of nature and artifice; the house is angled for it, the
unbroken lawn leads to it, the flanking tree plantations frame it, the
church on its hill enhances the middle distance, the Blue Mountains
close it – and the view from the opposite side, the east or garden front,
complements it by being so different. Set on a rather small plateau or
shelf of land, planted as a semi-circle of lawn and garden, this aspect
drops steeply to broken country, a billabong, and natural bushland,
which is more civilised in near view, much wilder in the background,
and all more intimate in scale than the sweeping vista to the west.

This eye for a site was not limited to great houses. It was as true
for many a modest farm house, but it is a skill that has been lost.
A 'view' today seems to mean only a large range of visibility, as from
the West Gate Bridge, or from aggressive houses rearing above the
landscape on the Mornington Peninsula or Mount Gravatt to peer
at equally aggressive neighbours. Skillion roofs are set at an angle
contrary to the slope; the flow of the landform is disrupted by trivial
shapes, or by brutal cut-and-fill to produce level building sites. Most
of the Yarra River has been filled along its banks, flattening out the
swamps and billabongs, and oversteepening the banks to leave the
river out of sight in a trench with steep and unnatural banks. Landscape architects have a little trick all their own called 'mounding'.

The creation of new landforms with big earth moving machines has exciting possibilities, of which the underground car park at the University of Melbourne gives an interesting example. It is also sometimes convenient to use mounds of earth to screen or to reduce noise. But the arbitrary tumuli or long barrows that now begin to appear in affluent suburbia – the long barrows of Mona Vale in the northern suburbs of Sydney are a major example – have nothing to do with natural landforms on this continent, although they bear some relation to glacial landforms in North America and Europe, whence the device has been copied. I hope also that we will have no more waterfalls beginning and ending nowhere – even the waterfall in Commonwealth Park in Canberra, on a generous scale and exceptionally well done, is ludicrous to my eye. No natural spring could possibly emerge from that granite bouldered construct on the limestone plains by the Molonglo.

Some public agencies have shown a new feeling for landform in the last decade. In Victoria, the Country Roads Board has created a fine mega-sculpture in the Wallan Bypass section of the Hume Freeway; failure of the road-bed has meant inadequate public recognition of this achievement. The highway is beautifully fitted to the land in long sweeping curves. The overpasses are tied securely to the hills from which they flow, and the road carries the traveller up and over the Dividing Range with kinesthetic pleasure. The State Electricity Commission (Victoria) now goes to great pains in the difficult exercise of siting its power lines. Fisheries and Wildlife have some interesting design successes, most notably the information building at Tower Hill near Warrnambool. This was designed by the late Robin Boyd, and the circular building with domed roof faithfully reflects the bare rounded hill forms behind and around it. It is unusual for a state agency to sponsor work of such distinction.

3. Study the soil.

Any gardener will improve the soil if he can, by digging in compost, adding gypsum to clay, and by fertilising. For an enclosed garden, it may even be legitimate to replace the soil entirely, with 'mountain soil' or an organic-rich sandy loam. Remember, however, that you are certainly robbing Peter to do so. In the larger landscape, excessive fertilising will mean that there is then a temptation to use plant materials that would not otherwise grow on site, and this may commit you to substantial long-term maintenance. There may also be ecological costs, and aesthetic ones. The fertilisers will add eutrophication risk to streams and lakes. Changes in vegetation may make a landscape more vulnerable to adverse conditions, reduce wildlife habitat, and look out of place against the bleached colour typical of so many Australian landscapes.

4. Interfere as little as possible with the natural hydrology.

To increase or decrease stream flow will lead to either erosion or siltation. Where the velocity of run-off is necessarily increased in one part of the system, for example by roads, this should be compensated by decreasing run-off elsewhere, for example by infiltration beds, reforestation, or retarding basins. There are now many devices for the systematic analysis and conservation of natural hydrological systems, and these give a better long-term return on investment than the very costly corrective devices required by ignoring them, a case where 'Design with Nature' is good practical advice. There are also some obvious aesthetic rewards for doing so.

5. Study the natural vegetation, and the existing vegetation.

The design of self-maintaining systems should be a general aim, although it can rarely be fully achieved, and there may be departures from it for specific, clearly defined purposes. One must also recognise the identity of cultural landscapes: the poplars of the middle Hawkesbury around Wisemans Ferry; the gentle vineyards of McLaren Vale; the great pine and cypress windbreaks of the rolling lava plains near Flinders in southern Victoria, almost black against summer-blonde pastures; the backyard almonds of Adelaide and the elms of inner Melbourne, where a eucalypt may look and be out of place. To grow only native plants is not a proper aim, which should be rather to grow appropriate plants – but the definition of 'appropriate' must rely on much physical and cultural information. One should nevertheless use local plant material, germinated from a local seed source, in the large landscape as a matter of general principle. Departures from this principle may often be legitimate, but should have an explicit justification. The variation in plant material is one of the strongest natural cues to changes in the local environment, but once again the forces of homogeneity are at work. In the Hume Freeway section praised above, there is one landscape inadequacy, and that is in this use of plant materials. A rather limited range of landscaping plant material has been used, drawn for its practicality and easy availability and familiarity, from around Australia. Perhaps one-third comes from south-western Australia. The Dividing Range is one of the great internal boundaries in a country that generally lacks marked differentiation, separating the southern coastal margins from the inland Murray Basin. This major transition is not recognised in the planting scheme on the Hume Freeway, which thus homogenises its route, and diminishes the *genius loci* in this respect.

It sometimes looks as if the rather limited range of imported exotic plants used to adorn our gardens and landscapes in the past has been replaced in the last decade or so by an equally limited range of native plants – native, that is, to Australia, but rarely indigenous to the site where they are planted. I am not an extreme purist, and am well aware, for example, that *Corymbia ficifolia*[2] grows much better in

Melbourne than it does in most of Western Australia, where its natural range is limited to a small area on the extreme south coast. There is in fact a vast range of Australian plants that have scarcely been tried in general cultivation – many of the rainforest trees, for example, thrive in the Royal Botanic Gardens in South Yarra, but are almost never to be seen outside them in Victoria – the species of *Lomatia* are a case in point. There is also a very great deal of work to be done in the design use of Australian plant material, a subject which men like Glen Wilson have pioneered. The use of repeated verticals, so easily achieved by close-planted species such as *Corymbia maculata* can give stunning effects, and there are many striking design possibilities which rely on the light canopy, fine and diverse foliage, subtle colour variations, sensuous trunks and irregular symmetry peculiar to so much Australian vegetation. All this should be explored for special effects. In the larger landscape, ecological principles should generally apply. They can also be very effective, soothing by their harmony in an urban setting, as Bruce Mackenzie has shown so well at Peacock Point.[3]

6. Respect the cultural landscape.

There are many good local and regional landscape practices: the whitewashed low wooden railing around the country race-track, for example, is preferable to the tubular steel with which it is sometimes replaced. Street names attached to the walls of buildings, rather than needing yet another pole rising from cluttered pavements, is an old and urbane practice in inner Sydney. The pepper tree (*Schinus molle*) is as much a part of the cultural landscape of Australian mining towns as any gum tree. The cultural landscape is made up of the sum of such details, reflecting our impact on the natural environment. Unfortunately, this principle cannot be applied incautiously, because much of the cultural landscape is not worth respect, a sad truth that applies not only to the dreary landscapes of part of the western suburbs of

Sydney, which are often subject to the scorn of aesthetes, but equally to most of the Barrenjoey Peninsula, where many of the aesthetes live, in an area of great wealth and breathtaking natural beauty among houses of equally breathtaking vulgarity. However, the hand of man has enhanced some landscapes: the Fleurieu Peninsula in South Australia, for example, and much of rural Tasmania. Such landscapes must be conserved, and their lessons applied elsewhere.

7. Analyse the *genii loci* of our landscapes, and celebrate them.
The landscapes of England have been loved, analysed, recreated, used as the background for poems and plays and novels for hundreds of years. Wessex is Hardy country, and the lakes are Wordsworth; East Anglia is interpreted through Constable, and Kent through Chaucer: this rich overlay of association deepens our experience and understanding. In Australia, Heysen invented the gum tree, and Tom Roberts showed us reddish landscapes, a change from the sombre colours of McCubbin, or the south-of-France palette of Streeton. But most Australian landscapes are unlimned and unsung. Dorothea Mackellar and her pop poem about loving a sunburnt country (which she did from a house on lush Pittwater with a rainfall of around 1300 millimetres) has probably done more to wean Australians from the hose than any landscape architect; programs like those of the ABC Natural History Film Unit have also had a major impact.

The view of some professional landscape architects that the way to get good landscapes is to get on with the job of design, and that words are all a waste of time, is clearly inadequate. Landscape architects will never play more than a partial role in managing landscape in this (or any other) country – but it can be a critical one if they are articulate, can say what they mean by good design as well as show it, can give meaning to words and phrases like 'compatible' and 'incompatible', 'in harmony with the landscape' and so on, by the capacity to

analyse in words – and photographs and sketches – the specific qualities of specific landscapes, thus showing us all how to pay homage to
the *genius loci*. This is a task that has barely begun.

These seven points are commonplace. Any landscape architect is likely
to have heard them all in the first few lectures of his first term of professional training. Some of them are put into practice on occasion, but
there are few practitioners who make a conscious attempt to apply all
of them all the time, with the outcome that some landscape architects
are helping to create a Hilton International Landscape, a bland, easily digestible setting that makes no demands, belongs to no place, and
makes the international middle-class traveller feel at home anywhere
in the world: the price that he pays is that he is really at home nowhere.

Moreover, much landscape management is in the hands of people
other than landscape architects – Shire Engineers, for example, who
may *not* be familiar with these simple principles and may need help
in applying them.

Notes

1   Ellis Stones was a Melbourne-based landscape designer. He began working for
     Edna Walling in the 1930s and his naturalistic rock-work style soon attracted a
     wider following. His magazine columns, TV appearances and best-selling book,
     Australian Garden Design (1971) cemented his reputation as Australia's first
     popular landscape designer: Anne Latreille, 'Stones, Ellis Andrew (1895–1975)',
     Australian Dictionary of Biography, National Centre of Biography, Australian
     National University, http://adb.anu.edu.au/biography/stones-ellis-andrew-11781/
     text21073, first published 2002, accessed 10 August 2019. [A.G.]

2   *Corymbia species* were classified as *Eucalyptus* until 1995, so *Corymbia ficifolia*
     and *Corymbia maculata* appear in the original essay as *Eucalyptus ficifolia* and
     Eucalyptus maculata, respectively. [A.G.]

3   Bruce Mackenzie, 'Alternative Parkland', *Landscape Australia*, no. 1, 1979,
     pp. 19–27.

5
———

MANAGING A RESOURCES BOOM, OR IN PRAISE OF COUNTRY BOYS

1982

THE GROWING COMPLEXITY OF THE JOB OF MANAGING the resources, people, economy and government of Australia in the face of rapid expansion is worth considering, although primarily as a reflection of a global problem. The most significant 'limit to growth' may indeed not be the external limits – the resource limits that have been discussed so widely – but what are now sometimes called the 'inner limits', the limits on man's capacity to understand and manage a society as complex as the one that lies before us. A growing unease in the face of such problems is reflected clearly in the history of the nuclear debate over the last decade. In the early 1970s the debate was mainly technical. Scientists were prominent in the debate, differing in a way that is common where there is no apparent conflict over objectives, but much technical uncertainty, over issues such as the means of safe storage of radioactive wastes, the risk of accidents and the significance of low-level radiation hazards. But the debate then extended to socio-economic problems, such as the dangers of terrorist use of nuclear devices, or of sabotage, or of nuclear war; problems of human fallibility; the problems inherent in the economics of nuclear power, and so on.

Thus critics of nuclear power have raised a series of value questions. What kind of society is implied by a nuclear economy? How centralised must it be, and how subject to corporate dominance? Will it dwarf the individual beyond what we can or should tolerate? What are the possible costs of a nuclear program to future generations? Who will benefit most, and who will run the greatest risks? Does any government have the institutional capacity to manage long-term risks? All these questions show doubt about the ability of government to manage such a complex system so as to exclude human error, at least at the most critical and vulnerable points. And how totalitarian would such a government be?

Continued growth and expansion will also generate much more mundane conflicts which, like all social conflict, will put increased pressure on our managerial resources, already overstretched. Some 'goods' are in limited supply, and increased demand means increased inequity in distribution, or rationing by other than the conventional methods of market prices. Some recreation resources already are overstrained, and others soon will be. Rottnest Island, Perth's favoured playground, has for years had a queue, requiring very early application, and distribution of the limited accommodation by ballot. Wilsons Promontory in Victoria and the Warrumbungles in New South Wales also now attract more than they can handle, and access to the snowfields will soon have to be controlled. Some fragile places like Fraser Island and Millstream oasis in arid Western Australia will also soon require strictly controlled access. Australians, not used to such controls, will resent them and do their best to circumvent them.

The supply of the best urban land is an example of a different kind. The favoured sites in Sydney and Perth, for example, are along the waterways, the beaches and the foothills, but these sites are already taken up for the most part (or have a high environmental cost, as in the case of the foothills, and a high travel and social cost, as in the further fringes of Perth's northern corridor). The cheap land on which Sydney and Perth must expand are the western plains of the Sydney Basin and the Bassendean sands respectively, both inferior to the choice sites. Thus growth magnifies inequity in a way which is more repugnant to the 'fair-go' ethic than merely not having enough money. Equitable societies can be self-managing in many respects. Inequitable ones require much greater inputs of institutional control. New Zealand, for example, has generally maintained law and order with proportionately far fewer police than the United States (except, of course, during some rugby tours).

Again, at the practical level, the problems of co-ordination increase greatly with increasing size and complexity. I think it would be generally agreed by those closely involved with the practice of government that the problems of co-ordination are the key problems of the day. In Victoria, for example, the powerful semi-autonomous agencies such as the State Electricity Commission, the State Rivers and Water Supply Commission or the Melbourne and Metropolitan Board of Works have been accustomed for many years to go their way in the pursuit of limited and well-defined objectives. Only in the last decade or so has it become clear that their actions often have major environmental, social and economic side effects that impinge on every arm of government and of course on the general public as well. Government today, irrespective of party politics, is generally inefficient and it seems to become steadily more so, despite the best efforts of some dedicated servants of the state. Melbourne's West Gate Bridge is a typical example – the bridge is a beautiful engineering structure, and the need to bypass the city from east to west has long been felt. But there is no adequate link to either the Eastern or South-Eastern freeways; no link on the western side to Ballarat and Adelaide, although West Gate Bridge should surely be the gate to the west; and the Johnston Street Bridge, opened as a toll-free bridge in partial competition with the West Gate Bridge (built by a different state-created agency) has virtually guaranteed that the big bridge will run at a loss for many years.

But examples are legion, not merely of failures of co-ordination, but also of inconsistencies at the policy level, sometimes even between different policies of a single agency. An environmental protection agency in one of the states recently produced a draft policy on noise control which would have had the intended effect of reducing industrial noise in the inner city – primarily by driving noisy industries to the city limits, where they could buy cheap 'buffer zone' land. This is not only contrary to the current planning strategy for the city in question, but by increasing the car trips necessary for the workforce it would increase the major source of urban pollution, increase the use of fossil fuels, add to the inflationary energy bill, and increase urban sprawl.

We now have a variety of techniques for understanding such complex interdependencies, and to help us make decisions that take into account the crazy angles revealed in the house of cards we have built ourselves – but these, not surprisingly, are also imperfect. Systems analysis, cost-benefit analysis and multi-objective planning are the straws that professionals lean on to try to impose a logical framework on behaviour which is often intrinsically inconsistent. They are often an advance or check on intuitive judgement, but in making explicit the assumptions that underlie intuitive judgements, and by taking account both of a range of factors that we might otherwise ignore, and also of the way in which these and other factors interact, they may seem to many people merely to add needless complexity to what should be simple. But in fact the issues to which such techniques are addressed are *not* simple; what the techniques do is to drag the complexities out into the light of day, so that we may attempt to assess them rationally.

Why has the world become so complicated? Has it really become more complex, or is it merely that we are now better at perceiving its complexity? Both, I think. The growth of ecology at both the scientific and popular level has meant that the word 'ecosystem' is now widely used. The concepts it embodies are reflected in pop-ecology slogans such as 'It is never possible to do only one thing', and 'Everything is connected to everything else'. It is not significantly true that *everything* is connected to everything else, and the effect of such slogans on some people is almost paralysing. It makes many young people feel nervous, helpless and inclined to quietism – yet it is true that ecologists have established some surprising and, at first sight, remote and improbable consequences from our actions. One example that is now familiar, but was at first startling, is the decline in numbers of the eagle in North America; as a high-level predator, the eagle has been the victim of successive concentrations up the food chain of toxic substances used in agriculture, to the point of interference with the bird's calcium metabolism. The outcome has been thin-shelled eggs that fail to hatch. This and a host of similar examples have given us a new insight into the complex interdependencies of the natural world. Natural systems have always been complex, whether or not they are disturbed by our species, and it is not the complexity that is new so much as our perception of it.

But the world has also genuinely become more complex, and there is good reason for this, in that man has steadily taken over more and more naturally self-managing systems, and substituted man-managed ones for them, to the point where he is now approaching, or has perhaps exceeded, his managerial capability. Consider, for example, the great rainforests of the tropics, which we are well on the way to destroying. They have functioned successfully for hundreds of thousands of years without management, without significant erosion or siltation of rivers or pollution, supporting a huge population of living things, including our own species. They have been full of a myriad insects working as part of a balanced natural cycle – but there were no insect *pests*. So soon as we fell the forests and plant our own crop varieties, however, we are overwhelmed with pests on which we will forever after have to wage unceasing war, a war moreover on unfavourable terms, because their capacity for evolutionary adaptation is far greater than ours. We have supposed in the past that our managerial capacities were without limit, or perhaps it might be better to say that we have never given serious thought to the question. Edward Goldsmith gives an interesting example. Date palms in Arabia are hand-pollinated. Suppose we decide that we should take over all pollination – either in the interests of greater control and efficiency, or because we had killed off the natural pollinators. Our decision would be irrelevant – we could not do it. In destroying our rainforests we are now adding huge tracts of difficult land to man's already overstretched managerial responsibilities. Can we cope?

The costs of increasing complexity are twofold. The first cost is the practical cost that follows our failures in co-ordination and management; the second cost is a social cost. To many intelligent people the difficulties of evaluating the full consequences of any major decision are so great that they withdraw, leave the decisions to the politician, and get on with their own individual lives. Australians as people are often contemptuous of the quality of their elected representatives. They seem to me to be at least the equal of politicians from most other countries, and there are some able and far-sighted men among them. Politics nevertheless by its very forms of tenure is preoccupied primarily with the short term, and is not well suited to analysing complex long-term problems. Only those who are too limited even to see the complexities seem easily able to make the difficult decisions, and they are the people who are often least suited to do so.

GEORGE SEDDON

Education for Management

Where do people with managerial skills come from in our society? Are such skills a mere chance of personality, or can they be fostered, either directly or indirectly? I have a proposition to put now that may surprise you. Improbably, many Australians with high-level managerial skills have a country background. In fact, a case could be put that rural Australia has produced talented Australians in a variety of fields in numbers that bear no relation to the rural–urban population ratio. If this is true, then it has consequences for education.

Consider Australian writers – Henry Handel Richardson, Patrick White, Miles Franklin, Joseph Furphy, Alan Marshall, Donald Horne. More than 70 per cent should come from the big cities to maintain the ratio, but the proportions are almost reversed. Try prime ministers – Fraser, Menzies, Curtin, Lyons. Then there are names like Bjelke-Petersen, Sinclair, Nixon, Anthony, Bolte, McEwen. My claim is not that they are all great statesmen, but that there are a lot of them, even given the rural gerrymander. Rural origins again predominate. Some professions are overwhelmingly rural. In 1970 I checked the place of birth of a large sample of members of the Geological Society of Australia, and found that they were more than 90 per cent rural. So were most biologists; lawyers, on the other hand, are a highly metropolitan group.

I have no hard data to support the claim that those with high-level managerial skills are likely to be of rural origin in Australia, but I have done a deal of informal checking among company executives, the managerial positions in the state agencies such as State Rivers and Waters, Soil Conservation, Forest Commission (these are all heavily rural); also the higher ranks of the public service. In all these fields one would expect four out of five to be big city boys. Not so.

Just what *are* managerial skills? All those skills needed to get complex and difficult things done, things that involve a range of actions and a range of people. Analytical skills are needed to take the scene apart, skills of synthesis to put it all together again. The capacity to make best-available-evidence decisions when decisions must be made, but also the instinct that tells when delay might bring critical new information. Skills of negotiation and motivation, to get others to play their part. A nose for trouble, that can anticipate and bypass it. The *will* to manage, make things work, get things done, rather than to take the role of amused bystander watching the passing parade.

There are, of course, many useful managerial skills, and many different kinds of managers. The thumb-nail sketch above is merely a device to lead to the next question: why should country boys – or girls – have more than their fair share of them? Consider the model of society with which they grow up. The country town is comprehensible, and the pathways to action are clear. Moreover, successful action is seen to be possible. Suppose, for example, the town wants to build a new wing to the hospital. You know who has to be on the committee: a couple of the bank managers, the town lawyer, perhaps, the Dalgety agent (who knows all the community and which ones have money), and a couple of farmers, preferably related to half the district, which is not too hard. You also know who to avoid – you can't, as a rule, have the Catholic priest, for instance, unless you have the other denominations too. You know how to get publicity. You know where the opposition will lie, and how to circumvent it. You know who will want to sell his land for the new wing, and which builder is likely to get the contract. In other words, an effective pathway of action can be plotted, and followed through.

There are other advantages. Country people have a special relationship with their environment. Especially if they are farmers, they accept responsibility for it and, if they own the land, they will expect to pass it on to their children in productive good health. Both literally and metaphorically, they can take a long view. At the same time they are also obliged to look closely at detail. If you don't learn to be observant, then you miss the detail by which you judge the well-being of the enterprise. Most country children, moreover, can watch both their parents work for their living, and are not fobbed off with 'Daddy is going to the office where he makes money'. They can actually see what he does, and thus once again learn to see the relation between effective actions and results.

I believe that our fundamental attitudes to social action tend to be formed in this way. City children may have different models. Some working-class suburbs – like Brunswick or Richmond in Melbourne – are very tight-knit, and there is a strong sense of community, but the community is incomplete. If there are thirty doctors practising in Richmond, not more than ten are likely to live there, and the professions in general are much under-represented. The possibilities for successful social action are much less in Richmond than in country towns; the cards are stacked against Richmond, and Richmond knows it. (For example, the South-Eastern Freeway, which serves Toorak and Malvern, was built along the Richmond side of the River Yarra, and not the Toorak side.) So Richmond people are likely to feel that 'you've got to change the system' before the local community can act effectively. Planning models of society derived from that sort of background are likely therefore to have an ideological basis, in contrast with the more pragmatic models derived from rural communities.

The great social revolutions, on the other hand, are almost inevitably urban. The French Revolution was based in Paris; the Cultural Revolution in Peking and Shanghai. Marx was very much an urban intellectual. Revolution is the extreme case, and the cities are also generally the centres of innovation and social change.

Children from the post-war middle-class suburbs – such as Glen Waverley in Melbourne, or St Ives in Sydney, or Applecross or Floreat Park in Perth – do not come from tight-knit communities at all, nor from complete ones – they are as incomplete socially and economically as Richmond, and much more remote from the commercial and industrial basis of their society. Although comfortable and secure, such suburbs are essentially the product of an *invisible* power structure, of decisions made elsewhere, and no cohesive model of community action would be apparent to children who grow up in them, other than a sense of rather remote determining forces, both bureaucratic and economic. Perhaps this is why the typical outcome of a resident group meeting in such areas is to pass a resolution that someone else – such as the state or federal government – should do something about the problem in question. However, because professionals are well represented in such communities, action may then go a step further by appropriate lobbying. Professionals do not as a rule wish to 'change the system' – they concentrate on making it work in their favour. Thus a planning mode I derived from such a background will have as a central feature that change in one community or area can best be brought about by manipulating forces in another. This may be greatly reinforced by the experience of attending a public school[1], which may generate a 'network' model of effective social action. Schools such as Melbourne Grammar or Shore or St Peters or Guildford are tight-knit communities, with a wide-ranging intake geographically, but a relatively homogeneous one socially, moulded rather strongly by a common school experience and personal ties *throughout the larger community* (which the Richmond boy will not have, nor will the country boy unless he went to a boarding school). Thus you always have connections, and if you want something done, 'give old Bloggs a ring'. Social action therefore consists in exploiting a network of informal and personal connections within the power structure of the community. Networkers are, of course, unlikely to be revolutionaries or ideologues. Public schools are strongly hierarchical, but one's rank in the hierarchy increases with age. When advancement is guaranteed by growing older, all one has to do is wait a little.

This typology of formative planning models is intended to be suggestive only. It is obviously incomplete – for example, strong horizontal linkages which transcend local loyalties must play a part with many minority groups such as the Jews, or some immigrant groups such as the Greeks and Italians. The Irish Catholics were a cohesive group fifty years ago, with a distinctive view about ways of encompassing social action. Then there are the great clans, like the Myer-Baillieu clan in Melbourne; or the 'five families' in Western Australia, intermarrying for four generations to conserve money and power; and some of the pastoral dynasties of South Australia and western Victoria. The latter, especially, cut across my idealised country town quite dramatically. Some country towns are rigidly stratified – Armidale, for example, or Hamilton. The graziers form their own network, which is, of course, also locked in to the public school network, and thus trans-local. A wheat town like Horsham is more democratic than a wool town like Hamilton but, even in Hamilton, the way things get done or not done is at least comprehensible and visible, even if the consensus model doesn't quite fit.

But my point is not to suggest either that there are only three formative planning models, or that all consensus managers come from country towns, all systems analysts from Richmond, or all networkers from Glen Waverley plus Scotch College. The point rather is to suggest that there are some fundamentally different biases towards planning and management, and that they may *in part* reflect the models of social action offered by different community backgrounds. The reader can then make his own list if he doesn't like mine. I would also want to argue that a complex pluralistic society has need of planners and managers who work in different ways – the 'networkers' certainly have their uses for quick and effective action, but at the price of bypassing community consensus (which you can rarely do in a country town). Equally, those who seek to gain an understanding of a particular action by analysing its relations with a complex structural system can play an enormously valuable part, especially in understanding and shaping long-term changes. An action that is inhomogeneous with the system in which it will have to operate is generally modified to perform the functions of the system rather than the functions for which it was originally designed, and this is the shortcoming of much *ad hoc*, problem-oriented management.

But when these necessary qualifications have been made, I would argue that the 'country town model' of social action is the most useful one for most managerial purposes, in that it involves a whole and relatively complete community, relies largely on powers and forces within that community, and, above all, generates a belief in the *possibility* of effective social action, whereas large cities tend to generate attitudes of passivity or resignation or amused detachment. Decadent societies – if I may risk a large generalisation – are often rich in witty observers of the passing scene, and are therefore very favourable to the growth of certain cultural forms, especially comedy and satire, but may suffer from a paralysis of the will. They are often highly urbanised. Imperial Rome worked so long as it could successfully recruit managers from the countryside; Londoners could run an empire so long as they could recruit raw Scots to manage it for them.

This shorter version of the original essay was extracted from pp. 37–46.

NOTES

1   In the Australian context, what Seddon refers to here would be called a 'private school'. [A.G.]

6

—

A SNOWY RIVER READER

1986

*In this piece Seddon grapples with the writing of his book on the
Snowy River. Published in 1994 as* Searching for the Snowy:
An Environmental History, *the book won a Eureka Prize.*

I HAVE BEEN EXPLORING THE SNOWY RIVER FOR FIVE
or six years, and studying river and records intensively in
almost every spare moment for the last three. I have come
to love the Snowy, and want to share that love by writing a
book about it, but I find that I do not know how. Some books have
almost written themselves, in the past, but this one does not write
itself at all, so I set down the words that follow in an attempt to find
out why I can't get on.[1]

There are problems. The first is that although the Snowy is in the
most densely populated south-eastern corner of Australia, its immediate setting is wild and inaccessible, and it has been little studied, so
there are great gaps in the information available; it is not possible to
give a definitive account of any aspect. Despite this, I have gathered a
wealth of information about the river and its natural and human history, but that leads me to my other problems: what to put in, what to
leave out, and how to organise my material. These problems in fact

forced me to attempt to define 'environmental history', to ask myself how it differs from other kinds of history, and why anyone should want to write it or read it. When I began I thought that the answers to these three conceptual questions were self-evident, but perhaps they are not. If environmental history[2] – by which I understand the reciprocal interaction between man and his setting, or more expansively, how we have changed a given environment through time, and how it has changed us – if environmental history is as significant as I think it to be, then why isn't there lots of it, with a well-established tradition for me to follow? I shall return to these lofty questions after I have explored further my primary problems about the Snowy.

The areas of ignorance or uncertainty are many. For example, little is known about the Aborigines of the region, and Josephine Flood's study *The Moth Hunters* was a pioneer work.[3] It has been followed by several further studies, but the information base is necessarily meagre, restricted to the partial accounts of early observers and to gleanings from the excavation of campsites. What we do know is that they were there, making a living along the whole length of the river, most of it now uninhabited.

Other matters are the subject of scholarly debate: interpretations of the geomorphology, the nature and timing of the so-called 'Kosciuskan Uplift', the discovery of Kosciusko itself, the evolution and recent history of the Bogong moth migrations; the role of fire, both natural and man-made, in the distribution of vegetation. Debate and controversy are a part of all scholarship, but the topics I have listed above have generated two opposing camps with little prospect of an easy truce, and the substance of the debates is not about values and points of view. It is more elementary, concerned with the facts and their interpretation.

Criteria of inclusion and exclusion are derived from central organising themes and by decisions about the intended 'audience' for a book. My major problem is the structural one and that alone makes it hard to decide what to put in and what to leave out, but there are subsidiary problems as well. For example, there is the question of privacy. The families who have lived along the Snowy are relatively few in number, and they know each other. One of the great-grandmothers of one family I describe was a convict, and there are others I know of. Most younger members of such families now accept their past calmly, but not all do, and one can see why, given the very firm social and economic stratification in much of rural Australia. The big land-owning families who came as free men, with some capital, have often established dynasties. They do not form a squirearchy and are rarely wealthy, but they generally have a fair level of education, usually in one of the Sydney schools, which gives them a metropolitan base, and many of them have travelled outside Australia. The families of the convicts and labourers of the early days have sometimes moved up or moved out, but others are still to be found as labourers, small landowners, small storekeepers and tradesmen and some of them are sensitive about their origins, so I have not recorded them by name.[4] There are also personal and social attributes that are worth recording, but again one must tread very warily. Some points can be made only in a general way: for example, many of the real bushmen are overweight. The old-timers like Bill Wroe and Whit Ingram are still slim and wiry, but they also still ride: straight as a ramrod on a horse, bow-legged and a little stooped on the ground. But nobody has ever walked much in this horse country, and now that the middle-aged have traded in their horses for a Land Rover, they drive *everywhere*, and their figures betray it. Male and female domains are usually very sharply defined. Muddy boots come off at the back door, and stockinged feet pad the house. The men wash up in the wash-house. The bathroom is for women, as the decor shows clearly. But it would be invasive to pursue these details to the point of attributing them to individuals.

Another major problem of selection is that of detail, and this is a problem at several levels. It is easy to use all the place names when writing of an area that is well known, but hardly anyone knows all the place names along and near the river, and to make matters worse, many places have several names: for example, the Pinch River is also the Moyangul, and so on. I find myself drowning in the detail, not just of names but of topography and geographic linkage – how one gets from A to B, for example. In trying to give a comprehensive view of the river from source to mouth, and of the history of its use, one needs further to call on the earth sciences and biology. Again, there is a problem in deciding how much a potential reader can be assumed to know. What, in short, needs explaining, and what can be assumed?

But these problems are minor compared with the problems of organisation. Considering the alternatives is a way of examining some familiar thought patterns and their limitations, and the exercise has also given me an oblique perspective on Australian history and society. I shall discuss the major options below.

1. Geographic sequence, following the river from source to mouth. The river itself is a geographic entity, and such a sequence would be appropriate to a travel book, but it is an awkward way of managing themes and history. The river is not a geological or biological unit; neither is it a historical, social or political unit. The Nile, the Rhine, Ganges, Mississippi all have historical, social, economic and political significance. The only big river in Australia of which that can be said is the Murray; it is perhaps true of the Tamar at a different scale. Australia is organised around ports, roads and rail, not along rivers. That is in fact one of the things that I have 'discovered' about the Snowy. It is *there*, a magnificent natural force. It has mythic stature, through one single poem. But it has no historical, social or political reality; *parts* of it have mattered a great deal in various ways at various times,

but only as a part of a different fabric. The most significant fact about the Snowy is that our society has never really known what to do with it. There is not even an accepted name for the area that I am discussing. 'The Murray Valley', and 'the Hunter Valley' are well known, but one cannot speak of the Snowy Valley – 'valley' is too gentle a word, a prosperous, fertile, smiling word, for the narrow, tortuous cleft in the rocks through which the Snowy hurtles to the sea. 'The Snowy catchment' would do, but might be taken to refer to the upper part of the river only. 'The Snowy Drainage Basin' is correct, but too formal for popular use, and in any case it is not much like a basin. There are names only for parts – the Monaro, the Byadbo, the Wulgulmerang and the Gelantipy plateaux and the Orbost flats, of which only the first and last are well known, and all five cover only half the river. It has no regional name because it has no regional function, for our economy and society. I shall call it all 'the Snowy', meaning more than the river itself: river, tributaries and hinterland.

2. Historic sequence, a chronology of events or their interpretation offers a conventional organising principle, but as noted above, the Snowy per se does not really have a history of its own. The lines of history do not run that way, although the events that have taken place there can be seen as part of a broader sequence, as we shall see.

3. 'Natural history' is a thematic sequence geographically applied: the geology, soils, flora and fauna are discussed in turn, with the opportunity to indicate inter-relationships. This is a standard scientific approach and it would work, although for a limited audience. The natural history of the Snowy has not been assembled to date, and such a compendium would undoubtedly be useful. It would be arbitrary in that the geological, pedological and biological boundaries do not coincide with those of the river catchment, but the river

is a natural hydrologic or geomorphic unit, and it is a major biological corridor. The river traverses greater ecological diversity than any other river in Australia, from alpine, montane, sub-arid grassland, sub-arid sclerophyll savannah to dense rainforest, and that is of biological interest.

This principle of organisation would be logical enough, but rather dull, because 'natural history' excludes people, whereas people are central to my story. Natural history forms a necessary part of a history of land use, that is, of one half of the man–environment interaction that I conceive as 'environmental history'.

4. History of land use requires a compound of organising principles, a chronology of events and a set of themes. This is a major concern, and a broad outline of such a sequence can be given easily.

There seem to be four or five broad categories of land use, that of the hunter-gatherers, that of semi-nomadic pastoralists changing slowly into a settled pastoral economy with service towns, roads, railroads and other services; and that of an urban industrial society which thoughtlessly murdered the river and now uses the corpse for recreation (perhaps this necrophiliac use is a fifth category). Much of the information about each of these phases is inherently unreliable, because each has been the subject of myth.

The Aboriginals have been 'observed' and presented as Noble Savages, primitive brutes or children; and, more recently, as Economic Man, driven to migrate hundreds of kilometres up the Snowy by his need for the supposedly protein-rich Bogong moth; or, alternatively, as Ecological Man, living in conscious harmony with his natural environment and a Lesson to us All.

The pastoral phase became a Heroic Age with Banjo Paterson and the *Bulletin*, and this was and is an urban construct, reflected today in, for example, the advertising for Marlboro cigarettes. Accuracy has never been important to this myth: The Man from Snowy River ads for Marlboro were mostly filmed in the South Island of New Zealand, which photographs better. Banjo Paterson also got much of his detail wrong. The real cattlemen from Snowy River were mostly illiterate, exploitative and very destructive. Large tracts of productive land were rendered useless within a few decades. But it is true that many of the men were magnificent horsemen and that they and their women-folk were remarkably resourceful to survive and bring up children in some of the most spectacularly broken and difficult terrain in Australia.

The Snowy Mountains Scheme ran the river west through the Divide for hydropower and irrigation in the Murrumbidgee and Murray valleys, now beset with major ecological and economic problems, despite the provision of virtually free water, paid for by urban power consumption. It was never properly costed, and it has been shown to be far from cost-effective. It was also dubiously legal at the time, carried out under the powers of the Defence Act. It had some social benefit in providing employment for 'DPs' ('displaced persons', many of them from the Baltic States) who were required to work in rural areas for a time because of the current decentralisation policy, at a time when rapid mechanisation was dramatically reducing the demand for farm labour. This 'melting pot' function, however, was vigorously promoted by the Snowy Mountains Authority and has become part of the myth. The death rate was high. The engineering and project management was generally of a very high standard, and it was undoubtedly of great psychic value for post-war Australians in seeing themselves as capable of great peace-time deeds at the national level, and it was thus promoted by the Department of National Development. The Scheme can therefore perhaps be seen as a sacrifice on the altar of national identity, like the other great human sacrifice at Gallipoli. We live by myth. Perhaps it also has some features in common with the engineering masterwork that gave us our cultural identity at Bennelong Point – not cost-effective, not functional, but worth it.

There was, of course, no environmental assessment whatsoever of the consequences of the Snowy diversion for either river system. The benefits of irrigation were taken to be self-evident at the time, and the Authority was able to boast freely that the additional irrigation water made available by the Scheme was 'free' – that is, paid for by the metropolitan consumer of electric power. It is now generally agreed that one reason why irrigation water has been so thoughtlessly used in the Murray Valley is that it has been too cheap. The Murray-Murrumbidgee is now deeply in trouble. The beheaded Snowy is dead from Jindabyne to the Quidong, where the Bombala and Delegate rivers form its functional headwaters today. Above the Quidong, you can step across the mighty Snowy, a cot-sized trickle in a king-sized bed. This is thus the history of a throwaway river.

Such an approach, that of land-use history, looks like an adequate framework at first sight, but problems persist. The first and most obvious is that each of these phases belong to different segments of Australian history, not just in time, but in their linkages; moreover, they are seen not to be significantly linked to each other except by the accident of geography, and partly for this reason each requires a different set of background information. However, that each of these phases seems discrete, with little to link one phase with the next, is true only if one looks for the links within the Snowy. That is a problem in writing most regional history – the major events are generated outside the region. The phases that I have listed are linked if we consider them as successive transformations of Australian history, itself a colonial response to 'four long waves of expansion and decline in the capitalist centre'.[5] Aboriginal land use remains discrete, until it began to be displaced by the pastoral economy, which was succeeded by mercantile capitalism, followed by industrial capitalism and by corporate capitalism. Three of these phases are exemplified very positively in the Snowy. The story of its European settlement is the story of pastoral expansion. The Snowy Mountains scheme is very much a product of industrial capitalism and of the values which upheld it. Without those values, it is virtually incomprehensible; with them it seems necessary, almost inevitable. The 'post-industrial' society, that of corporate capitalism, brought with it a new set of values; a quest for legitimation brought with it a concern, among others, for the environment, and hence support for national parks, while it also made available the leisure to enjoy them. With this set of values, it seems unthinkable that the Snowy should be seen other than as a great natural resource, to be jealously guarded as a national heritage. Within a decade, the river changed from a mere water supply, to be manipulated at will, with no inherent value of its own, to its current status – still largely unknown and unmanaged, but replete with heritage values. It says something for the flexibility of our sense of national identity that many people seem capable of maintaining both sets of values simultaneously regarding the Snowy: they can be proud of our great engineering achievement, and be thrilled by the grandeur of a wild river. It is an innocent pride. Major industrialisation came late to Australia, and it has had such a short and recent history that it may be hard to accept its demise, and in any case we have had few major engineering achievements other than Sydney Harbour Bridge and the Opera House, and these can be regarded as sources of national pride by non-Sydneysiders only when they are overseas. The complex history of the change in values from industrial capitalism to corporate capitalism is not to be traced within the Snowy region, and does not form a part of this essay, but it is certainly dramatised by the events recounted here, in that their consequences have the appearance of abrupt discontinuity at this regional scale.

The phase of mercantile capitalism is least dramatically represented in the Snowy, or rather, it is more often represented negatively, by the things that didn't happen rather than by the things that did. The major events were the consolidation of the pastoral industry in the Monaro by land purchase, the construction of fences, dams, substantial homesteads, roads and service townships. This story has been told well by Hancock in *Discovering Monaro*.[6] In the 1890s, Cooma was linked to Sydney by rail, by way of Goulburn. The other area of settlement was the Orbost flats, but this was several decades later than the Monaro. Orbost was linked by rail to Melbourne only in 1916 – or almost linked, as the rail stopped at Newmerella on the west side of the Snowy, where it stops today seventy years later. Thus both Cooma and Orbost were at the end of the line, and this symbolised their status, as far-flung outposts of metropolitan dominance. All the significant investment decisions were made in Melbourne and Sydney, and these determined land use, within the limits of its natural capability. It is tempting to see what in fact has happened – which is very little – as almost inevitable, given the remoteness of the area, but that is not so. The region might have had a very different regional history if different decisions had been taken outside the region. One national policy decision to affect the Monaro and the Snowy was the ultimate choice in 1909 of Canberra as the site of the national capital, overturning an earlier decision in 1904 to build it near Dalgety on the Snowy River. The 1904 Act, opposed by New South Wales, was therefore never put into effect; if it had been, the environmental history of the region would have been very different. Canberra has been a poor site for a national capital because it has no natural place in the regional economy of a thinly populated grazing landscape, although of course it has a great impact on the region. A similar city in the Monaro would have had a different kind of regional significance. The waters of the Snowy would doubtless have been used to generate hydropower, but the water would have remained in the Snowy. The major effect would surely have been to improve communications, by both rail and road to Eden and its fine harbour of Twofold Bay, and to Orbost in Victoria – thus to the growth of intensive agriculture in the coastal valleys, and of much more substantial development along the south-east coast of Australia.

It seems then that I have found a way of ordering my material into a history of land use, by looking for the links elsewhere. But that would be only half the story, 'a study of man's impact on his environment' (the subtitle of *Discovering Monaro*). But what of the interaction, which includes the impact of that environment on man? *Why* have we behaved in particular ways at different times? Such a question can be answered at many levels, and it can be broken down into smaller questions: for example, who liked the country enough to stay there in the first half century? The answer: the Scots, who are substantially 'overrepresented'. It is easy to speculate why. It is also easy enough to see why the rightness and greatness of the Snowy Mountains Scheme seemed beyond question in the 1950s. In fact, I have already introduced this theme, the impact of the environment on us, by using the word 'myth'. To use such a word is to signal concerns that go beyond social, political and economic history into the domain of cultural history. To understand the variety of behavioural responses to the Snowy we need to look at the ways in which it has been perceived.

5. Perceptual history is then a fifth option, offering a sequence of records of the way in which the river has been seen, by explorers, photographers, artists, natural historians, cattlemen, miners, engineers, hydrologists, bushwalkers. There have been almost as many rivers as there have been observers, and that is in the end why the river is 'incoherent'. There can be no single view of it, but I can give some samples.

One of the more interesting is that of the Reverend W.B. Clarke, who published an account of his geological explorations in 1860: *Research into the Southern Goldfields of New South Wales*. Clarke was a good economic geologist, and it is obvious that he much preferred field exploration to looking after his parish, St Thomas in North Sydney; but he feels obliged to justify his tastes, and therefore breaks into the rhetoric of 'the sublime':

The most gorgeous cathedral, filled with holiday worshippers, is not more pleasing in my recollection than that noble landscape by which we were surrounded, and the company of pilgrims who stood by me under a burning sun on the side of the hill, listening to my homely words of encouragement and exhortation. It is to be hoped that I may never be reproached with forsaking my calling to seek for the gold that perisheth, for the judgements of the Lord, which I proclaimed amidst the mountains, 'are more to be desired than gold, yea, than much fine gold.'[7]

Nevertheless, the fine gold was the object of his explorations, and purple passage over, he returns to professionally prosaic appraisal of the geology and the likely distribution of precious metals. Other passages combine the rhetoric of the picturesque with flat economic evaluation, for example:

This part of the course of the Snowy River is wild in the extreme, and the ranges about Walgalamarang, and all through to the south-east, towards the Deleget country, is a collection of broken, steep and almost inaccessible masses. It has never been thoroughly explored, though the most considerable portion of it is north of the boundary. On another occasion I approached this defile of the Snowy River from the south-eastward; it was there equally inaccessible. The amount of fluviatile and transported surface drifts must be enormous; and doubtless they contain gold.[8]

The 'picturesque' is also shaping rhetoric in a somewhat later account by W.H. Ferguson, also a geologist, of the Snowy gorges across the Victorian border:

The scenery is wild and rough and grand in the extreme. In no place else in Victoria are there such dizzy precipices, such sheer bluffs, or gorges with such vertical sides. In places the river is hemmed in between rocks which leave but a 30ft waterway. In others the waters of the stream ripple over the gravel beds with a width of 7 chains. In places the river is a wide still pool; in others it is a soaring rushing rapid, which plunges tumultuously over a bouldery 10ft drop ...[9]

In 1937, Arthur Hunt and Stanley Hanson made the first successful canoe trip down the Snowy all the way from Jindabyne to Marlo at its mouth. 'Don't be a fool, Arthur', advised one Monaro friend, 'there are places down there where even the blacks won't go.' But he went, took two months to make the trip, and described it for the *Sydney Mail* in three articles.[10] He also used the rhetoric of the picturesque, but it is a laconic bushman's version:

We had the crows with us, and we always imagined they were the same crows right through the trip. When we pulled our canoe out of the water for the last time, it was in the darkness of a wild, rough night, and the scream of the wind sounded like their disappointed curses.

Many times during the two months we were on the trip, one of us would pause, shake his fist at the crows, and say: 'You haven't got us yet, you black brutes!'

The Snowy River is a strange, lonely, and wonderful river, and breeds strange thoughts.

Stan, however, livened up the proceedings a little by finding a brown snake – one of the several we had seen that morning. He teased and tormented it, hitting it across the head with his hat when it struck at him.

He got a forked stick, jammed the snake's head hard on the ground, picked it up and played with it. When he put it down, I put an end to his childish fun with a large rock.

I think Stan was annoyed because I killed that snake.[11]

The harsh cry of the crows is the appropriate background music, and Stan's game with the snake is a smaller version of their game with the river, for which they show the grudging respect – almost love – that many Australians used to feel for a tough adversary, like Johnny Turk in World War I. After their first leg through the Beloka Gorge below Jindabyne, Hunt and Hanson spent a couple of nights at Dalgety, mostly in the pub:

We would meet someone for the first time and be introduced as one of the coves who were going down the river. He would say: 'You got this far, did you? How did you get on coming through the gorge?' We would tell him in as few words as possible.

Then would follow that long-drawn 'Ummmm!' which shows that an Australian is getting into gear to say something, and the little play would conclude: 'Yes, it's a bit rough up in there; but you wait till you get further down. You'll never get through. You'd better come and have a drink.'[12]

They did, but then continued with their trip, and were soon into the very rough country between Ironmungy and the McLaughlin River.

For the next four days we averaged less than a mile a day. We worked from daylight until it was too dark to see, very often going without our midday meal. It was a canoeist's nightmare. We were well behind time, and we began to have doubts that our flour and tobacco would last out until we reached Williams [homestead near Burnt Hut Crossing].

We slipped and fell, dragged, hauled and sweated.

We pulled our sleeping-bags on each night and were asleep before we had time to finish our after-supper smoke. We almost forgot what it felt like to be in the canoe; it was just portage, portage, portage through the roughest country it was possible to imagine.

There were no pools – only small falls, bad rapids, rocks, foam, and the dull roar of the river. We were reluctant to do any shooting as we were afraid of rain, which would have meant abandoning the canoe, as a few more feet of water in those gorges would have left us no room even to climb along the banks.

The banks were masses of boulders, with the sides of the gorge rising sheer in some places for hundreds of feet. Our hands cracked and bled, Stan's back was getting worse, the canoe was leaking again – altogether we had a pretty rough time.

We found that in one place the river completely disappears and runs underground for fifty yards. Very few people on Monaro know of this, and many were inclined to doubt the authenticity of the tale.

The truth of it was brought home to us when we camped near the Stone Bridge, as it is called, and had to walk 100 yards upstream before we could climb down to the water's edge to fill our billies. The blacks used this natural crossing when they were travelling backwards and forwards from what is now Victoria.[13]

I have quoted Hunt at length because his words bring the river to life for me far more than the purple passages of Clarke, and his tone of voice is rare in written accounts. It is exactly the tone of men who have lived by and worked around the river, but very few of them have put pen to paper. Miners, engineers and hydrologists have discussed the river and its surroundings in more prosaic and utilitarian terms, but even the rhetoric of utility tends to break into hyperbole. This is particularly well illustrated by Robert Menzies in a speech delivered at the opening of the Tumut Pond dam in 1958:

> In a period in which we in Australia are still, I think, handicapped by parochialism, by a slight distrust of big ideas and of big people or of big enterprises ... this scheme is teaching us and everybody in Australia to think in a big way, to be thankful for big things, to be proud of big enterprises and ... to be thankful for big men.[14]

Perhaps Menzies was correct in this assessment, in that, as I have suggested above, the scheme has probably had more psychological than utilitarian value, although it has to be said that Menzies was not one of 'the big men' when the Scheme began under Chifley; indeed, it was he who questioned its legality, although the Menzies government in the end saw the project through. Of course the Scheme was promoted on utilitarian grounds, even if they proved illusory, requiring a notable sacrifice of non-utilitarian values. The case for these non-utilitarian values was well put (again using the rhetoric of the sublime) by B.U. Byles, the forester who made the first major soil conservation study in the upper catchment, in what is now Kosciusko National Park.

The occasion was the proposal by the Snowy Mountains Authority and its big men to dam Spencers Creek, a high-level headwater of the Snowy, a proposal strongly opposed by the Academy of Science, but abandoned by the Authority on pragmatic grounds that the glacial moraine was too unstable for secure foundations. Byles' words: '*all* the water in the high levels of the park must not be converted to power; *some* of it must be left on the altar of the gods'.

Banjo Paterson also wrote in the romantic-heroic mode. All the writing about the river is in this vein, using the rhetoric of the picturesque or the sublime. Either that, or it is utterly prosaic, the prose of hydrologists recording water flow or the like. There is almost nothing in between. Perhaps because our society has not been able to find much direct utility for the river, our imagination seems unable to encompass it. The record is one of environmental abuse and lofty prose. Now that what is left of the river is dedicated to a non-utilitarian use, that of National Park, we may learn to see it in new ways. I have done so myself over the last few years, and the last principle of organisation I have considered is to record the sequences of my own discovery – physical and emotional – of the river.

6. The last option I have considered is therefore the autobiographical mode, sharing my own voyage of discovery towards understanding the river with the reader. This is often a good way of introducing a complex subject, bringing order out of confusion. Keith Hancock follows it in part in *Discovering Monaro*, maintaining an autobiographical flavour throughout the book, unobtrusive but always fresh and first hand. The author has tramped the high country, sat in the kitchens with mugs of tea and talked to the sheep farmers. He introduces this theme early, by unpacking the meaning of his title, *Discovering Monaro*:

a soil chemist or a botanist, a painter or a poet ... would all agree that the discovery of Australia, or of any Australian region, is not a once for all achievement, but rather is a continuing effort, whose end – if ever there is an end – still lies far beyond sight.[15]

The practical men also 'discover' the land through the lessons they learn in using it. The author then takes part in this process at two levels; he records his own discoveries as an individual, and tries to set them in a larger context of discovery.

The enquiry is this: 'How has man in Monaro used the land on which he lives?' Looking for answers to this question could keep a large team of experts at work for a long time; in this book, an historian makes his bid for a place in the team.[16]

Eric Rolls also gives an autobiographical flavour to the most successful environmental history to date in Australia: *A Million Wild Acres: A History of the Pilliga Scrub*. He lives in the district that is his subject, farms the land, walks in the 'scrub', and used kangaroo grass to deck out the church in which his daughter was wed:

We cut big bunches of its light brown heads on purple stalks to decorate the little Baradine church at our daughter's wedding which excitingly disrupted the finishing of this book. Several city guests stopped to pick bunches along the Coonabarabran road on their way home the next day.[17]

He sees with the eye of a poet, and can communicate what this land has meant to him, and what it has meant to others, including those who have hated it, or exploited it, or been indifferent to it. Neither Rolls nor Hancock, however, are fully autobiographical; they weave a fabric with several threads. Travel books are usually more literally autobiographical, in that the sequence is determined by the author's own journey. There have been some great travel books, most of them from the last century or the early decades of this, when the world was new, or at least difficult of access. *Travels with a Donkey in the Cevennes* (Robert Louis Stevenson, 1879)[18] seems a better title than *Travels with a Toyota in the Snowy* (anon, 1986?). In any case, I do not want to write a travel book, but an environmental history.

✳

I still do not know how to do it, but I begin to see how it should be done, and why it is rarely attempted. Half of it is fairly easy – to give a history of land use along the lines sketched out above, linking successive behaviours towards the Snowy lands with major determinants in Australian history, interweaving as much 'natural history' as is needed to make sense of the story. It is the second term in the interaction between man and land that presents intractable difficulties. I can show this influence in minor ways, for instance, the way in which the river and its topography have influenced patterns of settlements. In *Discovering Monaro*, Hancock does not do this. The last section of the book is called 'Two Landscapes' – but there are three landscapes in the Monaro, not two. The third, the Snowy gorge, has not been of much economic significance in this century, so one can see why it was ignored. But it is beyond doubt a third *landscape*, quite different from the other two, as the cover photograph of his book shows well, and its hidden presence exerts a powerful influence, even though it is not obvious. The presence of the gorge has in fact determined the settlement patterns and communication routes. It is skirted by a great arc of settlement and roads from Cooma south and east to Bombala, and south again to Delegate and Bonang, which is also the main link south to Orbost. It is a long way round, but the direct route south down the

Barry Way is inevitably much slower. The country within the great loop of the river is an island; its relatively limited accessibility has isolated it from the forces of change, and it therefore belongs in part to an earlier phase of history. This is even more marked in the small valleys that run to the river, pastoral fingers that probe the edges of the gorge, with only one exit, back to the palm from which they diverge.

That, at least, is the current effect of the gorge, but one of the most striking features of life in the Monaro is obscured by it. The current pattern is that of the motorised world. In the days of the horse, the river could be forded – most of the time – at a number of well-known and much-used crossings, from *El Paso* to *Ironmungie* south to the mouth of the McLaughlin and the Quidong, Burnt Hut, Warm Corner, and so on round to Slaughterhouse Creek, Gattamurh and Sandy Creek. These crossings were used for routine travel and to move cattle. Life was lived much nearer the river than it is now, because it was the only certain source of water in the dry months; and, of course, by crossing it one could greatly reduce the length of journeys (Bill Wroe had 25 kilometres to ride from *Spion Kop* to Delegate across Burnt Hut Crossing; it is more than 150 kilometres by car by way of Dalgety and Bombala).

It is also easy enough to show how the varying geology, soils and aspect of different parts of the region have created different opportunities, almost to the point of geological determinism – the soils derived from granites, basalts, diorites and limestone are used for grazing, while the soils derived from the Snowy River Volcanics, and generally those from the Ordovician shales and quartzites, are lean and hungry, rarely cleared. The boundaries of settlement correspond precisely with the geological boundaries.

This is worth pointing out, but it is the fine tuning of land use and its explanatory reach is limited. To say, as I have done, that primary land use around the Snowy has been determined by forces outside the region is almost to say that there is no second term, that the land has had little influence on us, that we have not listened to it, cannot comprehend it within our culture. I may seem, in short, to have built up a good case for not writing a book at all, to have shown that there is no subject, only an object. But that, in a way, is my subject. We do not own the Snowy River. It runs through an unwanted corner of the continent we have invaded. At best, our rights are custodial. True possession must be earned: that is possession by the imagination.

Notes

1   In the original essay Seddon acknowledged that he began to explore these ideas while he was a Fellow at the Human Research Centre at the Australian National University. Several of his colleagues made useful suggestions on a first draft, notably Ross King and David Evans of the School of Environmental Planning, the University of Melbourne; and Dennis Jeans of the University of Sydney. [A.G.]

2   In a recent paper in *Search*, 'environmental history' is used in a legitimate but quite different sense. Consider the following: 'Studies of recent environmental history, based on established geological and palaeo-ecological techniques, can be used to extend historical and instrumental records, to provide information, otherwise unobtainable, on long-term changes and rare events and to give multiple examples of environmental interactions' (R.J. Wasson and R.L. Clarke, *Search*, vol. 16, no. 9–12, 1985, p. 258). The 'recent' of this sentence is that of the geologist, and includes some thousands of years. Changes over this period may be in part man-made, but most of them will be due to natural causes such as climatic change. The emphasis is therefore on the physical changes themselves rather than on the human agents of change.

3   J. Flood, *The Moth Hunters: Aboriginal Prehistory of the Australian Alps*, Australian Institute of Aboriginal Studies, Canberra, 1980.

4   I have found some by direct enquiry, but I know of no detailed demographic study that goes beyond the work of Hancock (1972, p. 82, p. 112 and passim).

5   E. Mandel, *Late Capitalism*, New Left Books, London, 1975; M. Berry, 'The Political Economy of Australian Urbanisation' in D. Diamond and J.B. McLaughlin (eds), *Progress in Planning*, vol. 22, part 1, Pergamon Press Ltd, Oxford, 1984.

6   Sir W.K. Hancock, *Discovering Monaro: A Study of Many's Impact on His Environment*, Cambridge University Press, Cambridge, 1972.

7   Rev. W.B. Clarke, *Research into the Southern Goldfields of New South Wales*, Macmillan, Melbourne, 1860, p. 119.

8   Clarke, p. 123.

9   W.H. Ferguson, 'Report on Geological Survey of Snowy River Valley', *Geological Survey of Victoria Progess Report No. 11*, 1899.

10 A.L. Hunt, 'Down the Snowy by Canoe', *Sydney Mail*, 21 and 28 July, 4 and 11 August 1937, to which Klaus Hueneke drew my attention.

11 Hunt, 21 July, p. 51.

12 Hunt, 21 July, p. 51.

13 Hunt, 28 July, p. 15.

14 quoted in L. Wigmore, *Struggle for the Snowy: The Background of the Snowy Mountains Scheme* (Oxford University Press, Melbourne, 1968), p. 194.

15 Hancock, *Discovering Monaro*, p. 12.

16 Hancock, *Discovering Monaro*, p. 14.

17 E. Rolls, *A Million Wild Acres: A History of the Pilliga Scrub*, Thomas Nelson, Melbourne, 1981, p. 267.

18 Robert Louis Stevenson, *Travels with a Donkey in the Cevennes*, Roberts Bros., Boston, 1879.

7

———

CUDDLEPIE AND
OTHER SURROGATES

1988

AMONG THE WORDS THAT EUROPEANS HAVE USED to describe their sense of the Australian landscape, 'hostile', 'indifferent' and 'alien' are common. Of course the landscape was not, and is not, literally hostile, but it is literally indifferent to human emotion, and was certainly felt to be alien by the first settlers, and still is to some later ones. To make ourselves more at ease, more at home, in this landscape, we have used a variety of devices to build bridges between man and the natural environment. These devices are not peculiar to us, but some of their Australian exemplifications are.

One class of these devices I shall call, for the sake of a name, anthropomorphs. They are human constructs that aim to humanise the natural world, or at least link the two worlds. […] A prime example of anthropomorphs comes from May Gibbs. Born Cecilia May Gibbs in Cheam Fields, Surrey, on 17 January 1877, her parents had both attended the Slade School and had therefore had some training in art. They emigrated to South Australia in 1881 when May was four years old. They tried farming at Franklin Harbour, and failed, so her father became a draftsman for the Lands Department in Adelaide. He next took up land with a group, including his brother George, at Harvey in south-western Western Australia, but gave up in 1887 and went to Perth, where he first farmed at Lake Claremont. In 1889, he joined the Lands Department again as a draftsman, where he spent the rest of his working life. After a short time in a house on Murray Street in Central Perth, the family moved to 'The Dune' in South Perth, which then remained her parents' home for the rest of their lives.

In 1900, May made the first of three return visits to England (with her mother, with whom she fought on and off), and took art lessons at Chelsea Polytechnic. She returned to Perth at the end of 1901, where she got a few assignments as an illustrator, but was unhappy and returned to London in 1904. She was back in Perth in 1905, and worked for the *Western Mail*. She escaped to Uncle George's farm at Harvey as often as possible, and this formed a major part of her early 'bush' background. She returned to London yet again in 1907 – at the age of thirty-two, and again with her mother. She was employed by Harrap and Co for book illustrations, and met Rene Heames, who became her lifelong companion. Mother disapproved of Rene. The trio returned to Australia, first to Perth, but Rene and Cecie (May's mum) clashed, so the two young women went to Sydney, and set up house at Neutral Bay. May prospered in Sydney, won contracts with Angus & Robertson and the *Sydney Mail*, and established herself as an illustrator. She lived in Sydney for the rest of her life, where she died in 1969 at the age of ninety-two, by which time she was the author and artist of eight children's books and innumerable comic strips. She kept 'Bib and Bub' going until 1967, her ninetieth year.

She kept in touch with South Perth, and made several return journeys by sea, including a long holiday in 1918, which culminated in 1919 with her marriage to Mr J.O. Kelly, a well-educated and charming Irishman, more than ten years her senior – May was then forty-two – virtually penniless and virtually without occupation. He became her business manager, duties he performed indifferently, and remained a man-about-town. May was the breadwinner. They were married at the registry office in Perth during Easter in 1919, spent their honeymoon in Northam – where the bride absentmindedly signed the hotel register as 'May Gibbs' – and returned to Sydney. After six weeks in a hotel, they moved into a flat in Neutral Bay, where they were joined by Rene and Rachel, another long standing woman friend of May.

Her character is obscure, and it scarcely emerges from her only biography (by Maureen Walsh, 1985), other than that she was shy, strong-minded, unconventional and a shrewd business woman who managed to screw a 15 per cent royalty out of one publisher, the usual rate at the time being 10 per cent. However, this was probably simple economic necessity – she had to provide for a household of three or four for much of her working life.

Her best known book by far was *Snugglepot and Cuddlepie*, published by Angus and Robertson in 1918. It has never since been out of print. The gumnut babies had made their first unobtrusive appearance in 1913, incorporated in two separate publications. Soon after, she designed the gumleaf book mark, which is still on sale (I often use it as a token gift when travelling overseas):

> I thought of the Australian gumleaf, which was an ideal shape for a book mark and a pretty thing. If only I could make it interesting on both sides. In the middle of the night I awoke, and, in fancy, saw peeping over a long gumleaf, a little bush sprite with a gumnut on its head. I hand painted them and Lucy Peacock of the Roycroft Library sold them for me at 5s each. They became so popular, later we printed them and sold thousands for 6d each.[1]

She has given the gumnut babies dual citizenship in memory:

> It's hard to tell, hard to say, I don't know if the bush babies found
> me or I found the little creatures. Perhaps it was memories of
> West Australian flowers and trips to Blackheath.[2]

This is an interesting comment, and the evidence of the illustrations suggests that it is very exact. Her drawings are not generalised, but a precise record of the flora and fauna of the Hawkesbury Sandstone (Blackheath is in the Blue Mountains near Katoomba), preconditioned by an equally close familiarity with the flora of south-western Australia. These two flora are very closely related, given the distance that separates them, both very rich, and matched all down the line with the same genera and paired species. There is nothing else quite like them in Australia. The most surprising thing about May Gibbs is that she is such a fine naturalist. There is no trace of this in her background in South Perth or her trips back and forth to art school in London, and her biographer does not address the question. It was something of a Western Australian tradition for cultivated young ladies, from Georgiana Molloy to Barbara York Main and Rica Erickson, but she must also have had opportunity and some tutelage – perhaps from Uncle George at Harvey, but not, one would think, from her parents, whose culture seems to have been of the provincial salon.

Her gumnut babies seem to me to be primarily based on the marri, *Corymbia calophylla*, which has an exceptionally large, woody fruit (the gum nut), and long dark green, glossy, curving leaves with a prominent, reddish midrib, red leaf stalk, and 'fine regular parallel veins at 50–70° from the midrib. Intramarginal vein close to the margin'. These are all characteristic of the bloodwood group of eucalypts, including *C. ficifolia*, the red-flowering gum of south-western Australia, indigenous only on the south coast, but widely planted, with a nut even bigger than the marri. On the east coast, the red bloodwood (*C. gummifera*) is common on the Hawkesbury

Sandstone, and the spotted gum (*C. maculata*) is also very common along coastal New South Wales. But I think her gum nuts are based on the marri, such a distinctively beautiful tree around Harvey, the memory reinforced by *C. ficifolia* and the Sydney bloodwoods.[3]

The Banksia Men are certainly Western Australian, on the author's own authority:

> The Banksia Men arrived in this way. When I was out walking, over in Western Australia, with my cousins, we came to a grove of banksia trees, and sitting on almost every branch were these ugly little, wicked little men that I discovered and that's how the Banksia Men were thought of.[4]

Botanically, they fit fairly well with the large cobs of *Banksia grandis* common on the Swan Coastal Plain (or at least it used to be: Banksias have proven highly susceptible to *Phytophthora* infection around Perth). However, several banksias have similar cobs including the Saw Banksia, *Banksia serrata*, which is common around Sydney. The wiry, curling black hairs in which the body is covered are the twisted pistils of withered flowers. Only a few of these flowers are successfully fertilised. and these warty dry fruits or follicles make up the eyes, ears, nose and other features of the Banksia Men.

May Gibbs' comment that the image was formed in the West is illuminating on three counts. That she was out 'with my cousins' indicates that she was at Harvey, since her father's brother George was the only relative in Australia. That she had identified the Banksia Men shows that the anthropomorphic leap had been made well before she moved to Sydney; and that she saw the Banksia Men as wicked shows that she had invented that imaginative polarity of forces that drives the action of her narrative. In other words, all the primary ingredients of *Snugglepot and Cuddlepie* came from the West. Indeed, she must have become a naturalist at Harvey; she could not have done so living in inner Sydney with occasional train trips to Blackheath. Her knowledge of marine biology, which is evident in *Little Ragged Blossom and More About Snugglepot and Cuddlepie*, published in 1920, was also probably derived largely from the Swan estuary and Indian Ocean, although again reinforced by Sydney's coast. *The Medical Journal of Australia* reviewed this book somewhat unexpectedly:

> Apart from her charming humour and style, Miss Gibbs is a naturalist of class. She knows every leaf and twig of the Australian bush and judging from her knowledge of sea cornets, anchovies, anemones and the like, she would seem to have spent at least half her life down in the mysterious deep.
>
> The whimsical illustrations compete for supremacy with the text.
>
> Some of them are in colour, but all of them bring a sparkle of merriment into the eye and a chuckle into the throat. We wish this delightful little volume a happy voyage into every Australian home.[5]

One other incident seems drawn directly from Perth: Snugglepot and Cuddlepie pay a visit to White City; 'they had honey sticks and dew drinks at the refreshment stall. They went on the switchback over and over again.'[6] White City was a generic term for amusement parks with their canvas tents, and there was one in Sydney near Trumper Park in Paddington, but that was remote from Neutral Bay. 'White City' in Perth was at the foot of William Street, just across the water from South Perth, and by the ferry terminal.

If the genesis and perhaps the mood of her work are Western Australian, much of the detail is clearly not. Mr Kookaburra appears, for instance, and koala bears, neither of which were native to the West, although both have been introduced. There are many distinctive plants of the Sydney region, such as the scribbly gum, *Eucalyptus haemastoma,* which turns out to be the bush newspaper, or the New South Welsh Christmas Bell, *Blandfordia grandiflora.*[7]

The first book is like all the later books. It is full of inventive humour – like Lilly Pilly, for example, and her father, Mr Pilly. There are some good one liners, such as the following dialogue between Snugglepot and Ragged Blossom:

'I'm sorry I've no clothes,' he said. 'Where I come from they don't wear any.'

'That doesn't matter,' said little Ragged Blossom. 'It's better to be a kind Nut with no clothes than an unkind one all dressed up.'[8]

– sentiments which one might expect to hear on Swanbourne beach in the 1980s, but not from a Victorian maiden lady. She was clearly a conservationist well before her day, a trait which shows itself repeatedly, for example in the story and illustration of the possum caught in a trap[9], but she is too good a naturalist to talk about reverence for life – in fact, she is very off-hand about death and killing, both of which occur with some frequency in the book. At the very beginning of the story, a greedy Owl had carried off Snugglepot, thinking he had got a tasty pink mouse. When he saw his mistake he dropped Snugglepot, who fell through the window of an Ant's house.

A tired night-nurse saw him coming, but before she could do anything he had crashed in and killed several babies. This was a blessing for Snugglepot, but it was sadly hard on the baby ants.

'I'm so sorry,' said Snugglepot.

'It can't be helped,' said the Nurse.

'What will their mother say?' asked Snugglepot, brushing tears from his eyes.

'She won't know,' said the Nurse, 'we have three hundred babies in the house.'[10]

One ant more or less would hardly be noticed. The book is full of violence, but it is all narrated in an amused, matter-of-fact tone. Snugglepot and Cuddlepie sit on Mrs Fantail's eggs, go to sleep and break them all. Mr Lizard kindly brings a couple of replacements, but they turn out to hatch two young lizards. Mrs Snake is cast as a villain, along with the Banksia Men, but even she is not *really* villain-ous – snakes are merely snakes. Snakes eat small birds and frogs. The Kookaburra eats snakes. This calm and clear-eyed acceptance of eco-logical reality is one of the remarkable features of the book, greatly in advance of English children's books of a similar vintage, and it has occasioned both praise and blame.

'One day I received a letter, a very angry letter, saying that it was wicked to make drawings of these Banksia Men to frighten the lives out of children. He'd torn the page out of my book where Banksia Men were on it, and scribbled it all out and dashed it with a heavy pencil, and wrote me a very nasty letter.

I think getting accustomed – I mean, children getting accus-tomed – to ugly things like Banksia Men and that sort of thing, it strengthens them if anything, and then they find that they're not all bad, things are not so bad as they seem.'[11]

Most critics of children's books today would support her:

Gibbs has a firmer grasp on the grimmer realities of life for a five year old and for us over-fives, than comparable English writers such as A.A. Milne and Beatrix Potter. The dangers and nasty characters the intrepid bushbabies face emerge from darker regions of the subconscious than Milne's 'Heffalump' or the foxes and Farmer MacGregors in Beatrix Potter. The giant squid and giant octopus, dark holes and spiders, snakes and Banksia men of *The Complete Adventures of Snugglepot and Cuddlepie* focus on strangely recognisable images; the unspoken and nameless horrors of childhood. Not the least of May Gibbs' achievements is the way, however unintentionally, she releases and copes with these images from the collective unconscious of children.[12]

The humorous control is the main feature of all these books, and they seem very sane to me. May Gibbs' own life certainly raises some questions, and there is one feature of her illustrations that is almost obsessive – the presence, on almost every page of every book, of bare babies bottoms, nearly all males (the girls had stamenoid skirts, although these tended to ride up behind, too). Most good children's books have come from men and women who were not cast in the common mould, and May Gibbs is one of them.

This sample of anthropomorphs leads to no easy conclusion, since the primary question is 'What are they for?', and that is not easily answered, although there are some partial answers. They are a survival into the present of an animistic world view that may still have some value in the processes of growing up, by familiarising the unfamiliar, for children. They may have prophylactic value in giving names to nameless terrors. The most memorable children's books seem to do this – the Banksia Men belong to the same genus as the Red Queen in *Alice in Wonderland*. 'Off with her head' is also under comic control, so the delicious thrill of induced terror can be enjoyed in safety. Snugglepot and Cuddlepie themselves belong in a slightly different category, along with teddy bears: they are comforting surrogates for maternal protection, although by inversion. The child reassures teddy, and is thus reassured, and in like manner shows protective concern for poor little Cuddlepie. In short, these are all coping devices.

As for 'reverence for life' and 'conservation' – these phrases are vacuous as general terms. Life consists endlessly in making choices, rarely simple or easy ones, and the art, skill and ethical achievement of a life well lived consists in making more good choices than bad ones. May Gibbs does not show 'reverence for life', but she exposes cruelty and teaches a familiarity with the bush that is more likely to breed respect than contempt.

Notes

1 M. Walsh, *May Gibbs: Mother of the Gumnuts*, Angus and Robertson, Sydney, 1985, p. 96.

2 Walsh, p. 95.

3 *Corymbia species* were classified as *Eucalyptus* until 1995, so all of the *Corymbia* species mentioned here appear in the original essay as *Eucalyptus*. *Corymbias* are still eucalypts, even though they're longer *Eucalyptus*. [A.G.]

4 Walsh, p. 106.

5 In Walsh, pp. 121–122.

6 May Gibbs, *Snugglepot and Cuddlepie*, Angus and Robertson, Sydney, 1918, pp. 15–16.

7 Gibbs, p. 9; Walsh, p. 4.

8 Gibbs, p. 20.

9 Gibbs, p. 22.

10 Gibbs, p. 7.

11 In Walsh, p. 106

12 In Walsh, pp. 106–108.

8

—

THE NATURE OF NATURE
1991

THE PROBLEMS IN UNDERSTANDING HOW WE ascribe meaning to a key word like 'Nature' are deeply embedded in our cultural history – from which, of course, the word derives its complex of meanings, as with all words. We might begin with a warming-up exercise familiar to philosophers. What are the antonyms to Nature and the Natural? With what is it in contrast? The major ones are as follows: the natural and the supernatural (or the Divine); the natural and the unnatural; the natural and the human (as in Man and the Biosphere, or Man and the Environment, so that Nature becomes everything that is Not-Man). Finally, there is the natural and the artificial. Wool is a natural fibre, nylon is an artificial one, although both are man-mediated, as is even more obvious when we think of the advertising campaign claiming that sugar is a natural food and all those television advertisements showing waving fields of golden sun-flowers or whatever, about to be processed into margarine. Logically, butter and margarine are equally synthetic or equally natural, but the difference in feeling about the two shows clearly that we are already beyond the bounds of logic.

The first of the meaning-pairs (The Natural–the Supernatural) has first place in the history of western thought and it is still very powerful,

120

but it is no longer the primary contrast. The view that Nature was inferior to Super Nature, the Supernatural, the Divine world, co-existed with its opposite, that Nature itself is Divine, through most of the Middle Ages and beyond, while the view that Nature is an expression of Divine creative power has persisted to the present day. Contempt for the natural world – the contemptus mundi – was exemplified by the lives of the saints; in its extreme form, it denied value to the natural world, to the self, and to all pleasure, especially sexual pleasure.

However, this attitude was never uncontested. Since God was creator, and the Perfect Being, then his creation might be seen as Perfect, and the natural world, it might be argued, was fit, not for contemptuous dismissal, but for study and delight. These opposites were to an extent, reconciled by the concept of the Great Chain of Being. 'Everything, or nearly everything, that existed was thought of as necessarily existing, but as graded in value. The further away from God, the lower the value.'[1] Nature constituted an artistic order. Sir Thomas Browne puts it splendidly: 'Natura nihil agit frustra' [Nature does nothing in vain] 'is the only indisputable axiom in philosophy; there are no grotesques in nature, nor any thing framed to fill up empty cantons and unnecessary spaces'.[2] His reasons, however, are not ours: Nature does nothing in vain because it fulfils God's purposes, which are wholly focused on Man. God made the ants to teach us industry and thrift, the bees to teach us the principles of social order. That is what they are for.

That Nature partakes of the Divine is also a component of many non-Judeo-Christian theologies, especially in Asia, and also of the animistic world view of the Australian Aborigine and other groups, and to the extent that we see God revealing himself through Nature, it may also be a component of Christian theology. These are deep waters, but before we strike out for the shore we should note that the romanticisation of Nature as partaking of Divinity is a major component of popular culture today – and it is very common among idealistic students. It is expressed in phrases such as 'interfering with Nature' (which is supposed to be a bad thing to do) or 'Design with Nature' (which is supposed to be a good thing to do); and of course, in the more basic and long-lived phrases such as 'Mother Nature' and 'Nature Knows Best', beloved of the homeopaths. The trouble with all these phrases is not that they are wrong, but that they are fuzzy-minded. They all express a grain of wisdom, but a wisdom that is applicable in some situations, and not in others. As with all slogans, they do not carry with them any instructions that indicate when they should be used – criteria of application and misapplication. Consider 'Nature Knows Best' (presumably because Mother knows Best). As a general warning against interventionist medicos who have an inbuilt tendency to overtreat, this is wise. As advice to parents of a child with acute appendicitis, it is dangerous folly. Let nature take her course, indeed – as it did in a recent unnecessary death in the USA.

Consider 'Design with Nature'. As general advice to a society which has so often turned to engineering and technological solutions to biological and social problems, this is again wise advice. But there are just as many circumstances in which Nature is inimical to our purposes, and we therefore design against her (if one cares for this turn of phrase, which I don't). Think of Venice. For over one thousand years, the Venetians opposed natural forces with brilliant success. They needed the Venetian lagoon to remain at a constant depth. If it had grown deeper, the city would have drowned (as it is now doing). If it had become shallower, they would have lost the security that preserved them from invasion through all those many centuries. But lagoons are naturally ephemeral features of the earth's surface, normally filled in by sedimentation – and the Venetian lagoon was fed by three big, fast rivers rushing down from the

Dolomites and the Alps. So they took to pick and shovel and diverted all three rivers in a masterwork of engineering control. They did not Design with Nature – that would never have been possible. But they had a profound understanding of natural processes, and that is the real point – an understanding lost only in this century, when the deep water channels were cut through the shallow lagoon to the industrial Porto Marghera, thus dramatically changing the tidal flux and initiating major erosion.

Another version of Nature as partaking of the Divine was a component of the Romantic Revival. Wordsworth is full of it, although his version of Nature takes meaning largely from his detestation – in most moods – of London, The Great Wen, as Cobbett called it, a cancerous growth. For Wordsworth, Nature included agricultural landscapes, country folk and children. He did not draw our current distinction between 'natural' and 'cultural' landscapes: his primary distinction was between the 'natural' and the urban. In North America, Walt Whitman shared somewhat similar sentiments, but the Divinity of Nature is perhaps most fully expressed by the national parks movement and the language of John Muir and some early members of the Sierra Club. The mood is caught by the superb photographs of W.H. Jackson, and later, Ansel Adams. As David Lowenthal, one of our most subtle cultural-historical geographers has pointed out, Americans were acutely conscious in the nineteenth century that their continent lacked the great cathedrals and other architectural treasures of Europe, so they sanctified their natural monuments instead: The Grand Canyon and Old Faithful and Muir Woods and Yosemite were older and grander expressions of the sublime than anything Europe could show. We have constructed an 'Ayers Rock' cult in the same vein.

The view that Nature is Divine or Holy co-existed with and was in part reaction to its opposite: the view that Nature is the Enemy.

This has always been a part of the popular culture, with good rea-son, because ordinary people have always been the most vulnerable to the vagaries of natural forces. It has had strong expression in the high culture in periodic mode, like Halley's Comet. The two moods co-exist, but one is now in the ascendant, then the other, depending on a whole range of associated shifts in cultural mood.[3] Nature as the Enemy is expressed in phrases like 'Taming Nature' (of which we have done a good deal in Australia), or 'harnessing' a natural resource, such as the wind, or the tides, which are like a wild horse before we introduce the bit. The popular culture is rich in such phrases, and the gardening columns are full of them. 'Untidy trees' for example, or trees that have a 'poor habit', usually said of poor old *Eucalyptus macrocarpa*, and pruning to retain 'a good form' and so on. All of these suggest that Nature at the very least is undisciplined, and much in need of our control.

An interesting variant of the 'Nature is Hostile' theme is to be found in much natural history discourse of the David Attenborough kind. Imagine him – as one easily can – on the top of a high, windy snow-swept mountain, or in Tierra del Fuego or the middle of the Sahara, enthusing over some plant or animal and its ability to survive in what he calls 'this very harsh environment'. The truth, of course, is that since the plant or animal is adapted to that environment, it is not at all harsh for it: it is at home. But take that plant from the Sahara and put in in your temperate zone garden, and water it and fertilise it; it will almost certainly die. That is the harsh environment for that plant.

The view that nature is undisciplined and in need of control lies deep, and can lead to striking inconsistencies. I discovered one in myself recently. I regard myself as ecologically enlightened, but I still don't like to see dead wood on trees in my garden, and I hate to see my *Eucalyptus erythrocorys* disfigured with lerp. Yet I love birds.

A young ecologist a few weeks ago pointed out that lerp are good: they bring insects and the insects bring the birds. So I am learning to love lerp. After all, 'it's natural'.

However, the antonym pairs that seem to me to underwrite most current discourse using the word 'Nature' are 'natural–unnatural' and 'the natural' and 'the human', in which Nature is NOT-MAN. The idea of the 'unnatural' has been around for a long time, and although it grades into the 'Nature Knows Best' nexus of meanings, it usually carries specifically moral overtones, as in 'Sodomy is an unnatural practice'. That not many people use that expression today does not mean that the concept of the 'unnatural' has disappeared, but rather that its range of application has changed. Some will now say, for example, that celibacy is unnatural, or that it is not natural for a young girl to lock herself away in her room reading books all day, or whatever. The point, of course, is that what we consider to be 'natural' and 'unnatural' changes through time. Our concept of Nature is a cultural product.

This leaves me with what is today the most elementary meaning of Nature: the non-human world – it is in this sense that we talk of the conservation of nature, and understanding natural systems (a phrase I have used myself already). We could hardly communicate without some such distinction, since we could not talk about an undifferentiated cosmos, and one of the most basic distinctions is between the US and the NOT-US. Yet there are some major problems with this distinction.

It may be surprising to learn that this sense of the words 'Nature' and 'the natural world' are of fairly recent origin. Michel Foucault has suggested that the landmark is the publication in 1657 by Jonston of a natural history of quadrupeds. He uses this date to mark the birth of natural history. Before that date, there were just histories, for example, a *History of Serpents and Dragons* by Aldrovandi, or *An Admirable History of Plants* by Duret. Up to and including Aldrovandi:

History was the inextricable and completely unitary fabric of all that was visible of things and of the signs that had been discovered or lodged in them: to write the history of a plant or an animal was as much a matter of describing its elements or organs as of describing the resemblances that could be found in it, the virtues that it was thought to possess, the legends and stories with which it had been involved, its place in heraldry, the medicaments that were concocted from its substance, the foods it provided, what the ancients recorded of it, and what travellers might have said of it. The history of a living being was that being itself, within the whole semantic network that connected it to the world.[4]

The distinction that we make so easily between the knowledge derived from direct observation, that from reliable secondary sources, and that from sources that we regard as legendary or fabulous, did not exist. Thus the essential difference between Jonston and Aldrovandi is not that Jonston knew more. In a sense he knew less. The difference lies in what he left out.

The whole of animal semantics has disappeared, like a dead and useless limb. The words that had been interwoven in the very being of the beast have been unravelled and removed: and the living being, in its anatomy, its form, its habits, its birth and death, appears as though stripped naked.[5]

There has been a further change within our own times. Most of us now wish to see ourselves as a part of Nature, and this new sense of the interdependence of all living systems and their further dependence on physical cycles is a significant intellectual advance – but of course it undercuts the dualism of Man and the Biosphere or Man and Nature! Those signs on freeways, fairly common in Australia, that read 'Animals prohibited on this freeway' now seem comic, although we know that 'animals' means 'horses', and excludes ourselves.

Another aspect of this distinction is one of the enduring puzzles of philosophy, usually approached in the philosophy schools through an introduction to Locke, Berkeley and Hume. To parody the debate, which is all I have time for, Locke was a champion of the newly emerging scientific methods, based on observation and measurement. He was called an empiricist, and later, a realist, in that he believed that there is a real world out there, which we can learn about scientifically, while all the learned, wordy, theoretical debates were a waste of time: we should bum the books. But Bishop Berkeley, labelled an 'idealist', asked an unanswerable question. How do we know that there is a real world out there? All we have are our perceptions. We can never know what corresponds to them 'out there'. There may be no 'out there'. Thus the distinction between 'US' and 'NOT-US' is fallacious. Dr Johnson asserted the reality of the external world by kicking a table, thus splendidly missing the point, but nevertheless reaffirming the common sense of the ages. William Blake asks the Berkeleyan question, in poetic form:

'How do you know but ev'ry Bird that cuts the airy way
Is an immense world of delight closed by your senses five'.

The answer, of course, is that you don't, and can't, although as I watch a willy wagtail on my lawn, I wonder. To me, he seems to be playing and enjoying it immensely. He is also catching insects, and setting them up with his rapid movements, and perhaps courting an unseen mate. You can say I am projecting my own feelings onto his behaviour to say also that he is playing, enjoying himself. But you can't prove that he is not playing, and I can't prove that he is.

The battle between the idealist and the realist philosophers has not been settled, but the common sense view that there is a world external to ourselves continues to be held by ordinary mortals. Just what that world might be, however, has become increasingly uncertain over the years. We now know, for instance, that very few animals share our binocular colour discriminating vision; many organisms quite literally see a different world. One of the most conceptually sophisticated of contemporary landscape architects, the Frenchman Bernard Lassus, once began a talk with the following story, reported by a well-known French anthropologist:

> An African tribe was brought out of the dense jungle in which they had lived all their lives, in what used to be called French Equatorial Africa. When they came to the clearing, they at first tried in vain to shakes hands or clasp the arms in greeting, of people who were in fact many metres distant from them. In the dense jungle, if you could see other people at all, you were very close to them, and they therefore assumed that the figures they saw in the clearing were doll-sized people who were nonetheless very close to them.[6]

Lecturers in psychology sometimes use this story to introduce the study of perception, since it is a striking illustration of the way in which even our most basic perceptions, such as the judging of distances and relative size, which we take to be objective responses to the real world, are in fact conditioned by our prior experience. In a new environment, our prior experience may turn out to be irrelevant or even substantially misleading. Generally, we see what we need to see or want to see. When we go for a drive together, my son sees trees by the roadside, and Hondas, Mercedes, Pulsars and Holden Calais on the road. I see cars on the road, and *Eucalyptus polyanthemos* or

Eucalyptus melliodora by the roadside, and say to myself: ah, dry, stony, shallow hill soils, or deep alluvial loams, as the case may be. We have to learn to see: seeing is not like taking photographs. I still remember clearly how I learned to see zebra in tall grass in Africa. First I saw a little flick, which was a twitch of the tail, and then the zebra came into focus. The South Africans I was with just saw zebra, and if there were two stages in the process of recognition for them, they were so speeded up as to seem instantaneous.

Thus individuals perceive different worlds, and whole cultures do so on a greater scale. Whether or not we are philosophically realist, we are driven towards relativism by discoveries in science, including physics and psychology, and increasingly also by linguistic theory. The old chestnut about the Eskimos having a dozen different words for 'snow' has been around for years, but there are many other examples. The Australian Aboriginals from south-western Australia had about eight different words for 'burning-off', burning the bush, since they did it in different ways, at different times, for different purposes. In short, language structures our map of reality. The new relativism pervades contemporary culture. Semiotics, the theory of signs, for example: signs are susceptible to a range of interpretation. In much literary theory we find 'the text' and 'readings': there is a multiplicity of readings, and although some may be of wider interest than others, we are now wary of using words like 'misinterpretation'. A reading is simply a reading.

Scientists are not immune from such analyses. They strive for what we (usefully) call objectivity by focusing on the measurable and the repeatable and this can achieve a degree of paradigmatic consensus, but they too are a product of cultural conditioning. This is a subject of interest to me, because much natural science shows a bias towards the northern hemisphere, what I call Eurocentrism.[7] I have time only for a couple of examples. One striking example is the odd way in which the Australian flora is fitted to a classificatory system devised in Europe. There are some 600 species of one single genus, *Eucalyptus*, whereas there are only half-a-dozen representatives of one whole family, the Rosaceae, insignificant plants like the bidgee-widgee, *Acaena anserinifolia*. Had the Linnean system of binomial classification been developed in this hemisphere, there can be no doubt that the families would be different. The huge range of what are now the Proteaceae and the Myrtaceae would surely not be lumped into two gross families, while relatively insignificant groups like the rose and the lily would not have been accorded family status. The grass trees were assigned to the lily family for the first 150 years after their discovery by Europeans. They now have family status as the Xanthorrhoeaceae. Dr Laurie Johnson has also proposed a break up of *Eucalyptus* into a number of new genera, but his proposals are slow to be accepted.

Part of the problem is that North America belongs essentially to the same biogeographic province as Eurasia, to which it was linked by land during part of the Pleistocene, as the fauna and flora show (oaks and elms, wolves and bears etc.), and this has tended to confirm the Eurocentric bias of the natural sciences. The point is beautifully illustrated in a short article by Stephen Jay Gould from Harvard, with the title 'What Is Wrong with Marsupials?'[8] The answer, of course, is that there is nothing whatsoever wrong with marsupials, except that they have long been regarded as second rate citizens. From the outset, they were looked on as freaks; the platypus was actually called a 'lusus naturae' [freak of nature], and the first specimen sighted in Europe was regarded with suspicion, the compounded work of a practical joker (a view which, as we have seen earlier, could not have been entertained by Sir Thomas Browne). When it became clear that the marsupials were real enough, Darwinian evolution became the practical joker, and the following story emerged: Australia and South America were isolated from the great linked land masses of Africa-Eurasia-North America, and so the relatively primitive marsupials carried on in a kind of sheltered workshop, immune from the fierce competition of a free-market ecology prevailing in these more aggressive lands. When a land-bridge was at length established between the Americas, the placental mammals dashed across it, and the backward marsupials of South America were soon displaced by the more efficient placentals. Only in Australia were they able to dodder on.

Those relatively few biologists who have done research in this field tell a quite different story. It is now thought that reproductive differences had nothing to do with the success of North American over South American mammals in the Tertiary. The North Americans would have won out even if they had been marsupials themselves. Their adaptive advantages were in locomotion and feeding characteristics, derived by chance from pre-adaptation – that is, they had already begun to adapt to climatic changes which were felt earlier in North America than in South America. This does not mean that they were more highly evolved, but only that they were better adapted. As for the Australian marsupials of today, the first point is that they are as 'new' or recently evolved as the fauna of all the other continents. They are not ancient relics at all, but post-Pleistocene, a response to climate change, as everywhere else. Only Africa and Asia retained a substantial representation of the Pleistocene megafauna – large animals – that we had and lost; but of course even so the elephant and giraffe and camel are not Pleistocene but Holocene species. They are just a little closer to their ancestors. Our marsupial fauna is nothing like its ancestors.

Moreover, the marsupial fauna of Australia is a miracle of adaptation to an environment that is mostly arid and has very high climatic variability. The amazingly efficient production line of marsupials may involve the presence of three sequential stages of offspring associated with their mother at the same point in time. An almost weaned young kangaroo (a 'joey') may be still going back occasionally to the pouch to suckle, when a newly arrived diminutive sibling can already be in the pouch and while a very early embryo is waiting ('embryonic diapause', a physiological block to development) in the uterus for its turn to grow.

Other evidence that life in the pouch is not a second-class solution for 'unsuccessful' primitive mammals can be found in the degree of sophistication of marsupial milk production. When both older and younger joeys are feeding in the same pouch, the mother is producing two different types of milk: one richer in proteins secreted from the nipple where the younger joey is feeding, and one richer in lipids for the nipple used by the older joey. A four-star catering performance, which makes lactation by 'higher' mammals look like a fast-food line.[9]

*

Whether or not there is a world out there independent of our perceptions of it, we cannot escape the variability of those perceptions. The ways in which we perceive, imagine, conceptualise, image, verbalise, relate to and behave towards the natural world are the product of cultural conditioning and individual variation.

One of the rewards of the study of philosophy is to strengthen our defences against abstract theorising: we should be searching for clarity rather than for theory. The important question usually is 'what do we mean when we say … ?' or 'where have these words been before, and what aspects of our past do they trail behind them?' It is important because linguistic structures are conservative, and they pattern our thinking. The feminists have taught us that we need to struggle to escape sexist language, but that is only one example of cultural bias perpetuated by language. The examples of Eurocentrism are another, but only one of many. Our ethical and our aesthetic pronouncements are probably the most suspect from our present point of view.

For the purposes of this discussion, our current intellectual dilemma, one that has many practical consequences, is that we conceptualise 'Nature' in three ways – ways which are not mutually compatible in logic. They can be crudely located along an axis measured off by degrees of internalising and externalising Nature. At one pole, we see ourselves as a part of Nature, a concept at which we arrive through evolutionary theory. Man is collapsed into the biosphere, rather than set outside it. At the other pole, natural systems are seen as self-regulating and self-maintaining. Extreme forms of this conceptualising are the theory of the Selfish Gene and the theory of Gaia, both of which see Man as of very minor significance in the scheme of things; his pretensions to externality, responsibility and some degree of control are irrelevant. The more common forms, however, are those implicit in much ecological writing, which is preoccupied with 'natural systems', 'the balance of Nature', and so on. Human intervention is conceptualised as disturbance, almost always seen in a negative light, which clearly externalises us from Nature itself. We operate on Nature.

Somewhere in the middle, very uncomfortably sited, is the most common conceptualisation, of Man both as a part of Nature, yet at the same time responsible for managing it. The paradoxes of conservation arise from this uneasy compromise – wilderness areas, for instance, are managed to protect them from 'disturbance', i.e. human intervention, but how? – by human intervention, of course. And, for whom? Well, for us; for 'natural man' rather than 'techno man', but there is still only 'us'. These paradoxes are endemic, and I could give many more examples. Nor are they restricted to the natural sciences. A central preoccupation of physics and also of linguistics, for most of this century, has been the relation between the observer and the observed. There is no securely privileged external viewpoint in physics, and this undercuts all traditional concepts of the very act of observation. In linguistics, we have learned that there is no point outside language from which we can observe language. Hence the poststructuralists began to ask: 'But what is the structure of structure?' and so began deconstruction. As they may, at this very point, begin to ask, 'But, ah! What is the nature of the Nature of Nature?'

NOTES

1   D.S. Brewer (ed.), *The Parlement of Foulys by Geoffrey Chaucer*, Manchester University Press, 1972, p. 28.

2   Sir Thomas Browne, *Religio Medici (1642)*, Clarendon Press, Oxford, 1972, p. 16.

3   Geoffrey Blainey, *The Great See-saw: A New View of the Western World, 1750–2000*, Macmillan, South Melbourne, 1988.

4   Michel Foucault, *The Order of Things: An Archaeology of the Human Sciences*, Tavistock Publications, London, 1970, p. 129.

5   Foucault, p. 129.

6   Bernard Lassus, Five design proposals (1975–1980), translated and introduced by Stephen Bann, in 'The Landscape Approach of Bernard Lassus', *Journal of Garden History*, vol. 3, no. 2, pp. 79–107, 1982, p. 79.

7   George Seddon, 'Eurocentrism and Australian Science: Some Examples', *Search*, vol. 12, no. 12, 1981, pp. 446–450.

8   Stephen Jay Gould, 'What's Wrong with Marsupials?' *New Scientist*, 2 October 1980, pp. 27–28.

9   Piero P. Giorgi, 'What's Wrong with Marsupials' in Giovanna Capone (ed.), *Contributions to Intellectual Life in Australia and Italy*, Longo Editore, Ravenna, 1989.

9

—

VENICE AND THAT
SINKING FEELING

1994

ONE OF THE WORLD'S MOST REMARKABLE achievements in environmental management and urban design is that of Venice and the Venetian Republic. It is a great story of adaptation – by men to the exigencies of a special and in many ways very difficult environment, and also of the adaptation of the environment itself to man's own special needs, which in this case included an insatiable thirst for quality in the city buildings – all of them, not just those of the wealthy.

All the world recognises the beauty of Venice, but the long, sustained effort to adapt and manage the lagoon and its hinterland is not at all well known. It was one of the finest examples of landscape planning in the broad sense for well over 1000 years. Only in the last 140 years or so have all the lessons been forgotten.

One primary objective, pursued from the thirteenth century onwards, was to stabilise the lagoon. Lagoons are essentially ephemeral features; their usual fate is to be filled in by river-borne sediment. Venice itself is built on the remnants of the delta of the Brenta River, flooded by rising sea-levels at the end of the Ice Age. Over the centuries, the Venetians systematically diverted the rivers (by pick and shovel) to the north and south of the lagoon; the major ones diverted to the south were the Brenta, which delivers more water than the Murray, and the much smaller Bacchiglione, which runs through Palladio's city of Vicenza (my favourite city in Italy); to the north, the Sile, Treviso's delightful little river, and the Piave – another major river, rising in the East Tyrol, and the site of bloody battles during World War I. The ways in which these great engineering feats were executed were ingenious: the Sile, for example was diverted by canal into what had been the bed of the Piave, and then into the sea near Jesolo, while the Piave itself was diverted into the bed of the next river to the north, the Livenza.

The tides could not wholly be regulated – disastrous high tides, *le acque alte*, have occurred sporadically throughout Venetian history – but they were controlled in some measure by strengthening the sea walls of the *lidi*, the sand bars that fringe the lagoon on its seaward side. The many entrances between these *lidi* were in time limited to three; these are the Chioggia, Malamocco and Lido entrances. The sea walls were the last of the great works of the Magistrates of the Waters. They were begun in 1744, took thirty-eight years to complete, and cost some forty million Venetian gold ducats – hardly surprising, since they were built of great blocks of white marble brought from Istria across the Adriatic, the customary Venetian source of marble. These walls are around 5 metres thick at the base, and some 7 metres high, replacing wooden palisades that needed constant repair.

Venetian hydraulic engineering was not perfect, and there were costs, but it worked adequately for most of the history of the Republic. One cost was their elimination of one of the distributaries of the mighty Po, the Po di Tramontana, which emptied into the lagoon north of Chioggia at the southern end of the lagoon. It delivered vast quantities of silt, and was rapidly turning its environs into a *laguna morta*, flooded only at high tides, stinking mud through the rest of the cycle. In five years, thousands of labourers cut the Sacca di Gora, a channel from the Po Grande, the main river distributary, into a bay of the Adriatic east of Pomposa, and water no longer drained through the Po di Tramontana into the lagoon. The results for the lower Po Valley and the Delta were disastrous; silting accelerated, the Delta increased three times in area in two hundred years, and the severity of flooding increased. But none of that worried the Venetians. They had protected their own lagoon.

Perhaps they protected it too well. One school of hydrologists today argue that at least some incoming sediment was desirable, to compensate for the lowering of the lagoon floor consequent on compaction under the weight of centuries of deposition. There certainly is a problem today, but its origins are complex, and the system of management by diversion worked well for nearly one thousand years. It was essential to Venice, and she knew it. She had close at hand the example of Ravenna, a great Roman and Byzantine sea-port, now high and dry. The Venetians, moreover, were sailors, and they knew the great cities along the Aegean coast, such as Ephesus and Miletus, long beached like stranded whales.

The lagoon was her chief defence, and she was never invaded until Napoleon ended the Republic. It was also her only transport system, both externally and internally. Finally, it was her major source of protein: sea-food sustained the Venetians. The level of the tides has always been critical to her functioning, as Ruskin shows so well in *The Stones of Venice*; a few inches lower at low tide and Venice begins to stink, many canals are no longer navigable, and the lower landing steps become intolerably slimy; a few inches higher at high tide and water would come in the doorways, the level becomes too high to get under many of the bridges, and the buildings begin to erode. That is part of what is happening now. Venice may be sinking. It is certainly eroding.

It is besieged by a range of problems. First, there are *le acque alte*, the exceptionally high tides. These are sporadic natural events, a recurrent feature of Venetian history, always destructive and costly. They generally happen when the spring tides or naturally high tides coincide with strong and persistent winds from the south-east – the sirocco – push and funnel the sea water up the Adriatic between Italy and Croatia. The horrific floods of 1966 were of this kind, exaggerated further by exceptionally heavy rain throughout much of northern Italy. The water reached 2 metres higher than normal high tide level, the Piazza San Marco was under water, and waves were breaking against the Ducal Palace. The damage was estimated at forty billion lire.

This was nevertheless an extreme event – recurrent, but infrequent. Various remedies have been proposed, and a good deal of money spent on inflatable barrages, designed to block the three entries of the lagoon when exceptionally high tides threaten. But there are other, less dramatic, but more insidious, problems. One is chemical corrosion, both from sulphur dioxide and other pollutants in the air, which attack the very stones of Venice, and from similar industrial and domestic pollutants in the water and the mud. Venice is built on piles driven into the mud. Great logs cut from chestnut trees have lasted well in the anaerobic environment of the mud, but now it is heavily laced with chemicals which may be beginning to attack the piles.

There was subsidence attributed to the withdrawal of water from some 20,000 deep artesian wells, used to supply the city and industry on the mainland. Many of these wells are now capped and water is supplied by aqueduct. There may also be slow subsidence of the lagoon floor caused by long-term compaction of the great layered wedge of sediment that underlies it. The lagoon floor is certainly being lowered, but whether this has one or several concurrent causes is not clear. It is undoubtedly subject to erosion, and this seems to me to be the key problem.

Why should the lagoon floor be eroding? In brief, because no sediment is coming in to replace the sediment now lost daily by tidal scour. The rivers remain diverted. Sand from longshore drift, which once balanced tidal scour, no longer enters the lagoon because of the long moles protecting the three entrances to the lagoon. And tidal velocity is much greater, because the ship channels have been deepened (Malamocco to 13 metres, the Lido-Giudecca channel to 11 metres). Moreover one quarter of the tidal marshes, which used to dissipate tidal energy, have been filled, for industrial land at Porto Marghera, for the new airport Marco Polo, and so on. Thus more water rushes in and out during the period of the tide, into a significantly reduced lagoon, from which the natural baffles of reed and marsh have been almost eliminated.

Venice conserved and managed its other natural resources as well as it managed the lagoon, and for the same reason – it knew it needed to. The myth of an inexhaustibly bountiful Nature was never a part of the Venetian world view. For instance, it needed a constant supply of good timber for ship-building at the Arsenale, chestnut for the galleys, beech for the oars. Her only reliable sources were the forests above the Canale di Brenta and the Altipiano di Asiago and Monte Grappa, and these forests were conserved with great care throughout the Republic. The forests of Dalmatia also supplied timber, but less reliably. Timber was always in short supply, but that was seen as a reason for conserving it rather than overproducing from a wasting resource. The chestnut forests of the Brenta lasted until after World War II. They were then all felled within twenty years, and are not now regenerating. Fishing was regulated. Stone came from the quarries at Istria and the Euganean Hills, transported through a canal system. Stone is not a renewable resource, but the quarries were regulated.

The country estates with their Palladian villas – such as Villa Barbaro a Maser, the Pisani Villa at Stra, La Malcontenta, both on the Brenta, Villa Contarini, and so on – were well managed, and the estate workers were generally well cared for by the standards of the day.

The city itself and urban life was also well regulated, by the most stable government Europe has ever known, on which the American constitution was substantially modelled. Urban scale was preserved by regulations on building height. Civic and social life were accommodated in the public open spaces – campi – which came in all sizes from the Piazza San Marco to the Piazetta dei Leoni, Campo Luca, Campo Santo Stefano of middling size, and small ones like the Campo San Lio. There were also internal courtyards. These spaces allowed light into the buildings and air circulation, and they collected water in the central well. The markets were well run, and civic administration was at a high level. Venice instituted the census, and maintained it for hundreds of years. Taxes were fair. It was a tolerant city; Venice never burnt a heretic. Its urban services were, and still are in many ways, a marvel of adaptive talent. The taxis, the ambulance, the fire brigade, the police, all go by water.

It was, and still is, mostly a 'hard' landscape, made of stone and water, although there is a surprising number of private gardens full of greenery. (*Magnolia grandiflora* is common, some huge old *Wistaria sinensis* are to be seen and roses do well, too.) Street trees are rare, although the zattere at Dorsoduro are lined with Russian Olive and standard Oleander, almost trees, and years old. There is no *cosmetic* landscaping, and this is perhaps the most important design lesson Venice has to teach. Get the functional relations right, the scale, the spaces, the proportions. They are what create good urban landscape.

Today, it has nearly all gone wrong. The lagoon is heavily polluted and eutrophic, the fishing is in decline, the city is eroding and decaying, the chestnut forests have been felled, the Veneto is subject to a vast monoculture of maize, the sick fields are suffering from an over-dose of superphosphate, so the canals are clogged with green algae, which decay and stink, the very underpinning of the city is under attack, and that splendidly resilient civic pride has gone; all is now geared to the tourists, who swarm like locusts. Mountains of their garbage in its hundreds of thousands of plastic bags is carried out to sea and dumped daily, into that self-same Adriatic to which Venice once renewed her marriage vows yearly with a gold ring, the marriage bed now a garbage dump.

There is adequate knowledge to understand most of these problems and to offer solutions. The eutrophication is due to excessive use of superphosphate on the plains of Lombardy. We have encountered similar problems in some of our estuaries, and tackled them, and are on the way to solving them – in the Peel-Harvey Inlet, for instance. I have explained to the Venetians that we are much better at solving the problems of incompetent agriculture in Australia because we have been practising it longer, while they took it up only after the last war.

Now the Venetians hardly know where to begin, because there is no political–administrative system that corresponds to the plains of Lombardy; an informal association began to emerge only last year, to tackle common problems. But even if it were strong, there is no equivalent in Italy to the field officers of our Departments of Agriculture, who can go the rounds and talk to each farmer. In any case, the current form of agribusiness is itself the outcome of a political system, the EEC, which is heavily protectionist.

The solution to the erosion is to close Porto Marghera or drastically to reduce ship size, to fill in the deep channels, and probably also to re-excavate some of the filled land and to shorten the moles to allow some sediment to be carried in once again by longshore drift. One could even dump sand from barges, but it is always better to harness natural processes where that is feasible. Most Italian ports are suffering from decline. As Europe has turned inwards, transport has moved to heavy lorries – not a wise choice. As the environmental costs become more obvious, there will surely be a new investment in rail-freighting; the passenger trains have already had their renaissance. The ports too may revive one day, but there is no sound future for Porto Marghera.

As for mass tourism – the answer is simple, if difficult to impose. Restrict entry, as we now do to many national parks after determining their carrying capacity. Yosemite is one; even Wilsons Promontory has a strict ration of campsites other than that of Tidal River, and would-be backpackers need to book long in advance to get one of the seven sites at Roaring Meg, for instance. Venice is not the place for Pink Floyd, or for Expo. Happily, she will now be spared the latter. One Pink Floyd was enough.

Can we learn anything from Venice, or is it so special as to be irrelevant to our circumstances? If we acknowledge that Venice is in itself a lesson in urban landscape, we can still ask 'What is the lesson?' We are in part asking about pathways and forces, in part about shared community values, in part about the way in which a shared design framework evolved, to which many could contribute without that restless striving for originality and the immediately distinctive that characterises so much design today. The concentration on the central functional relations is probably the key. Design marginalises itself if it is concerned primarily with palliatives, as it so often is. Words like 'screen' or 'conceal' or 'soften' all indicate this approach. We would not need to 'soften' buildings with trees, for example if we got the buildings and the spaces right. Cities ought not strive to be gardens, or rather, they should strive first to be cities.

Finally, our coastal cities might care to institute the office and the powers of the Venetian Magistrate delle Acque. Listen to his edict:

Whereas the waters of the Venetian lagoon, its channels and marshes and sandbars, are a natural defence to the city, as the moat and city walls of less happy cities, any man who is found to damage them in any way will be considered an enemy of the State, like one who destroys the city walls elsewhere, and will be dealt with by the full severity of the law.

Inscription in bronze on the walls of the Arsenale, erected under the authority and name of the Magistrate of the Waters.

Had Shakespeare read it? Had, at least, John of Gaunt?

This precious stone set in a silver sea
Which serves it in the office of a wall
Or as a moat defensive to a house
Against the envy of less happy lands

Would that he were still empowered to deal with those who have transgressed his edict – with the full severity of Venetian law, that of the Serenissima Republica di Venezia. For Venice was a marvel to the world.

'Venice and That Sinking Feeling' is the second of two parts of a longer essay, 'Two Centres of Excellence in the Mediterranean', extracted from pp. 88–92.

10

____

FAREWELL TO ARCADY, OR GETTING OFF THE SHEEP'S BACK

2003

Sheep and Land Use (All We, Like Sheep, –)

ONE OF THE MISFORTUNES OF AUSTRALIAN colonisation was that the Bigge Commission took place during a period when the geodetic survey and a set of attitudes that went with it was in its ascendancy and Australia was in its infancy. A continent was ruled up by straight lines, even the state boundaries for the most part, ignoring natural features, creating artificial political units and property lines that are often inimical to sensible land management. Most of our farm boundaries are in the wrong place. Early surveyors had little understanding of land capability. That was not their job. Nor, of course, was it to establish what the stocking rates for each land unit should have been. Range management is a recent science which had its beginnings in Utah, followed by the Taylor Grazing Act of 1934 in the USA. Range management in Western Australia had its beginnings in the Pilbara in 1951 (where Henk Suijdendorp began his work), followed in the Wiluna area in 1955 (under David Wilcox). Until very recently there has been no restriction on the number of stock that could be carried on a given lease. In Western Australia, the Land Act of 1912 stated the minimum numbers of stock that should be on the land; there was no instance where maximum numbers were recommended.

Those responsible for allowing settlement in the 'outback' were persuaded by their European heritage that a more or less constant level of production was possible; droughts were perceived as being an intolerable nuisance, but not at all the norm. The administration of the day not only failed to suggest safe stocking rates or best management practices for the land: they did worse in New South Wales and Queensland, where they were bent upon establishing small land holdings under the misguided belief that it was possible to define 'home maintenance units' or 'homestead blocks' 'sufficient to provide for the needs of a man and his family'. In the first half of the twentieth century whole tracts of land were subdivided into grossly inadequate parcels capable, so it was thought, of supporting a man and his family. The obsession with home maintenance units did not extend further, but its legacy is one of severe economic depression and land degradation in the west of New South Wales and south-west Queensland. All the states still suffer under the failure of administration and government to recommend safe stocking capacity and best management practices to lessees, who were left to fend for themselves until the 1960s, and then advice given was largely ignored. It is useful to remember that in talking about leasehold land in Australia, we are talking about half a continent, so the issues are significant.

The millennium is an arbitrary occasion of no natural significance whatsoever, the outcome of several bureaucratic-political decisions based on inaccurate information, in which it mirrors some of our land-use practices. The Catholic Bishop in Perth, Bishop Hickey, wished to celebrate the millennium in October 1999, on what he claimed to be the technically correct date. Putting the millennium to one side, I think most Australians today are nevertheless in reflective mood, ready to look back, assess both our successes and our failures, and ask ourselves what changes we need to put in place for the future. So I now want to put forward a proposition, which is that we not only should, but, in a global context, must concentrate on the things we do well and quit the things we do badly.

The following questions should be asked of every land use in Australia:

- Does it have a high environmental cost?
- Is its product decreasingly competitive on world markets?
- Does it incur significant import costs (e.g. by way of items like superphosphate, farm machinery, diesel)?
- Does it require significant direct or indirect subsidies from the public purse (e.g. high infrastructure costs, such as roads and communications, disaster relief, medical and educational services)?

If the answer is 'yes' to most of these questions then we should seriously consider discontinuing the land use. If we do so, we must then urgently address two other questions:

- What are the social costs for the families practising the land use to be phased out?
- How can a major land use be phased out without accelerating rural depopulation? What alternatives can be generated? (I am strongly supportive of the view that 'Keeping People on the Land' is important, although not necessarily doing what they do now. We need to be highly creative in finding ways of keeping people in rural Australia.)

Getting off the Sheep's Back

The land use that is urgently in need of review in the sub-arid range-lands of Australia is the grazing of sheep on leasehold land. (The grazing of cattle on leasehold land is a different story, and in Western Australia it belongs primarily to the Kimberley rather than to the Pilbara; the product, moreover, is still saleable.) The raising of sheep on pastoral leaseholds is an historic land use, and a great deal of sentiment is attached to it. Many of the pioneering pastoral families showed enterprise and courage, and still do.[1] Many of them also amassed considerable wealth, and retired to mansions in Peppermint Grove, Toorak, Vaucluse and North Adelaide. But that wealth could not have been acquired without a double exploitation: that of cheap labour (Aboriginal) and virtually free land, a public resource used for private gain at negligible cost to the exploiter, but leaving a legacy of costs, by way of rehabilitation, to the future taxpayer.

Sentiment remains strong. Our culture includes images of the drover, the shearing shed, the merino on the face of a coin and, of course, of the swagman. 'Australia rode to prosperity on the sheep's back', the saying goes. We should have got off long ago. The saying never had more than a limited and partial measure of truth; it is better rephrased as 'Australia has enjoyed limited periods of modest prosperity through the near-destruction by sheep of a fragile native vegetation'.

Looking up from the ground, a sheep is four little mobile jack-hammers, pounding to dust the thin skin of an old land that had known only the gentler limbs of the kangaroo. In much of pastoral Australia sheep have caused a loss of both vegetative cover and topsoil that may now be beyond our capacity to repair; the *Oxford-Hammond Atlas* claims that 'About one quarter of Australia's range and crop land has become irreversible desert'.[2] This is an overstatement, as regeneration of the Ord Catchment after destocking shows, with similar results in several other areas, but the damage has nevertheless been great, and 'regeneration' limited to adequate plant cover.

There is still a place for sheep bred for the table, and a specialised market for super-fine wools, both of which can be met from relatively small and robust areas like the Yass Tablelands, parts of Victoria and the Midlands in Tasmania, but the environmental costs of running sheep on the leasehold lands of much of pastoral Australia outweigh current and easily foreseeable future economic returns.

Can we discontinue pastoral land use in the more degraded and/or the less productive areas without depopulating the land? The immediate answer at least for the Pilbara, the area I know best, is very clear: to withdraw the pastoral leases would begin a dramatic improvement in environmental values, but would make very little difference to the population of the Pilbara, and hardly any to its economy. It would be cheaper to pay a few leaseholder families to control vermin, act as firewardens and perhaps run a few of the better homesteads for accommodation than to continue to lease land at 50¢ per hectare, which is only slightly more than half what it costs the state to administer the system ($780,000 costs for a return of $490,000!). The current population of the Pilbara is around 41,000, of which approximately 90 per cent is engaged directly in mining and indirectly in support infrastructures, services and tourism support facilities.

The pastoral industry could not possibly support towns like Newman or Karratha in Western Australia, Broken Hill in New South Wales or Mount Isa in Queensland, and the very expensive roads, airports, electric power and water supplies that sustain them. Tourism has been a valuable by-product of mining, but is viable only if the resource industries pay for and maintain the infrastructure, either directly or indirectly.

The towns such as Newman and Karratha (and Mount Isa) already serve tourists and a slice of the retirement population, who head north in droves every winter, and both these uses could be expanded, especially retirement. The towns might also become a base for research and information industries: some branches of medicine that can best be carried out away from the allergenics and pulmonary irritants of a metropolis; research on the chemical properties of native plants; astronomy; geological and mineral research; production or processing that makes use of the evaporative power of the sun, of which salt production at Dampier is our current example. I want to emphasise here that high-level technological skills are essential to our very survival in this country. None of this would be easy, and it needs creative thinking.

So does the future of quite large areas of Australia, which currently depend on mining. There seems to be no national policy for these areas. If there were, we would be looking critically at what happens to mining royalties and the taxes on the resource companies. They should be earmarked at least in part for helping to create some sort of sustainable future for arid and sub-arid Australia, rather than disappearing without trace into the ever-gaping maw of general revenue. We should be beginning to behave as if we planned to stay in a wide brown land, and not just huddle around its coastal margins.

The Politics of Wool

Libby Robin has explored the history of Australian nationalism built on wool in an outstanding paper, 'Fleecing the Nation': her illuminating window on the past was the wool seminar convened by Sir Keith Hancock that ran in Canberra from 1957 to 1959.[3] In the first half of the twentieth century, the Australian economy had become dependent on a single commodity, the method of marketing was seen as of national significance, and 'the interests of the woolgrowers were "the interests of the nation"'.[4] That these interests had coincided with those of the 'mother country' and were substantially propped up by British investment were so taken for granted that they were seen as immutable, part of the natural order of things, which left Australia extraordinarily vulnerable to a change in the market.

Robin also probes the 'silences' of the wool seminar, taken as a snapshot of widespread attitudes at the time. By the 1950s, the merino was an allegorical key to 'Australian-ness', provided of course that you were of British stock and were white. The merino was said to breed 'pure'. Given concerns at the time about miscegenation in the years of the White Australia Policy, it was not just the Australian economy 'but also a particular type of culture that was riding on the sheep's back'.[5] Such social considerations were excluded from the seminar. The claim about the 'purity' of the stock has also had unfortunate pragmatic and economic consequences. To breed true is to produce offspring with certain characteristics identical to or within a very narrow range of those exhibited by the parents. So it is a very subjective term, contingent entirely on what are considered desirable characters. In strict genetic terms, heterozygote (non-genetically identical) individuals don't 'breed true' even for fibre diameter. Nevertheless, merinos and the other breeds have bred far too pure for their own good. The wool industry has by far the worst record of all Australian animal industries in terms of improvement in desirable characteristics. Milk production has been increased from cows by 300 per cent since 1940, and most of that increase is since 1960. The productivity from chickens and hens has increased by 350 per cent in the same time, whereas the productivity from sheep has grown a meagre 43 per cent since 1900.[6] So to 'breed true' has the implication of fossilising, to fail to improve adaptive fitness, and that is exactly what has happened.

Given the declining terms of trade in agriculture since the mid-1940s (returns increasing at a slower rate that the cost of inputs), to insulate wool growers from these realities through the floor price scheme maintained so assiduously by a small power group of growers was to bring the industry to its knees.

The environmental considerations were also among the 'silences' of the Wool Seminar. That sheep were an alien introduction in the Australian environment could hardly be recognised; the sheep was seen simply as a 'benign fleece-producing machine'.[7] Yet doubts were of long standing: as early as 1847, a son of John Macarthur had questioned those who acted 'as if this fine country had no higher destiny than to continue a sheep walk forever'. By 1937 soil erosion was widely recognised, and Francis Ratcliffe had delivered stinging reports about the overstocked arid-zone leaseholds that were losing topsoil at an alarming rate. Dust storms at times darkened the sun in both Sydney and Melbourne. I can vouch for the latter from personal experience.

Yet the Golden Fleece belonged to a different universe of discourse, and it is now time to explore that discourse, one that generated and has sustained the pastoral myth. If we fail to understand the power of this myth, it is hard to see how a once successful industry has been allowed to become at the same time so destructive environmentally and so uncompetitive economically. For it is the myth that has allowed a small group to insulate the industry from necessary change, to guard it zealously from scientific breeding to suit a variety of physical domains, and from producing wool with qualities tailored to specific purposes. Power has remained in the hands of the families who have owned eight or nine key studs; an oligopoly who have been intensely conservative, jealously protecting their interests even to the extent of influencing research funding that might have had the outcome of weakening their control. So now for the sustaining myth that has allowed such things to happen to us.

Australian Arcady

Et ego in Australia vixisse

The pastoral is one of the most enduring literary forms, and it is also one of the most urban. It has flourished in highly urbanised societies, notably Rome, and from the seventeenth century on in the centralised economies of Western Europe and their capitals such as Paris and London. Australia is one of the world's most highly urbanised societies. It is therefore not surprising to find that it has been powerful here, too, although not so much as a literary form, but rather as a set of attitudes. Without it the success, for example, of an indifferent, even absurd, painter like Norman Lindsay would be inexplicable. So would landscape preferences, still current, that have their origins in the great estates of the eighteenth century built up during the Enclosures in Britain. So would our tolerance as a society of the continuing environmental damage to half of Australia through inadequate rangeland management. So, above all, would be the near-collapse of a wool industry that should still have significant natural advantages, but lost its competitive edge because of a myopic oligopoly in the well-watered south-east of the continent. That the rest of the world would continue to come begging for our wool, at whatever price that seemed attractive to us, turned out not to be one of the eternal verities.

The Greek poet Theocritus is commonly described as a Sicilian or Syracusan, but the date and place of his birth is uncertain, as is the date of his death.[8] But it is known with confidence that he spent most of his adult life in Alexandria at the court of Ptolemy Philadelphos, and that he was at his prime around 270 BC, when Alexandria was considered the largest city in the world, with a population of around one million inhabitants. Diodorus the geographer gives a figure of 300,000 free population, nearly all Greek speaking and usually with

Greek names, although not all of Greek origin. There were usually two or three slaves and other non-citizens for every citizen. He also says of the city that 'it surpassed all others in size, wealth and beauty'. It was undoubtedly the world centre of trade, exporting grain above all, papyrus, a range of medicinal drugs, spices and perfumes, among other things.[9] Its trade dominance was aided by its superb strategic position, with a good sea harbour on the Mediterranean, and equally good access to the Nile Valley and its wealth of produce through Lake Mareotis and a network of freshwater canals.

There is a distinguished and continuing scholarly literature on the pastoral mode.[10] Most scholars agree that there is a high degree of consistency about pastoral poetry and that, for example, Milton's *Lycidas* is 'far closer to its classical models than is, say, Shakespearian tragedy to Sophocles'.[11] Part of its perennial appeal is its escapist quality: it exists in a timeless present and the action is situated in a *locus amoenus*, a pleasant place, not too hot, not too cold, free of flies and mosquitoes, in which the shepherds and shepherdesses, all of course young, comely and healthy, can run around with few or no clothes. The qualities of the pastoral world most commonly cited are its simplicity, leisure and freedom. The latter is a freedom from the ballast of civilisation: 'the life of politics and the public calendar is a prison house',[12] while the shepherds embody a simplicity far removed from the turmoil of the city. 'The pastoral character must be limited in insight precisely because he is free and need not ferret out mysteries or solve problems.'[13]

Pastoral Care in Australia

The Polish explorer or traveller in south-eastern Australia, Dr John Lhotsky, met shepherds – but no shepherdesses – on his travels in 1834.

He came across them, always alone with their flocks, in the Upper Murrumbidgee area (south of Michelago in the southern Australian Capital Territory). There is a sorry account of a convict shepherd dressed in rags because his master had failed to supply him with the 'slops' (clothing) required by the government:

> In this lonely place we were met by a prisoner, belonging to a neighbouring station, who, barefooted and covered with rags, reminded me forcibly that I was in a land of banishment and expiation. I asked him how he came to be so badly off, he replied that the slops were issued very irregularly, and was besides of the very worst description. He was also all over affected with the Syphilitic disorder and told me that many men were in the same situation, without any surgeon at hand. I shook my head, as it appeared to me as if some demon sentenced to perdition was addressing me in this valley of desolation.[14]

Lhotsky goes on to say that 'As I was now beyond the limits of the colony, I found myself quite in a new situation, even so far as social life is concerned. I had lived before under absolute monarchies and under commonwealths; here I found myself surrounded by absolute anarchy and lawlessness'. He then describes a sly grog shop he saw in Michelago, noting that the restrictive regulations are not likely to be observed where there is nobody to enforce any law whatever.

> In such places, the convict stock-keepers, shepherds, runaways, bushrangers, &c. congregate, to dispose of stolen property, especially cattle, to some squatter or another, which latter nuisance has just now reached to an unprecedented degree in this colony. There, fighting and disorder of all kinds is going on, for which there is no redress – no stoppage.[15]

So freedom from 'the ballast of civilisation' does not ensure a life of simplicity and natural goodness: the ordered structure of society has its uses. Eric Rolls, who is a country person, also knew the loneliness and the dread of a life of isolation, recorded when he was sixteen in an extraordinary verse under the title 'Death Song of a Mad Bush Shepherd':

> Must I take my sheep to water?
> Must I take my sheep to slaughter?
> There has been slaughter but there is no water,
> For Drought has been and Fire her daughter,
> Oh Lord give us water, for I am tired of slaughter,
> and the creeks are forlorn without any water ...
>
> At night I am racked by the howl
> Of some unseen, shapeless owl.
> For an owl is no owl but a monstrous ghoul, this
> unseen owl is a monstrous ghoul;
> A monstrous owl is a shapeless ghoul and Lord,
> I am tortured by its howl ...
>
> And now the plovers cry,
> Telling me to die,
> When plovers fly by night and cry, when plovers cry
> at night and fly
> O God I know I surely die – there is a death-note
> in their cry.[16]

Eric Rolls is more often celebratory of country life, but in the other classical mode, sometimes called Boeotian or Hesiodic (after a place, Boeotia, and a poet, Hesiod), and this has an equally long literary history. Virgil uses both modes, often giving an (apparently) unvarnished account of life on his farm. Patrick White used the Hesiodic in *The Tree of Man*, in prose rather than verse, with a bleaker vision than that of Virgil (who was, in effect, a hobby farmer).

The 'Boeotian' could also be understood satirically or comically as it was by the Athenians, who regarded their neighbours as figures of fun; Dad, Dave and Mabel are Boeotians. Hal Porter saw the sheep themselves as creatures from the French Court of Louis XIV, with high heels, powdered faces and curling perukes, a witless caste dressed for a Theocritan idyll, but dramatically miscast in the Boeotian landscape of the French Revolution, awaiting the guillotine:

> They teeter with an inane care among the skewbald stones,
> plead each other's prison names in grey bewildered tones,
> and thrust their faces – powdered, pale and bilious with unease –
> against the wires of the fence, like haunted internees;
> 'Here and here, man, m-a-a-n'.
> About them die the sun-scarred miles, the dams of muddy milk,
> the fences sutured on mirage, the ranges ripped from silk;
> before them, from the gravel road, their murderer assesses,
> their thief examines haughty teeth and parts the clumsy dresses:
> 'Here and here, man, m-a-a-n.'[17]

Porter's elaborate trope works at several levels; above all, it shows that the sheep are out of place, but it also evokes the acute vulnerability and the aloof, aristocratic air of many sheep (the Border Leicester, for example). The sun-scarred miles and muddy dams are their creation much as pre-revolutionary France was ravaged by its luxury-loving nobility. His image has an especial poignancy in Fremantle, a major export centre for the live sheep trade, where the tumbrils roll past daily with their hapless victims crowded against the bars, on their long journey to the bright knife.

Sheep are not merely the dumbest of the dumb brutes: they are the least romantic of animals, as anyone who has had to deal with foot-rot or fly-strike, cutting maggots out of the living flesh, or knackering the lambs, or even rounding them up, will attest. There has been little attempt to romanticise them in Australian or any other literature, to my knowledge, except, of course, when they are stage props for The Good Shepherd, which we will come to later. What has been romanticised end-lessly is the Arcadian setting, along with the values and behaviours that it is perceived as legitimating. These values and behaviours of Arcadia are best exhibited in Australia at the beach, our own *locus amoenus.*

So it is not the literary form proper that has played such a large role in Australian culture, but the pastoral setting, Arcadia, and the values that go with it. One has been the tendency to locate health, happiness and virtue in the country, and vice and misery in the city. This has long been an English literary tradition. There is a suite of associated myths and attitudes: that of the Golden Age, including its Edenic version, and the appropriation of the pastoral imagery by the Church, which has played a part in Australia in sanctioning a par-ticular form of land use and of individual wealth accumulation. There is a splendid example in *Geoffrey Hamlyn*, one that uses the rhetoric of the Old Testament to legitimise invasion of the Snowy country:

'There are a cattle down there, certainly,' I said, 'and a very large number of them; they are not ours, depend upon it: there are men with them, too, or they could not make so much noise ...'

'I'll tell you what I think it is, old Jeff' said James, 'it's some new chums going to cross the watershed and look for new coun-try to the south. If so, let us go down and meet them: they will camp down by the river yonder.'

James was right. All doubt about what the newcomers were was solved before we reached the river, for we could hear the rapid detonation of the stockwhips loud above the lowing of the cattle; so we sat and watched them debouche from the forest into the broad river meadows in the gathering gloom: saw the scene so venerable and ancient, so seldom seen in the Old World – the patriarchs moving into the desert with all their wealth, to find a new pasture ground. A simple primitive action, the firsst and simplest act of colonisation, yet producing such great results on the history of the world as did the parting of Lot and Abraham in times gone by.[18]

These are cattle rather than sheep, but the pastoral imagery is especially potent. The heifers following the 'lordly bull' and the whole range of patriarchal rhetoric of pastoralism (*Cattlemen of the High Plains*, etc.) became part of a masculinist culture that has taken (is taking) a long time to throw off. The understanding of the mythic perceptions embedded in this passage is complex, because dispossession (of the indigenous people) and possession (by invaders) become fused. Kingsley invokes the image of Abraham leading his flocks to new pastures, like Moses leading his people to the Promised Land. By using the word 'desert', he has clearly absorbed the doctrine of *Terra Nullius*: the land was empty, and the birthright of these intrepid Britons, who took it with God's blessing. He was merely keeping a promise to them. It is easy to see in this passage how the word 'squatters' changed its meaning in Australian English, from 'illegal occupants of Crown Land' to 'a natural aristocracy claiming their birthright'.

The heyday of the visual expression of Arcadia was celebrated in the exhibition of paintings that went under the name *Golden Summers*. It was a clever name, with overtones of a Golden Age, and yet perhaps also a tacit admission that the great wealth of the society that could supply patrons for painters was derived from real gold. But whence came the gold in the paintings themselves, that special quality of light sought by Sir Arthur Streeton, the light that seemed to gild all it touched? The answer is that it came from dust in the air, dust from the Western Plains, denuded of vegetation, the topsoil pulverised by sheep and cattle and blown to the coast. Today it would be called 'particulate matter', and would consist largely of industrial pollutants and unburnt hydrocarbons from vehicle exhausts. In Streeton's day it was dust.

Arcadian imagery was part of the cultural baggage brought by some of the more affluent early colonists. It had been greatly reinforced in Britain by the Enclosures of the eighteenth century, promoting an idealised landscape of trees and grass. The new settlers found Arcady in eastern Australia, often prepared for them by the Aborigines (who found the settlers unsettling); in came the alien sheep, the lawn-mowers of the day, and up went the place names, from Camden Park on. 'Parks' had social status. Landscapes of trees and grass were created also in parts of the new cities. One of the more enduring and debilitating legacies of the pastoral idyll in Australia is its effect on gardening and landscape preferences. The Greek Arcadia in the Peleponnesus has a green flush in late winter, but for most of the year it consists of stony brown hills with a few scattered holm oaks. But the literary Arcadia got greener as it travelled north and west, and it is the 'green cabinet' that was imported to Australia. It is a costly image in a dry land. Landscapes of trees and grass are still much admired, but lacking an understorey they are essentially rather sterile from an ecological point of view. They favour a near-monoculture of medium-sized herbivores, whether kangaroos or sheep, both essentially unstable, like all monocultures which are the outcome of human intervention.

There are Arcadian overtones in many accounts of Aboriginal land use; the Dreamtime is yet another Golden Age. The romanticisation of hunter-gatherer cultures has been given some substance by claims, for example, that Aboriginal land use in south-western Australia yielded a more varied and healthier diet for less labour than that of the British colonists for most of the nineteenth century, who were obliged to import food.[19] In more general terms, anthropologists have used the phrase 'primitive affluence'. Behind this looms the Fall, that change in human history, taking place at different times in different places, when our species turned from a hunter-gatherer and pastoral economy to an agricultural one. Thus began the commitment to unceasing labour and sweaty brows, but also the possibility of increased density of population, and, in time, urban cultures that gave leisure to some and saw the birth of 'civilisation', which is epistemologically the culture of cities. So the agricultural labours of the fellahin made it possible for Theocritus to write his pastoral idylls, for Ptolemy Philadelphos to admire their enviable simplicity from his palace windows in Alexandria, and for Banjo Paterson to ride with the 'western drovers', sharing the 'pleasures that the townsfolk never know' without leaving his lawyer's office in Sydney. Today he would have a share in the ownership of a vineyard in the Hunter Valley or Margaret River. None of them would care to be a shepherd.

Australia has had one good shepherd, though. His name was Thomas Chapman. He was the youth who in 1849 stubbed his foot on a rock while minding sheep near Amherst, some 60 kilometres north-west of Ballarat. It had gold in it, 38 ounces of it. He took it to Melbourne, and set off the gold-rush that challenged the power of the wealthy Western District squatters, at least for a time. Chapman has never quite made the stage as a national hero, however. An itinerant vagabond stole the limelight. 'Waltzing Matilda' has long been Australia's unofficial national anthem (no-one knows the words of 'Advance Australia Fair', other than the last line, on which we all come in strong). The jolly swagman has been a kind of folk hero because he was an untrammelled free spirit, in contrast with the grasping pastoralist and his paid minions of the law. They are called 'troopers', which has military overtones, so the expropriation of the land is seen to be maintained by force, while the squatter is mounted on a 'thorough-bred', which makes genetic claims. The squatter was doubtless a 'pure Merino', a term used for a time for the Australian free settler of British origin, with no convict taint, and preferably an upper-class free settler, the usual meaning in the Darling Downs in Queensland. These are the forces that confront the happy-go-lucky swagman (he was not 'jolly' in the original A.B. Paterson version of 1895; the word was added in the early 1900s). The swagman was carefree until he was sprung, and the poem catches a yearning for a less structured life that most Australians still respond to. There is something to be said, then, for the Arcadian dream, at least for the weekends. The capacity to enjoy our leisure outdoors in fairly simple pursuits is one of the good things about Australians. But we need to rid the pastoral idyll of the sheep. So there are many reasons for the swagman's status as national hero. As well as being free of that 'ballast of civilisation', he was nomadic, thus responding to the natural rhythms of an unpredictable continent; he was egalitarian, a quality now in retreat; he denied the 'right to rule' of an acquisitive oligopoly. Above all he killed and ate the jumbuck.[20]

Notes

1　For a good account of the values of pastoralists, see J.H. Holmes and P. Day, 'Identity, Lifestyle and Survival: Value Orientation of South Australian Pastoralists', *Rangelands Journal*, vol. 17, no. 2, 1995, pp. 193–212; and J.H. Holmes and L.D.P. Knight, 'Pastoral Lease Tenure in Australia: Historical Relic or Useful Contemporary Tool?', *Rangelands Journal*, vol. 16, no. 1, 1994, pp. 106–121.

2　*The Oxford-Hammond Atlas of the World*, Oxford University Press, Oxford, 1993, p. 18.

3　Libby Robin, 'Fleecing the Nation', *Country and Calling: The Journal of Australian Studies*, no. 62, 1999, pp. 150–158.

4　Robin, p. 152.

5　Robin, p. 155.

6   Data from Professor David Lindsay, Dean of Agriculture, UWA.

7   Robin, p. 156.

8   T.B.L. Webster, *Hellenistic Poetry and Art*, Methuen, London, 1964, p. 81.

9   P.M. Fraser, *Ptolemaic Alexandria*, 3 vols, Oxford University Press, Oxford, 1972, p. 133.

10   e.g. C.J. Glacken, *Traces on the Rhodian Shore: Nature and Culture in Western Thought from Ancient Times to the Eighteenth Century*, University of California Press, Berkeley, 1973; David Norbrook, *Poetry and Politics in the English Renaissance*, Routledge & Kegan Paul, London, 1984; Anna Rist, *The Poems of Theocritus*, University of North Carolina Press, Chapel Hill, 1978; Thomas G. Rosenmeyer, *The Green Cabinet: Theocritus and the European Pastoral Lyric*, University of California Press, Berkeley, 1969; Charles Segal, *Poetry and Myth in Ancient Pastoral: Essays on Theocritus and Vergil*, Princeton University Press, 1981; Webster, 1964.

11   Webster, p. 1.

12   Rosenmeyer, p. 54.

13   Rosenmeyer, p. 55.

14   John Lhotsky (1834) in Alan Andrews (ed.), *A Journey from Sydney to the Australian Alps*, Blubber Head Press, Hobart, 1979, p. 147.

15   Lhotsky, pp. 79–80.

16   Eric Rolls, 'The Death Song of a Mad Bush Shepherd' (1939) in John Thompson, Kenneth Slessor and R. G. Howarth (eds), *The Penguin Book of Australian Verse*, Penguin, Mitcham, Victoria, 1958.

17   Hal Porter, 'The Sheep' (1957) in John Thompson, Kenneth Slessor and R. G. Howarth (eds), *The Penguin Book of Australian Verse*.

18   Henry Kingsley, *The Recollections of Geoffrey Hamlyn*, 1859.

19   Brian de Garis, 'Settling on the Sand: The Colonisation of Western Australia' in *European Impact on the West Australian Environment 1829–1979*, Octagon Lectures, University of Western Australia Press, Nedlands, 1979, p. 14.

20   Seddon noted that 'In writing this article I have had help from several people, especially David Wilcox on rangeland management, David Lindsay on animal production and the social forces that have led to near-stagnation in the wool industry, and Ted Lefroy on practically everything else, right down to current surfing parlance. Their comments on an earlier draft have been paraphrased and incorporated in the text, which I acknowledge here. I am very grateful to all of them. They remind me of what is still good about working in universities.' [A.G.]

GARDENS IN CONTEXT

11

SWAN RIVER LANDSCAPES
1970

'Winds and waves work with a careless and graceful hand: and,
should they in some places carry away a portion of the soil,
the trifling loss would be amply compensated for by the additional spirit, dignity, and loveliness, which these agents and the
other powers of Nature would soon communicate to what was
left behind.'

Wordsworth, *Guide to the Lakes*

MAN'S ATTITUDE TO NATURE VARIES FROM ONE
society to another, and also according to individual temperament: regard for our landscape reflects
basic attitudes which have been characterised in
many ways. An old distinction that I find fruitful is that between the
vita activa and the *vita contemplativa*, the life of the active and the
contemplative man or woman. The contrast is dramatised in the New
Testament story of Mary and Martha (Luke 10: 38–42): 'Now it came
to pass, as they went, that he entered into a certain village: and a certain woman named Martha received him into her house. And she had
a sister called Mary, which also sat at Jesus' feet, and heard his word.

165

But Martha was cumbered about much serving, and came to him, and said, Lord, dost thou not care that my sister hath left me to serve alone? bid her therefore that she help me. And Jesus answered and said unto her, Martha, Martha, thou art careful and troubled about many things: But one thing is needful: and Mary hath chosen that good part, which shall not be taken away from her.' Martha merits sympathy. Someone has to remember to bring matches on the picnic, and her competence and efficiency is often taken for granted. However, Martha and her children are secure in their own regard and although they are not often the stuff of great literature, they dominate most societies through control of social, political and economic power. Leisure, of which literature and the arts are among the fruits, is made possible by their work. Yet Martha has a problem. She doesn't know what to do with leisure. She can't be still, she can't let things alone. If her sons become scientists, they are forever putting nature through her paces, doing experimental genetics, cutting things up in the laboratory, undertaking great engineering projects which harness water-power, tame the wilderness, reclaim the foreshores of rivers. 'Tame' and 'harness' and 'reclaim' are all good Martha-words, stressing man's dominance over the environment. 'Reclaiming the foreshores' has quite a different ring to it from 'filling in part of the river'.

Mary's children are not often scientists at all. 'Be still, and know that I am God' (Psalms 46: 10) has meaning for them. If they do turn to science, they are likely to be ecologists, naturalists who are more concerned to see than to change. They are conservationists. But the word 'conservation' can be made to mean many things, and there is a problem here, too. 'Conservation' is a great Mary-word, but it may mark hostility to all change, sheer nostalgia for the world we knew when we were twenty, not because it was better, but because we were twenty. Some 'conservationists' are fundamentally hostile to human society, an attitude that comes out clearly in Mary-words such as 'spoiled', and has been well put by Edward Hyams in discussing the ideal English garden, which, he says, 'is not meant to have any people in it any more than the beholder of a landscape painting is meant to get inside it'.[1] I find this statement profound as an analysis of the quality of imagination that has gone into the making of some great English gardens; and also both touching and absurd.

This preliminary categorisation is, of course, too simple. There are no Marthas, and no Marys: all of us have something of both in our make-up. But the contrast in attitudes is clear, and I see it as fundamental in our handling of landscape. In classifying landscapes which have been moulded by the hand of man, my basic contrasting terms are 'transformationist' and 'Arcadian'. Let me explain them. By 'transformationist' I mean the landscape that Martha has worked on, where the natural scene has been remade, and the hand of man is everywhere evident. By 'Arcadian' I mean the landscape in which the hand of man is everywhere concealed. These terms are to an extent arbitrary: their use and limitations as classificatory terms will become apparent as we proceed to examples. I choose 'Arcadian' because Arcady was a real place, a mountainous district in the Peloponnesus of Greece, and I wish later to contrast Arcadian landscapes with the 'paradise garden' (this term has been borrowed from Hyams) which has no natural analogue. But the word 'Arcady' in literature has meant more than a part of Greece: it is an ideal of rustic simplicity and pastoral content. In Arcady, shepherdess and swain live and love in a landscape that is naturally harmonious and well proportioned. The Arcadian landscape architect in a later age has this natural harmony in view.

It might seem at first sight that the contrasting term to the transformed landscape, the one that has been wholly made over by the hand of man, should be the wilderness landscape, the untouched natural scene in which man has played no part at all. But this is a third category. Man changes the environment by his presence and any settled population will make many changes in the natural scene. Both the transformationist and Arcadian landscapes are in part man-made: the contrast is in the intent to show or to conceal the hand of man.

[…]

The basic precept of the eighteenth-century landscape gardener Humphry Repton was this: 'First study well the genius of the place', and this is the heart of the Arcadian approach to landscape, and it is sufficiently distinct from all of the transformationist modes, which begin by sending the *genius loci* packing. There are many variants of the Arcadian landscape, but these cannot be named because they are local landscapes, directed by the genius of the place. An Arcadian approach to the landscapes of the Swan River will not aim at reproducing the landscapes of Stourhead or the Lake District or Sicily or even Arcadia. It will begin with a study of the Swan River, and to this we now turn.

NOTES

1   Edward Hyams, *The English Garden*, Thames and Hudson, London, 1966.

12

A CAPTIVE JUNGLE, OR
RAINFOREST IN SOUTH YARRA

1984

This is an extract from the first in a series of four related essays on rainforest, published in Landscape Australia, *1984.*

WILLIAM GUILFOYLE, THE FOURTH DIRECTOR of the Royal Botanic Gardens in Melbourne, from 1873 to 1909, is generally credited with the creation of the Gardens as we now know them, a series of landscapes of great delicacy. Guilfoyle's labours can be described under two main heads.

First, he gave the Gardens structure. He said of the Gardens as he found them that '... landscape beauty seems to have been sacrificed to correct geographical classification'. Guilfoyle immediately set about reorganising the rows, lines and isolated specimens of [previous director Baron Ferdinand] von Mueller into free-flowing arcs and irregular, rather tightly packed clusters that organised the whole of the grounds into a series of great, informal, open-air rooms, which carry to this day names such as 'Princes Lawn', 'Tennyson Lawn', 'Southern Lawn', and so on (there are ten of these major spaces). The contrast is very apparent in comparing the plan of the Gardens in

169

von Mueller's day with the Guilfoyle plan. The walls between these great rooms give structure to the Gardens. They are not, however, like the walls of a house – they twist and turn, rise and fall, change colour with the seasons, are at times an impenetrable barrier and at other times a light filter with views beyond. There are gaps, vistas, narrow dark alleys opening out into a broad prospect, with more glimpses beyond, and always the promise of something hidden, something more to come. This basic form is naturalistic, a refinement of the copse and spinney, meadow and woodland glade of rural England. Structurally, it is quite proper to describe Guilfoyle as working within the eighteenth-century English landscape tradition of Kent, Repton and Capability Brown.

But that is only the half of Guilfoyle. The other half is very much the Victorian plantsman, son of a line of nurserymen who filled English gardens with new plants from all over the world – mostly China and Japan – in the nineteenth century. After his initial inspection of the Gardens, Guilfoyle was 'greatly surprised to find that one of the chief defects was an almost total absence, in some cases, an entire one, of such flowering shrubs as camellias, azaleas, rhododendrons, etc. … which every lover of flowers must admit are essential …'[1] So, in effect, there can be no garden without camellias and azaleas, said Guilfoyle, thus establishing a truth which Melbourne gardeners took to be self-evident for the next eighty years. In the course of his admirable reorganisation, he had his men shift a number of low shrubs – gardenias, myrtles, jacobinia and the like – into positions of prominence, claiming that they had been 'quite overshadowed by useless indigenous scrub such as acacias and leptospermum – hakeas, eucalypts and melaleuca'.

In this, Guilfoyle was remote from the eighteenth century. Capability Brown, Kent and to a lesser extent Repton, used the native trees of the British Isles, especially elm, oak and beech. They avoided variegated and coloured foliage – other than the infinitely subtle variations in green of the trees named above. Flowers were kept to the kitchen garden. The azaleas and other flowering shrubs at Stourhead and the other great gardens of the eighteenth century were nearly all introduced during the nineteenth. The Victorians craved colour in their gardens, and Guilfoyle used it skilfully. He also had a remarkable flair for contrasting texture – thin and vertical palm trunks against vast subtropical figs, oaks and araucarias, plumes of pampas grass against a sombre backdrop of dark green. In this he is in the first rank.

Yet his effects are not quite like those in late Victorian or Edwardian gardens in England, where there were a number of distinct trends, such as the wild gardens, woodland gardens and great herbaceous borders of William Robinson and Gertrude Jekyll, the architectural gardens of Lutyens, and the massed bedding displays of municipal gardeners and other horticultural spendthrifts. Guilfoyle's work is equally remote from that of the eighteenth-century landscapists, to whom his resemblance is superficial only. Their basic intention was to idealise the natural English landscape. Their vistas culminated in views of fertile farmland and picturesque villages (moved to improve the view if necessary, but still real villages). Their landscapes were in natural ecological balance, and were essentially self-maintaining; sheep grazed the sward, and there was no watering. Guilfoyle's garden is not at all in ecological balance with the natural environment; it is not an idealised English landscape (apart from the Oak Lawn), and it is assuredly not an idealised Australian landscape. It bears little resemblance to late Victorian gardens in Britain, except perhaps for the conservatory, that common appendage of the nineteenth-century large house in which a craving for the exotic and luxuriant could be satisfied more easily than the English winter allowed in the open garden. Guilfoyle's garden in South Yarra bears some resemblance both to Bogor, the great botanical garden established by the Dutch in the East Indies, and to the gardens at Singapore created by the English; that, I think, is the key. Much of it is an idealised *tropical* landscape – not like any real landscape of the tropics, but representing a North European dream of the tropics, like the dream worlds in Henri Rousseau's painting, built on a limited experience in the Jardin des Plantes in Paris.

Northern Europe has had three persistent dreams of place; the first, of the Mediterranean, the second of coral islands in the Pacific, and the third, of tropical jungle. All three are essentially Romantic, and were especially potent in the nineteenth century. The Mediterranean dream is in Byron, Shelley, Norman Douglas's *South Wind*, Lawrence Durrell's novels, the classical education of the Great Public Schools, *Zorba the Greek*, a run of BBC serials – the Sons of Zorba, so to speak – and a phalanx of Nordic flesh encumbering remote Aegean beaches. The coral sands and nodding palms are in R.M. Ballantyne's *The Coral Island*, R.L. Stevenson's tales, *Bali Hai*, and hundreds of B-grade movies.

The dream of the tropics is in Henri Rousseau, Conrad, Henri Fauconnier's *The Soul of Malaya*. This is not the tropics of Indonesians, of Malays, any more than the dream Mediterranean is that of real Greeks and Italians and Maltese and Turks. They are exotic northern myths, and that is the mood that pervades Guilfoyle's remarkable creation. It is not, of course, jungle – primary or virgin rainforest is fairly open and easy to move through – it is *jungle edge*, as seen from a clearing, or better, from a river. It is there that the foliage is banked in, great tapestried walls, dense, impenetrable, green, shining, infinitely varied in texture. It is rainforest seen from the Tweed River, on the border of New South Wales and Queensland, where the Guilfoyles had begun to establish themselves a nursery, and the sugar cane that was later to supplant the rainforest.

Michael Guilfoyle described their journey up the river by boat in
November 1869:

> The scenery is beautiful, beyond imagination and wild fowl
> lovely to behold.
>
> Among plants which attracted my attention as we sailed
> along were some lovely specimens of *Acmena pendula*,[2] the
> graceful drooping boughs of which, like willows, gracefully
> curved over the green banks of the water's edge. The bright
> green foliage of the *Castanospermum* or Moreton Bay Chestnut,
> the stems of the branches of which, clothed with their gorgeous
> yellow and red flowers, were often visible. But far more beau-
> tiful than anything I have ever seen were the specimens of the
> flame tree, *Braclrychiton acerifolium* in full bloom. A mass of
> the brightest scarlet, enough to dazzle one's eyes would now and
> then present itself, perhaps backed up by the dark foliage of a
> huge *Ficus*, of which I noticed several species. Many fine tree
> ferns were seen – they have a beautiful effect when their bold
> grassy green fronds are surrounded by darker foliage. *Seaforthia
> elegans*, one of the most graceful of Australian palms, is pretty
> well distributed throughout the forests, but the *Corypha* or
> Cabbage Tree palm, is rarely seen. *Chamaedon* or walking stick
> palm is very plentiful, and *Calamus australis* or Lawyer palm –
> a sort of rattan – with other plants of struggling habit, form the
> brush which covers the fertile district for miles. *Ipomaea pen-
> dula*, varying in colour from the deepest shade of purple and
> lilac to white, literally covers some of the taller trees – the effect
> is beautiful. Higher up the river, I was surprised to find *Barkleya
> syringifolia* which is a splendid shrub. Its heart shaped, lively
> green foliage contrasted with its spikes of golden yellow flowers,
> was a sight worth seeing.

The botanical richness of the land, and the way in which nature has sheltered it, amazes me.'[3]

Guilfoyle also travelled as botanist to the South Sea island cruise of the HMS *Challenger*, so he had extensive first-hand knowledge of rainforest. That is the image that remained in Guilfoyle's mind's eye, I believe. The point may be established in a mundane way by looking at the main structural elements in the Gardens. There is a total of about 600 palms; forty-one specimens of Moreton Bay fig with 110 figs in all; 192 lilypillies; eighteen camphor laurels and 164 southern conifers (hoop pines, kauris and the like). The number of trees from the northern hemisphere is relatively small given the background and tastes of Melbourne's early citizens, shown for example by the almost universal use of the English elm as a street tree, and as the dominant tree in the Fitzroy, Flagstaff, Treasury and Carlton Gardens. There are only seventy-five English elms in the Royal Botanic Gardens; oaks total 100 in all, and pines of all species, eighty-one.

The Temple of the Winds, overlooking the Yarra at the north-western end of the Gardens, is a revealing Guilfoyle creation, in that each of ten pillars is topped by a capital composed of staghorn fern, rather than the classical acanthus, the staghorn being one of the dramatic epiphytes of Tweed River rainforest which so fertilised Guilfoyle's imagination.

Guilfoyle did more than plant tropical trees. He consciously set out to create a tropical landscape throughout the major viewing axis of the site; that is, from the Eastern Lawn across the Central Lake to Princes Lawn beyond, with Government House rising above a luxuriously forested horizon; and the same view in reverse, looking east from the upper boundaries of Princes Lawn. His intentions are described in his Annual Report for 1875:

Before commencing to obliterate these walks, I began to form groups in which tropical and subtropical plants will eventually be the prominent features. Through these, dispersed with a view to landscape effect, glimpses will be afforded of the clear lake, studded with islands, the careful plantation of which will materially add to the diversity and charm of the landscape. On this lawn I am endeavouring to imitate as much as possible tropical scenery. Most people will agree with me that it is far easier to lay out a *new* garden than to remodel one in which blunders have been made, not only in the general layout but in the planting of trees and shrubs. It should always I think be the aim of those in charge of public gardens not to reproduce vegetation which may be seen in other portions of such gardens – but to bring before the public, in special spots, scenes of beauty not to be found elsewhere, by representing plants of a different character to those more or less common to the locality.[4]

The intentions are brilliantly realised, but in a most individual way – the landscape bears little relation to any real tropical landscape. It is rather a northern European conception of what the tropics *should* be like.

In my view, neither the greatness and originality of Guilfoyle's achievement nor its costs have been adequately recognised in Australia. He is generally described as a man who worked – albeit in the colonies and in the second half of the nineteenth century – in the great landscape tradition of eighteenth-century England, but this is at best half true, and it obscures his originality. Without question, he handled space – vista, water, reflection, mass, bulk, glimpse and, again, vista – in that tradition. But he was intensely Romantic in his intentions, almost to the point of Surrealism. The rich, the exotic, the contrasts in colour, texture and form, from the spiky squat-trunked palms he loved to the dense velvet-green backgrounds he gave them, are quite remote from the Age of Reason. He created a dream world from the resources of a unique sensibility. To say that Guilfoyle was perhaps too fond of palms is to misunderstand Guilfoyle.

This creative achievement has had a price. Melbourne has one of the world's great landscape gardens, but it is not among the great *botanic* gardens. The herbarium and scientific functions of the Gardens are carried out well, but they have become divorced from the pleasure garden, which has only a limited educational and scientific function. R.T.M. Pescott, a former Director of the Gardens, concludes a chapter in his valuable book on Guilfoyle with these words:

> It is important to note that, at the close of this second period of development, none of the old Mueller concept remained. It is perhaps significant to comment that when Mueller died in 1896 there was no remaining visible expression of his earlier labours in the Gardens.[5]

His collection of pines, for instance, was scattered over all of the Gardens. Trees are grouped and placed according to the canons of art, not those of systematic botany or ecology.

Although the animals of the jungle are missing from the 'Captive Jungle' in South Yarra, there were animal and bird cages near the southern border of the lagoon in 1873, displaying monkeys, pheasants, pigeons, parrots and native animals. Guilfoyle had them removed to the grounds of the Acclimatization Society at Royal Park, later to become the Zoological Gardens, although he tolerated some free-ranging emus. The Fern Gully was then extended after disposing of the enclosures.[6] This strict segregation of botanical and zoological gardens throughout the western world is one of the curiosities of nineteenth-century cultural history, one that is now in reverse as the zoos try to recreate or simulate natural habitats. Horticulture and the management of exotic animals require different skills, so on practical grounds the separation of function achieved by Guilfoyle is logical, but a tropical aviary would nevertheless be an ornament to the Gardens, and might be used as a display that shows the interdependence of plants and animals. On the other hand, one should also record that the Gardens as Guilfoyle designed them carry a large and diverse population of 'wild' animals: eels, possums, feral cats, tortoises and a great variety of birds. This eclectic but rich population is undoubtedly a reflection of the equally eclectic but rich variety of habitats recreated by Guilfoyle's design.

My conclusion with respect to Guilfoyle is that perhaps his most important contribution to landscape was his creation of an idealised tropical landscape. It is the jungle edge, as seen from a clearing or river, that Guilfoyle sought to reproduce in South Yarra. The serious student of landscape needs to understand a good deal about rainforest and its plants if he or she is to understand Guilfoyle and his Garden; but the obsession with rainforest species is not peculiar to Guilfoyle or Melbourne. It is equally apparent in the Botanic Gardens in Sydney, Brisbane, and, to a lesser degree, Adelaide. It shows in many public plantings even in summer-dry Perth, and it reflects a set of cultural attitudes in the last century that have not yet been much studied.

The odd tendency in Australia to see Guilfoyle as a latter-day Capability Brown rather than as the intensely Romantic late Victorian that he in fact was, has obscured his originality, yet he is nevertheless also representative of his age and of our Victorian forebears, who were both attracted and repelled by rainforest. Indeed, as in other matters, our Victorian grandparents had a double standard about the trees of the rainforest; they planted them in their parks and gardens much more widely than we do today, especially the evergreen figs, cabbage

palms and the *Araucaria* species. They liked the captive, but the rainforests themselves were savagely exploited, and so far as they appear
in verse and prose, were seen as satanic. The great, spreading roots of
the Moreton Bay fig, for example, become sombre and reptilian; in
Christopher Brennan (1913), rainforest becomes a landscape of evil:

> the savage realm begins, of lonely dread,
> black branches from the fetid marish bred
> that lurks to trap the loyal careless foot,
> and gaping trunks protrude a snaky root,
> o'er slinking paths that centre, where beneath
> a sudden rock on the short blasted heath,
> bare-set, a cavern lurks and holds within
> its womb, obscene with some corroding sin,
> coil'd on itself and stirring, a squat shade …[7]

Something of this attitude of dread persisted into our own century;
when Judith Wright went to live at Tamborine Mountain she became
one of the great fighters for rainforest, but it is still rendered as a peni-
tential landscape:

> To reach the pool you must go through the rainforest –
> Through the bewildering midsummer of darkness
> lit with ancient fern,
> laced with poison and thorn.
> You must go by the way he went – the way of the
> bleeding
> hands and feet, the blood on the stones like flowers,
> under the hooded flowers
> that fall on the stones like blood.[8]

The details are literal, as Brian Elliott points out: the darkness at midsummer; the fern; the poisonous giant nettle trees (*Dendrocnide excelsa*).[9] The blood on the stones is the scarlet flowers of species such as *Brachychiton acerifolius* and *Castanospermum australe*, unseen until they fall from the canopy above to the forest floor. The precision renders the beauty, but it is still full of menace. It took Australians a hundred years to learn to love a sunburnt country, and perhaps that struggle made it too hard for us to encompass its contrary at the same time.

An interest in rainforest is now fashionable; conservation battles rage, while our surviving pockets of rainforests continue to shrink. Even among dedicated conservationists, substantial *knowledge* of any of our rainforests is still rare, largely because of their great complexity. Botanic gardens such as the Royal Botanic Gardens in Melbourne can clearly play a major role in education and conservation, by familiarising people with some of the species and their characteristics, by reproducing ecological associations, by conserving endangered species, by working on and demonstrating the horticultural possibilities of rainforest species, and by the specialised research work of the herbarium. The Zoological Gardens at Royal Park are well ahead of the Botanic Gardens in discharging their educational role. In the Botanic Gardens, the public pleasure gardens on the one hand, and the invisible research role in the herbarium on the other, have been too much divorced (partly because of the direction given by Guilfoyle). The Gardens now need the resources and encouragement to bring them together again, by assuming a major educational role.

This shorter version of the original essay was extracted from pp. 192–196.

NOTES

1   R.T.M. Pescott, *W.R. Guilfoyle 1840–1912: The Master of Landscaping*, Oxford University Press, Melbourne, 1974, p. 86.

2   Names in current use for these species are as follows: *Acmena pendula* – probably *Syzygium floribundum*; *Castanospermum* – *Castanospermum australe*; *Seaforthia elegans* – *Archontophoenix cunninghamiana*; *Coryphora* – *livistona australis*; *Chamaedon* – *linospadix monostachya*; *Ipomea pendula* – *lpomaea palmata* (?). The other species have retained their names. These plants are well represented in the gardens.

3   Pescott, p. 46.

4   *Annual Report of the Melbourne Botanic Gardens, 1875.*

5   Pescott, p. 99.

6   Pescott, p. 82.

7   C.J. Brennan, 'The Quest of Silence', verse IIII, *Poems*, G.B. Philip & Son, Sydney, 1913.

8   J. Wright, *The Gateway*, Angus & Robertson, Sydney, 1953, p. 59.

9   B. Elliott, *The Landscape of Australian Poetry*, F.W. Cheshire, Melbourne, 1967, p. 320.

13
———

THE SUBURBAN GARDEN
IN AUSTRALIA

1990

1. Beginnings

THERE IS A GREAT VARIETY OF SUBURBAN GARDENS in Australia, and I shall offer a crude taxonomy presently, but first let us try for some common characteristics. Typically, the suburban garden is *negative space*, what falls between two very positive boundaries. One is the boundary of the block, looking out. It functions as a moat, defensive to a wall – the wall being that of the house itself, looking in. The 'garden' is what is left between, a kind of no-man's-land, scarred by earlier events. The block has been surveyed, the bulldozers have done their work, cleared away the trees and topsoil, the builder has come and gone, leaving a rubble of plastic odds and ends, broken tiles, dropped nails, shattered concrete. This is the birth of the suburban garden.

There are other ways of designing and building, but they are rare in Australia. One is to survey the site, orient the proposed building in relation to the topography, keep the trees, whether indigenous or from an earlier garden, and maintain the land form, rather than flatten it. All of this happens at times in relatively affluent new

181

developments in forested areas like parts of Sydney's North Shore, parts of the Dandenongs, the Loftys and other Hill Stations on the urban periphery. But it costs the developer more, and requires care, so it is not common practice. Another way to build, more common than our way, is to take the block of land itself as the design unit – a common example is that of the building as boundary, with an internal courtyard, so familiar in Europe and Latin America. But our building regulations do not encourage this, although it often suits our climate. So we buy a block, flatten it, and plonk a house in the middle.

Why? The answer lies primarily in the way our cities have been surveyed and our building regulations drawn up, but behind these codifications lies a set of attitudes, substantially English in their origins, and far from simple. Dickens catches the territorial imperative of the suburban English, that intensified sense of a defensive space between house and the external world, and 'explains' it by implication, in *Great Expectations*. Pip visits Wemmick in Walworth, in nineteenth-century suburban London:

Wemmick's house was a little wooden cottage in the midst of plots of garden, and the top of it was cut out and painted like a battery mounted with guns.

'My own doing,' said Wemmick. 'Looks pretty; don't it?'

I highly commended it. I think it was the smallest house I ever saw: the queerest gothic windows (by far the greater part of them sham), and a gothic door, almost too small to get in at.

'That's a real flagstaff, you see,' said Wemmick, 'and on Sundays I run up a real flag. Then look here. After I have crossed this bridge, I hoist it up – so – and cut off the communication.'

The bridge was a plank, and it crossed a chasm about four feet wide and two deep. But it was very pleasant to see the pride with which he hoisted it up, and made it fast; smiling as he did so, with a relish, and not merely mechanically.

'— At the back, there's a pig, and there are fowls and rabbits; then I knock together my own little frame, you see, and grow cucumbers; and you'll judge at supper what sort of a salad I can raise. So, sir,' said Wemmick, smiling again, but seriously, too, as he shook his head, 'if you can suppose the little place besieged, it would hold out a devil of a time in point of provisions.'

'I am my own engineer, and my own carpenter, and my own plumber, and my own gardener, and my own Jack of all Trades,' said Wemmick, in acknowledging my compliments. 'Well, it's a good thing, you know. It brushes the Newgate cobwebs away.'

Dickens has taken the popular saw, that 'An Englishman's home is his castle', and pursued it, through Wemmick, to the point of affectionate burlesque. The parody of territoriality – the drawbridge – is put in context by 'it brushes the Newgate cobwebs away.' London was Europe's greatest metropolis, and English cities were the first to industrialise, which both intensified slum crowding and created the affluence which offered an alternative to all but the poorest, by building detached and semi-detached houses, each within its little plot of land, in the new suburbs. The acute territoriality is a response to crowding. But Dickens' fantasy shows too other aspects of English social life. Everything in Wemmick's abode is scaled down, not something created in itself, but a minute version of something grander. This may be seen, perhaps, as illustrating the nature of English class structure, in which the aspirations of even the lower of the lower middle class are modelled on those of their superiors. A robust peasant and labouring class has its own cultural values, but these were eroded in southern England by the pervading force of the middle classes. Finally, Wemmick is Robinson Crusoe (a very English figure), dreaming the dream of self-sufficiency, using his *back* garden productively. This too may be in part a response to the insecurity of urban life in the first half of the nineteenth century.

Much of our background comes from Wemmick's Walworth: the omnipresence of middle-class values, the scaling down, the productive use of the back yard and its sharp differentiation from the front yard, and above all, that strong consciousness of the individual boundary, not nearly so common in other cultures: the Americans rarely fence their front yard, even at the sides; while most Europeans live, as they always have, in apartment buildings with a shared internal courtyard in a building complex often fronting directly onto a piazza or other public open space. The individual has some rights in each of these spaces, but different ones, and so the 'drawbridge mentality' has less encouragement in a milieu that offers a gradation from the private to the communal.

11. The Cadastral Survey

Another major cultural force that underwrites suburbia and its gardens in Australia is the cadastral survey, that rectilinear grid imposed at various scales on an entire continent by the geometers of a remote imperial power in the nineteenth century, squaring off this old, irregular landscape to impose an order convenient to an authoritarian colonial administration. It is so much a part of our lives that many Australians are scarcely aware of it as a massive imposition, yet a glance at the map shows only two natural boundaries at state level, the Murray River, and the Tasmanian coastline. The survey grid is a characteristic of empire; the Greeks used it in their colonies in southern Italy, and the Romans carried it throughout their imperial domain, ruler straight. The grid was usually set to the positions of the compass, the cardio (north-south) and decumanus (east-west) of the Romans – of which Hoddle Street and Victoria Parade in Melbourne are an example, set by Victoria's colonial surveyor as the axis of his grid nearly two millennia after the Romans. The British took it wherever they imposed their rule: Ireland, India, North America. It was convenient for the movement of troops, for making a census, for imposing taxes. It has the logic of a central administrative power, but it ignores natural features, and has often had a heavy cost in Australia, where, for example, most farm fences now turn out to be in the wrong place. There are a few early subdivisions which run to a different logic – the narrow river frontages and long narrow blocks running back from them at Guildford, also at Hahndorf in South Australia. Much of early Sydney has an irregularity of form that is the product of a topography that could not be ignored because it was so rocky and so steep, but also because there was an improvised and adaptive quality to its first phase of settlement.

But regularity is the rule in suburbia until the curves of Canberra became popular. Thus the legendary 'quarter-acre block'. This notion is so much a part of our self-image that perhaps it is worth giving the background. First, we might note that although the quarter-acre block was fairly common, it was never standard, either in Perth or elsewhere in Australia – there was great variation in size both in and between cities. The 'classic' quarter-acre was 100 links (or 1 chain) by 250 links (or two and a half chains), with a frontage of 66 feet and a depth of 165 feet (roughly 20 metres x 50 metres – 1000 square metres). This was the standard subdivision in Dalkeith and Nedlands in Western Australia, for example, but blocks in South Perth were subdivided at the same time (1916 onwards) at 32 perches, which represented four fifths of the Dalkeith standard. In Claremont, an older suburb than Dalkeith, frontages were generally narrower (often 55 feet) but many blocks were deeper, 180 or 200 feet. The critical point is that most suburban houses everywhere in Australia other than the innermost cities had big back yard spaces by world standards. The measurements and their names – chains, links, perches – are alien and bizarre to those brought up with a decimal system, but they were so important in the production of Australian suburbia with all the values and design habits this form has engendered, that they are worth a footnote in themselves. The measurements have an ancient and practical origin. An acre, for example, was the land that one man could plough with one horse in one day; as a strip of cultivated land, it could be conveniently measured out by 2 chains in width, 5 chains in length. The system lasted because it was familiar and convenient. The 'chain' was valued, culturally because it was the length of a cricket pitch, practically because it was both imperial and metric – 66 feet, but 100 links. In short, it was a magic number. Roads, for example, were commonly one chain wide. When they curved, the width had to vary. The surveyor could then use trigonometrical tables to calculate the variation from 100 links by shifting a decimal point. It was a physical chain until well into the twentieth century – first the Gunter chain, later a steel band. Many country towns, especially in New South Wales, were laid out in 10 chain square blocks, and then subdivided into housing blocks that were 1 chain wide and 5 chains deep, half an acre, and very deep (for example, Tumut). The system began to be metricised in the Eastern States from the 1920s – the ACT, for example, used a metric foot – but it persisted in Western Australia until the introduction of the metric system in the late 1960s. And that is why so many of us now live, in a city, on a block of land of the length that a man with a horse could plough a straight furrow, and the area that one man with one horse could plough in one quarter of a day.

There would never have been much point in ploughing the infertile sands of Nedlands, but the form remains, with all its virtues and its costs. Intellectuals in Australia sometimes under-rate the virtues, which are very real – the spaciousness, the privacy, the room for children to play and for adults to entertain, room for the pool, and room to be Wemmick, your own engineer and carpenter and gardener. All of this is seen as a great privilege by the crowded urban dwellers of less happier lands. The costs are also great: above all the costs of servicing such a low density, which makes public transport grossly uneconomic and thus leads to car-dependence, with all its problems, including the isolation of young women with children, and of the elderly and of young teenagers – all those *without* a car become locked in their green prison.

The aesthetic cost is also great. In a suburb such as Nedlands, the natural diversity of landform, soil, vegetation and aspect has all been wiped out except in a few privileged streets such as Viewway, and the grid then emphasises the monotony. But we crave diversity, so that a spurious man-made diversity has been imposed, lacking any natural logic. And so that which should be diverse has been made uniform, while that which should be, if not uniform, at least homogeneous – the built form and the continuity of landscape style – has become heterogeneous. But we should turn now from the boundary characteristics and other general features to a crude typology, beginning by asking what goes on within the block.

iii. A Functional Typology

A way of classifying gardens is to ask what they are for. To a group of upper-middle-class gardeners the function of a garden might seem to be self-evident, but in fact there is considerable diversity of function in Australia, and the primary functions have changed substantially through time. There is, or was, also a sharp distinction between the function of 'the back yard' and 'the front garden'.

When I was young in the 1930s, and for several decades on either side, the function of the typical Australian back yard in the cities and country towns could be known easily from a list of its contents. It had all or most of: a woodheap, often with a rickety woodshed with a low roof of galvanised iron, and a fence for the back wall; a washhouse, with two tubs and a copper with a grate beneath it to heat the water and a wire rack to hold the Velvet soap and Reckitts blue; a clothes line; one or more tanks on wooden tankstands, with mint and parsley under or near the dripping tap in a cut-down kerosene tin; a dunny against the back fence, so that the pan could be collected from the dunny lane through a trap-door; there might be a kennel for the dog, although he often slept under the verandah; there was sometimes a crude incinerator, often an old oil drum, although rubbish was also burnt in an open bonfire. There might be chooks, usually in a chook-house along the back fence, and sometimes a sleep-out, usually a verandah enclosed with fly-wire, but sometimes free standing. A lemon tree was nearly universal.

In short, the back yard – and remember that 'yard' and 'garden' come from the same root – provided a number of essential domestic services, now centrally supplied. And of course it also had a few fruit trees and a 'vegie patch'. In the 1930s, the garage appeared, usually in the back yard, at the end of a long, narrow driveway, later migrating to the front yard, where it skeletonised to a car-port, and at length was built into the house. Sewerage meant that the outside dunny was replaced (or often merely supplemented) by an indoor toilet. The Hills Clothes Hoists sprung up like skeletal mushrooms in suburban back yards. Then the brick 'barbie' went in, and at last the pool. The function of the back yard changed from production and service to recreation, and in the more up-market homes, to display, which used to be one of the functions of the front garden; some of its characteristics now moved round back. It would be wrong, however, to think that these changes are universal. Perth, for example, is still only 73 per cent sewered; Brisbane slightly less. And the old, untidy back yard used to store junk, fix the car, or build a boat or play cricket and football on the cape-weed lawn is still alive and well, with its own cheerful vitality.

iv. Some Common Garden Types in Australia

1. The Nostalgia Garden

This comes in two forms. First the Hill Station garden, found in the Dandenongs and Mount Macedon, Mount Wellington foothills outside Hobart, and elsewhere in Tasmania, the Loftys outside Adelaide, the Blue Mountains, and Mossagong – that conurbation that now stretches from Mittagong to Moss Vale outside Sydney. It represents a total rejection of the Australian environment, and its transformation into something else. It represents a class culture, the product of money, travel and education. Some of the best gardens in Australia are to be found in the Hill Stations, but they are not Australian gardens, and although some of them are very valuable in their own right, they are largely irrelevant to garden design in Australia, since they choose to grow all the plants that in general cannot be grown well here, and in ways that are not generally available either.

The second common nostalgia garden is the 'cottage garden', now very popular in the professional suburbs like Hawthorn and Kew in Melbourne, North Adelaide, Claremont in Perth. They are also a class taste, and some of them are very attractive. They are pseudo-historical, commonly setting off Victorian houses behind picket fences, but rarely bear much resemblance to Victorian gardens *in Australia*. That hardly matters. Since many of the perennials and shrubs used have a Mediterranean origin, it is possible, although not very common, to design such gardens to be in reasonable balance with the natural ecology.

2. The Tiny Suburban Garden

This is the common model, almost universal in middle-class suburbs, and common enough both in working-class ones and in the wealthy one like Toorak. Its object is not so much ostentation as respectability, the garden equivalent of brushing your hair and having clean underpants. Neatness is the primary virtue; shrubs are clipped, lawns are cut, edges are trimmed, weeds are expelled. I suspect that these gardens have considerable psychological significance for most Australians: they are not only an outward mark of respectability, but they also give an opportunity to control our immediate environment, perhaps almost the only opportunity most people have. That the control should be so strict perhaps indicates that the natural environment is still alien to many suburban Australians.

3. The Nice Show of Colour

This is a special version of the above, with more effort; the tidy garden is 'brightened up' with annuals (usually). In Perth, colourful annuals like *Nemesia*, the Iceland Poppy and Sweet Peas are popular. The garden experts like Kevin Heinze, Allan Seale and Don Burke tend to encourage such displays, and why not? We are looking at one of the popular arts, and also at an activity that generates innocent pride in the exercise of horticultural skills. In general, these displays require a substantial input of fertiliser, chemical spray and snail bait, but they are not necessarily prodigal of water: in Perth and Adelaide they are late winter and early spring beauties, which coincides with the natural growth rhythms. A few people are coming to recognise that this seasonal flush is natural, and that it can be produced without *Nemesia* and Sweet Peas. The annual *Helichrysum* species, *Brachycome iberidifolia*, *Brunonia australis* can also give sheets of spring colour and reseed themselves each year, without the fertiliser; and there are perennial ground covers like *Gazania rigens* var. *leucolaena* and others from South Africa and elsewhere that will flower in sheets in spring and protect the soil the year round.

Both the 'tidy suburban garden' and 'the nice show of colour' are also nostalgia gardens, in their own way, but with a different class origin. My next common type also has a nostalgic component. It is the

4. Italian Garden

By this I do not mean the kind of garden that expatriates have made in Italy (like Bernard Berenson at *I Tatti* outside Florence). I mean the gardens that Italians make in Australia. Middle-class Australians tend to mock them, but I find them as much a legitimate personal and cultural expression as the 'tidy suburban garden'. These also come in two forms. The one I like best is simply productive, with tomatoes and onions and egg fruit in the front garden, along with a grape-vine on a Cyclone arbour. The other version is the hose-down garden, with paving, statuary and water: it often goes with terrazzo paving and a fat white concrete balustrade to the verandah. This type of garden has some significant virtues: it is easy to keep clean, and well adapted to our climate and lifestyle, in that it is not wasteful of water or fertiliser, and there is a recognition that lawn, summer flowers, azaleas and the like are extravagantly inappropriate here. There are no weeds, and therefore no weed killers or pesticides fouling the environment. And the easy maintenance leaves time for leisure, hospitality and social interaction, which are characteristic of most Italians.

5. *The Collection or Prize Specimen Garden*

This is a garden type in which horticultural passion over-rules design criteria, and is thus not so much a style as an emphasis, which can find diverse modes of expression: the collection can range from species tulips or cyclamen to a dozen different 'forms' of *Grevillea thelemanniana* (yes, I have a friend who has the latter – one form is called 'Wynyabbie Gem', I think). Many of us are plant snobs – there is undoubtedly a pleasure in having things that have rarity value – and this is wrong only if it leads to contempt for the common plants that grow easily. The 'collector' may work on varieties of one genus, or rare plants of many kinds, or grow prize specimens of a chosen plant: show roses or gerberas, for instance. Horticultural skill and the pride of achievement are the driving forces. They are difficult to reconcile with good design, which has different objectives.

6. *The Native Garden*

This title might be incomprehensible outside Australia, but its meaning is clear enough here: it refers to a garden made of indigenous plants. It is thus not strictly a style, merely a choice of plant material, but Australian plants are so distinctive in their form, colours and texture, and also in their horticultural requirements, that such gardens are inevitably distinctive. However, the simple term, 'Native Garden', conceals great diversity in form, plant material, history of use and design, and the subject deserves a paper all on its own. To give a few examples of this diversity: first, only a handful of purists actually restrict themselves to indigenous plants, plants from that area. I have been re-establishing the indigenous vegetation on a limestone hill in Fremantle, using *Callitris preissii* and *Melaleuca hugelii*, but could not resist adding a couple of *Araucaria heterophylla* which do so well in Perth. The Norfolk Island pine is 'native', more or less, but assuredly not indigenous, it comes from nearly 5000 kilometres away. The Norfolk pine is one of a group of 'native' trees and shrubs that were accepted very early into the common Australian garden vocabulary, and planted along with the roses and the geraniums – trees like *Tristania conferta* (the Brush Box), *Ficus rubiginosa* (the Port Jackson Fig), *Melia azedarach* (The White Cedar), and shrubs like *Chamaelaucium uncinatum* (the Geraldton Wax). On the other hand, shrubs like its close and very beautiful relative, *Chamaelaucium ciliatum* (the Albany Wax) or the stunning *Verticordia chrysantha* have been propagated commercially only recently.

In the last century, rainforest species were often domesticated; in the last thirty years, 'native plants' *tends* to mean plants of the heathlands, which generally are conspicuous in flower. This has been partly reinforced by the design work of the later Edna Walling gardens, and even more the work of Ellis Stones, who used mossy boulders and railway sleepers with his heath plants, creating subtle gardens that were said to be 'a recreation of the Australian bush'. This they were not – railway sleepers are not common in the Australian bush – although he certainly studied and learned from the natural scene. In my view, however, the primary design influence, albeit unconscious, was American West Coast, which is to say, a Japanese influence interpreted by Californian landscape architects.

There have been several other important contributors to the effective design use of Australian plant material, including the Canberra Botanic Gardens, the Melbourne and other Botanic Gardens, including Kings Park, Bill Molyneux at Austraflora, Gordon Ford,

Rodger Elliot; one of the finest designers is Kath Deery at Karwarra in the Dandenongs. This is a rather Victorian list – one could add names like Bruce Mackenzie, Jean Verschuer, Marion Blackwell – from the other states and the ACT. Despite much progress in the last decade, which includes a dramatic increase in horticultural skills and commercial availability, there is still much to learn, and I believe that this is by far the most significant growth area in garden design in Australia, not for nationalistic reasons, and not because of the myths of 'low maintenance', but because the design possibilities are so exciting, and still underexplored.

v. Conclusion

There is much to learn about the design and maintenance of Australian gardens, although I believe that some of the advice we get from our 'gardening experts' in the media is inappropriate. Enormous advances have been made in horticultural science here, so plant *performance* is better understood, along with horticultural needs, selection and positioning. But maintenance should also have an aesthetic component. We seem to have two schools. The obsession with tidiness is still very common; with native plants we need to accept some degree of 'untidiness' – leaf litter, asymmetries, and so on, but this should not lead to the other school 'put them in and leave them alone'. To show their form and texture to best advantage I believe that native plants need as much loving care as exotics, but of a different kind – pruning to reveal form, for example, by removing internal twiggy growth that obscures the branch patterns. In the intimacy of the courtyard garden it is possible to experiment with form (the Japanese garden in the Japanese Studies courtyard at the University of Western Australia is an interesting example, in which pruning is used to emphasise and create form, rather than to mutilate it).

Gardening is still a passion with many Australians, and although our cities are changing in so many ways, it is hard to doubt that they will not continue to garden, provided they still have a place to do it. The free-standing house with space before and behind has been the Australian dream. That too is now changing. Units, strata titles, duplexes, apartments, row housing, infill housing, penthouses, town-houses, all are names for denser living with reduced outdoor spaces. Australia, for better or worse, or both, is becoming urban, and the generous old back yard may become a threatened species. I should be sorry to see it.

14

—

THE AUSTRALIAN BACK YARD
1991

WHEN I WAS YOUNG IN THE 1930S, AND FOR several decades on either side, the function of the typical Australian back yard in the cities and country towns could be known easily from a list of its contents. It had all or most of: a woodheap, often with a rickety woodshed with a low roof of galvanised iron, and a fence for the back wall; a wash-house, with two tubs and a copper with a grate beneath it to heat the water and a wire rack to hold the Velvet soap and Reckitts blue; a clothes line; one or more tanks on wooden tankstands, with mint and parsley under or near the dripping tap in a cut-down kerosene tin; a dunny against the back fence, so that the pan could be collected from the dunny lane through a trap-door; there might be a kennel for the dog, although he often slept under the verandah; there was sometimes a crude incinerator, often an old oil drum, although rubbish was also burnt in an open bonfire. There might be chooks, usually in a chook-house along the back fence, and sometimes a sleep-out, usually a verandah enclosed with fly-wire, but sometimes free standing. A lemon tree was nearly universal: other trees varied with climate – almond trees in Adelaide and Perth, plums and apples in Melbourne, choko vines and bananas in Sydney and Brisbane, a mango in Cairns, figs and loquats almost everywhere. For a few weeks, there was gross overabundance of fruit, and much trading ('I'll take some of your plums if you take some of my apples next month'). Blackbirds, Ceylon crows and starlings grew fat (except in Perth). They didn't mind the fruit fly grubs and codlin crawling in the apples. In the country towns, there was a good chance of a pepper tree (*Schinus molle*), which left a grubby latex film on your hands and clothes when you climbed it. In Kalgoorlie, where water came in a pipe from the Darling Scarp, the shower water was drained out to a banana plant. Sometimes there was a patch of coarse grass, couch or buffalo, for the kids to play on, but there was rarely any special provision for the young, who played under the tankstand, in the woodshed, in the back lane, or in the driveway – which was good for cricket. Swings and sandpits all came later, as did swimming pools and barbecues.

I don't think there was much regional variation, and not much change either, over a period of fifty years or more. Wooden slatted fern and orchid houses were fairly common in Brisbane, and staghorn ferns were common even as far south as Melbourne. In Tasmania, the wash tubs might be made of Huon pine, in Victoria of concrete. Drier places like Mildura might have two tanks for rainwater rather than one. Some people had a vegetable garden – onions, peas, beans, cabbages, lettuce – and a compost heap to go with it. There was often junk piled up somewhere in the yard, since councils did not come round to collect it. From the late 1930s onwards, there was sometimes an old car body, enlisted by the young as play equipment. The advent of the car was a major change, adding a driveway, perhaps a garage, and a new activity (washing the car). In the last thirty years, changes have come thick and fast. The basic functions of the back yard have changed, but we will come to that later.

Not all back yards were the same, of course, but the variations were not so much regional as a reflection of differences in social standing and ethnic background. The Italians grew tomatoes, onions, oregano and tarragon, zucchini, fennel, olives and wine grapes, and sometimes 'rolled their own'. So did the Greeks, who also grew tomatoes, and two or three different kinds of basil, although any but the most common herbs (mint, parsley, thyme and sage) were hard to get in Australia before World War II, and the herb garden of today's fashionable middle-class suburban cook was unheard of. The Chinese, as always, cultivated every inch of ground available to them; Tom Hungerford gives a good account of such a garden in South Perth in the 1930s.[1] Greeks and Italians to this day often grow vegetables in their front yard as well as their back, in inner city suburbs like Richmond in Melbourne and Leichhardt in Sydney. The back yards of the German settlers in the Barossa were more orderly and better cared for than the Australian average, but not essentially different in function.

The vegetable garden probably showed the greatest variation. A raised bed was made for growing vegetables in many areas, but not all, reflecting the regional practice in the British Isles from which the settlers came. This neat raised bed, bordered with wood, brick or beer bottles gave good drainage. Narrow rectangles with gravel paths between gave good access. The bed itself was built up with compost, and mulched with straw and horse dung. I have seen survivors in Port Fairy in Victoria, an Irish town, and in Hobart, but the formal plots are now not so common; although vegetable beds are still often mounded, they are rarely bordered.

The other variation was social. Rich people had much bigger back yards, often with stables, a tennis court on the double block beside the house, more fruit trees, a bigger vegetable garden, a cutting garden for flowers for the house. Yet rich or poor, most of the domestic functions still had to be met.

Function is the key word. The back yard, equally in the town and the country, was complementary to the house in providing resources for living: storage, water, fuel, washing facilities, food input and food output (by way of the dunny and the compost heap). It also served as a male domain, while the house was female. The women did the washing, and perhaps the flower garden if there was one, but the men chopped the wood, usually lit the copper on washday, looked after the vegetables and washed up in the wash-house, as country men still do. The bathroom inside was for the women, and men continued to use the outhouse long after a toilet was installed inside. Glen Tomasetti faithfully records all these rituals and uses in *Thoroughly Decent People*, in which she is describing East St Kilda in 1934.

> Schooled to the remote privacy of the outhouse, no sewerage would induce Bert to have or use a lavatory in a bathroom. He continued to use the wash house for shaving and scrubbing in preference to the bathroom which, unless he needed something from the medicine chest, he entered only twice a week to have a bath.
>
> Bert was up at half-past six and Lizzie at seven. She didn't have tea in bed on Monday morning because it was washing day. Bert had filled the copper with water and, since he had lit the fire under it for so many years, he now lit the gas.
>
> While the men and boys played cricket in the drive with a kerosene tin for stumps, a good old bat and a tennis ball, the girls went inside to help Lizzie get the tea.[2]

So the suburban back yard served as play space, and for imaginative children, a magic carpet that could become many things. But that is not what it was *for*. In being a necessary adjunct of the house serving domestic needs, it was essentially rural, a gesture towards functional self-sufficiency, not complete, but not totally dependent on a web of urban services as we are today. The suburban back yard was not fundamentally different from the country back yard in

Australia. Indeed the main difference was only that the country back yard usually had more junk – because it was harder to get rid of.

The suburban Australian back yard had no equivalent in any Italian city, or inner London or Dublin or New York or Tokyo, nor does it today. They never had the space, and the domestic functions had to be served in more compact ways. In London, there was no woodheap in the tiny 'area', as the space was called, but coal in the cellar, reached from the street. In Rome or Hong Kong, washing hangs from upstairs windows. The cities that have something like the suburban Australian back yard are those that have grown in the last one hundred years or so, swelled by a migration of rural people to the city: cities of country-men and women. Some are rich, some are poor; Los Angeles is a rich example, but full of Dust Bowl farmers who walked off the land in the Depression. Port Moresby is an example of a poor city, made up of villagers who have to keep up a degree of self-sufficiency because urban services have not kept pace with their arrival, and who need and want to keep up a degree of self-sufficiency because they are culturally attuned to it: certain foodstuffs that must be fresh, or that cannot readily be obtained, or that should not be touched by other possibly malign hands. Most squatter settlements on the outskirts of Third World cities have these characteristics – because the squatters come from a culture of self-sufficiency, and because in any case, there is no choice.

Similar forces applied in our suburbs. The dream of almost every immigrant was to acquire land, no matter how little, but production on the quarter-acre block was also a product of living conditions characterised by poor supplies, no refrigeration, indifferent urban services – and poverty and shortage, as in the depressions of the 1890s, the 1930s, and much of World War II.

But if there is a functional continuum from country back yards to suburban back yards on the quarter-acre subdivision, there is a break as we move in to the inner city. These areas have a different history, especially in Sydney and Melbourne – although they now represent only 2 per cent and 1 per cent respectively of the housing of those two cities, they represent a distinctive urban form and culture.[3] They sprang from rapid population growth in the second half of the last century.

In some inner city areas, especially in inner Sydney, densities were very high. By 1891, the 3500 people of Darlington were housed in 672 five-to-six roomed houses built on 62 acres. The density per acre was 61.88, but this is less than the density of habitation, because it takes no account of space used for shops and offices, and therefore not available as residential. Paddington had 44.11 persons per acre, and Redfern 46.86. Several wards of the City of Sydney had a high average of persons per inhabited dwelling. In the ward of Bourke, there were 8.2 persons per dwelling (often of only four rooms) in 1891. 'In Long's Lane, off Cumberland Street, seven houses shared one water tap'.[4] The back yards were miniscule and filthy, with a water closet at the back door.

They were lucky. A court in the Rocks – Miller's Buildings – of fourteen houses, each of two rooms less than 3 square metres, had four closets for the fourteen houses, which were estimated to house about sixty people. In 1889, the investigating committee 'found on the doorstep, a heap of human excreta, covered with an old straw hat'.[5] In 1900, 303 people contracted bubonic plague, and 103 of them died. This at last brought these conditions into the limelight and led to slum clearance and better sanitation in inner Sydney.

In 1890, however, working-class housing in Sydney was thought by those few who had studied it to be worse than that of London, which was generally agreed to be worse than anywhere else. The loss of inner residential land to industrial and commercial use increased the density of a growing population, trapped by poor public transport, crowded into a decreasing area, served by an incompetent local government, in a steep sandstone terrain that of itself made the provision of adequate urban services difficult.

Water supply and sanitation had been difficult in Sydney from the outset: in 1851, only about 1000 houses of an approximate 8000 in the Sydney Corporation area were connected to mains supplies. Many houses in the 1850s had wells and cesspits side by side. A report in the *Sydney Morning Herald* said of the inhabitants of Parramatta Street that:

> they cook in dirt – they eat in dirt – and they sleep in it, they are born, bred and they die in dirt; from the cradle to the grave, they pass through life in filth – society tolerates it, and they look upon it as their inheritance.[6]

'Marvellous Melbourne' was little better than Sydney in the colonial years. Bernard Barrett has given a detailed account of the slums of Collingwood, and the uses to which back yards were put there.

> In the mid-nineteenth century privy outhouses were usually constructed over or near a cesspit. Cesspits were of varying degrees of sophistication. In the 1850s and 1860s the typical cesspit on Collingwood Flat tended to be at the primitive end of the scale – a mere hole dug in the ground. It was probably never emptied; when it became filled with solid matter, it might be covered over with earth, and the timber superstructure would be moved a few yards away to a new hole.[7]

They grow good tomatoes in Collingwood back yards today.

The Board of Works was created in 1890, with the responsibility of providing water and developing a sewerage system. Melbourne had already established a clean, continuous and publicly owned water supply by 1853, while London's system did not reach this stage until 1899, but Melbourne was well behind in establishing a sewerage system. London had made cesspools illegal in 1847, although it then ran its sewers into the Thames. Adelaide began constructing a sewerage system in 1878, and Sydney shortly afterwards. Hobart and Melbourne constructed their major works in the first years of the twentieth century. The inner suburbs of Perth were sewered at a leisurely pace, as befits the more relaxed lifestyle in the West, between 1906 and 1920, with the main outlet at Claise Brook in East Perth. 'Some wealthy households installed their own septic tanks. Most made do with the double-pan system and dry-earth closets until the sewerage pipes reached them'.[8]

Brisbane was the last of the capital cities to sewer, on a timetable like that of most country towns. The construction of Brisbane's first sewerage project began in 1916, but did not proceed until 1923, so that:

> pan closets were still operating in central Brisbane in 1923 – and they still operate (along with septic tanks) in many Australian country towns and outer suburbs today. In 1960, it was estimated that half a million people lacked mains sewerage in the Sydney metropolitan area alone.[9]

Perth in 1988 was 73 per cent sewered.

Australia is often described as one of the world's most urbanised nations, but this is misleading. For most of our history, most of us have been living in a suburb. Our culture still has a semi-rural flavour, although things are changing. And our back yards reflect it. In fact, our back yards faithfully reflect the history of the word 'yard', on which the *OED* has a long entry. First, there is a range of Teutonic words (OS. *gard*, yard, farm, MHG. *garte*, G. *garten*, garden, Goth. *garda*, enclosure) and so on. It goes on to say that 'close affinity of sense is exhibited by the words derived from the Teutonic root ...' The primary sense is that of 'enclosure' – of which the circle is the most economical form, used by cattlemen from the Bantu to early Australian bush-drovers, whose roughly circular corrals can still be found in quiet decay south of the Monaro. The basic enclosure was either to keep cattle in, or keep them out. It was sometimes qualified by a prefix – farm yard, vineyard, orchard. In short, the word was used for a multifunctional enclosure, generally attached to a house, basically rural in origin. There is a similar set of words derived from an Indo-European root *ghort*, viz, Gr. Xopros farm-yard, feeding place, food, fodder, L. *hortus* garden, *co-hors* enclosure, yard, pen for cattle and poultry; but there are phonological difficulties in the way of equating both groups of words. Whether they can be equated or not, it is interesting that both sets of words have a similar range of meanings.

So there is something primitive about the Australian suburban back yard, both word and thing. Indeed the word itself is faintly archaic, more used, at least unqualified, in North America and Australia than in the British Isles. The verb form, used as in 'yarding cattle', is given as '*colonial and US*', with a quotation from Kingsley's novel, *Geoffrey Hamlyn*: 'Well, lad, suppose we yard these rams'. There are few rams to be yarded nowadays in St Kilda or Double Bay, few outhouses or woodheaps or chooks or coppers, and not many vegetable gardens, either, although the lemon tree seems to be assured of eternal life. Self-sufficiency is no longer desirable to most people.

Does the suburban back yard described above go back to founding days? Denis Winston, the Foundation Professor of Town and Country Planning at the University of Sydney until his retirement in 1974, emphasised both space and function as follows:

With wide streets went large building plots; even the town-lands
in Adelaide had originally one acre plots: horses, cattle, hens and

pigs had to be provided for so that good yard space and extensive out-buildings were general. Even today Australians expect that a family home should accommodate the two cars, with trailer or caravan, and have room for the children's tent as a summer sleepout; and many home sites relatively close to the centres of the main cities are still big enough for this.[10]

In Perth, there was a fine debate in Council in 1876 on pigs. The Medical Officer thought they were injurious to health and the Attorney-General proposed that no-one should keep a pig within 50 yards of his neighbour's house – which would have had the effect of allowing them on the large blocks of the wealthy while forbidding them on the small blocks of the poor – but George Shenton and James Lee-Steere defended the poor man's right to keep a pig, and they won the day.[11] Pigs were finally banned forever in 1886 as insanitary, to be replaced by far more insanitary rubbish tips. This was part of the move towards centralised services that has characterised the growth of cities everywhere.

It is this that has deprived the back yard of its utility, or, more accurately, changed its functions. First, the coming of sewerage, then the advent of the motor car brought significant change, the car requiring a garage, also used for storage. There was sometimes an entry from the back lane (the dunny lane) into the garage in the back corner; if not, there was a long drive from the front, eventually paved, usually with two concrete strips and a well-trimmed grass median. The garage was usually behind the house. Later it grew in size, to accommodate two or three cars (and a trailer, and a boat, in homes that are more affluent but not necessarily wealthy); and it moved forward flush with the frontage, of which it became an integral part, rather than an afterthought.

In the late 1940s and '50s, the old clothes line went and was almost universally replaced by a horizontal windmill of steel and galvanised wire, known as the Hills Clothes Hoist (which began production in 1945); later, electric driers and retractable washing lines replaced the Hills Clothes Hoist in design-conscious back yards – or, rather, back gardens, because this is what they were becoming. I asked a middle-class, middle-aged English friend to describe the back yard of her childhood home in Surrey; she replied, with mild affront, that they did not have a back yard, they had a garden behind the house. This was a class distinction that applied in Australia also to a degree, but as the nation has become more uniformly suburban and middle class, the distinction is blurred. Perhaps it is more accurate to say that people make statements of various kinds by the way they use the land around the house. Especially in country towns, the old back yard lives on. Others still use their back yard as a functional space, still primarily male, for working on the boat, maintaining the vehicle, fixing the trailer, stripping the paint off doors and mantel pieces – it is still a service yard, although the services have changed. The atmosphere is casual, male, untidy, relaxed, spontaneous, and in its way, creative. It is emphatically for use, not for display – and it is still common. I have seen some prime examples in South Fremantle recently.

However, the trend is all the other way. The back yard has become back garden, for recreation, adult-dominated family use, and for showing off to one's peers. The following advertisement from 1988 is typical of middle-range homes now being offered in the new suburbs. It is not in the exclusive, luxury class of Claremont or Peppermint Grove, but is able to offer many of the same 'features', because the land is cheap.

> At the rear of the home there is a large and shady patio area, complete with gas barbecue. The rear garden is terraced and leads up to a paved area and a sparkling free-form swimming pool. The area is beautifully landscaped with palms and shrubs, being sheltered by a shade covered pergola.[12]

In becoming display space, the back yard has added a public function to its private one, and thus acquired a characteristic of the front garden. We have not looked at that yet, but front and back are a dialectical pair, defining each other negatively, and to understand either, we must look at both. Once again, Glen Tomasetti sets the background with her Bert and Lizzie in East St Kilda, 1934. First, what Robin Boyd called 'arboriphobia':

An enemy on one boundary, inoffensive people on another and friends at a short distance was a pattern repeated in the suburbs. The Larkins fulfilled the requirements for enmity. Their garden was neglected. Their flowering gums, planted right on the fence, dropped leaves and nuts on Bert's drive. Hanging low after rain, they wet his head when he parked the Vauxhall beside the house.[13]

With this enmity to trees goes a mania for pruning, which is still alive and well.

Arthur didn't believe in pruning soft-fruit trees. Bert did. He loved pruning, cutting back and lopping. He often walked round the garden working a pair of secateurs in his right hand, looking for dead flower heads and wayward twigs. When the day came to prune a tree, he started the job joyfully, cutting back to the last possible spot from which new growth might shoot. The sight of a tree, just after he'd pruned it, was as painful to Lizzie as the sight of her was to him, after she'd had a new permanent wave.[14]

By implication, Tomasetti later attributes both these behaviour patterns to a pioneering mentality by showing Bert's reaction to natural bushland.

They were passing through bush and it depressed him. He could see no beauty in it, no beauty at all. It represented only back-breaking labour. He thought of fire because he'd really like to put a match to it and see it swept away, leaving the land for man's use. That didn't happen after a fire of course. The bush recovered. The grey-green leaves of the gum trees with their ragged bark and the spindly wattles not yet in flower all filled him with dull melancholy; work, monotony, work. The bush had nothing to do with Bert's understanding of the glories of nature.[15]

This hatred of trees is still common. The following letter from a suburban newspaper in 1989 is not unusual.

Those damn box trees! I must admit I call them stronger things than that. Well, I've just spent another one and a half hours raking leaves. When are the Subiaco council going to do something about them? The streets and footpaths are an absolute disgrace. We know the council has a thing about cutting down trees but why not revert back to pruning them round and every year but on both sides of the street? Surely in the long run it would be cheaper than the major job it will be one day. I thought I would try if you can't beat them join them, but we like a tidy yard and a drive and the road sweeper would need to come every day to sweep them away. Subiaco and Shenton Park would certainly never win a tidy city or street award.[16]

Mechanical sweepers which suck up leaves from roads, footpaths and grass are common in Perth. Although the hungry sands of the Perth metropolitan area are notably deficient in organic matter, the leaves so collected are rarely composted, even in educational institutions.

A passion for neatness is the most striking characteristic of Australian display gardening, either institutional or private. Edges are trimmed, leaves are raked, flowers are staked, concrete hosed down, shrubs trimmed and clipped, trees pruned. The bounteous, brimming, rambling, over-blown, careless garden is still rare – with reason, in that it is actually harder to maintain in Australia, where growth is rapid, and the overgrown garden soon becomes no garden. But the driving forces behind this mania for neatness are highly conjectural. It is not peculiar to Australia – it is to be found in New Zealand, parts of the north of England, parts of Canada, less so in the US. It may in part represent the pioneering spirit, but it is clearly also a cultural inheritance, as its distribution shows. There is a strong component of what is variously described as 'keeping up with the Joneses', 'peer group pressure' or 'civic pride'. In pre-World War II Australia, ordinary, decent people kept up appearances, not without considerable effort, to maintain their self-respect; freshly ironed shirts for the school children and a tidy front yard kept the flag flying. But the mania for neatness also represents a discourse with the environment. Our houses and their immediate surrounds are one of the few areas in our lives where we have real power, make decisions and put them into practice. Perhaps it is this sense of control, especially among those who have limited control of their own lives in the outside world, that leads Bert to prowl the garden, secateurs in hand, looking for something to 'manage' by imposing his will. If there is a distinctively Australian component in this behaviour, which on the whole I doubt, it is a rejection of the endless leaf litter and the asymmetry – the *untidiness* – of the Australian bush. Perhaps that fear of the redback spider lurking under the toilet seat, waiting to strike when your defences are down, was seen as a malign outsider from the bush, a fifth column from that harsh natural Australia we have fought to control or exclude – since the fear was quite out of proportion to the occurrence.

Since it was always semi-public, a place to work in, but not for recreation or living, the front garden has changed less than the back yard, but it too has been subject to the vagaries of fashion. Some of the changes are shown in my last quotations from Glen Tomasetti:

'You look like having a good show of dahlias,' said Keith. 'They're always good after they've been lifted and you can stake them as you re-plant. You ought to have more dahlias instead of all those annuals and borders you plant: not worth the work.' 'Valerie likes them for picking,' said Keith solemnly. He wasn't interested in gardening but did what was expected of him, only declaring his independence by growing different plants from those favoured by the family into which he'd married. Instead of hydrangeas, standard roses, dahlias, snapdragons, a lemon tree and stag ferns for the shady side, he'd tried lupins, delphiniums, holly-hocks, begonias and his lawns were pure English grass, fine and soft. He'd just bought two azaleas for the south side of the house and he knew his father-in-law would disapprove of this unnec-essary expenditure. Bert, the son of a goldminer turned farmer, could spend happily only on essentials. When boots or chairs or a pocket knife had to be bought, he went for quality because it was economy in the long run. But gardens were to be made from other gardens, from cuttings, corms, bulbs and roots of buffalo grass. You had to buy a lemon tree, standard roses and grass seed for bare patches.[17]

The azaleas and English lawn grass mark the availability of a more abundant water supply, and a more reckless attitude to its use, with hose and sprinkler rather than bucket and watering can. The disci-plines of scarcity are relaxed. Not only water is abundant and used wastefully. Fertilisers, pressure-pack sprays, pelleted snail-killer, all add to the convenience of gardening, as take-away foods, full of fat, sugar and salt, add to the convenience of eating. Gardening has become a conspicuous element in the consumer society.

A recent book asserts the following:

The gradual infiltration of native plants into our suburban gardens, and the corresponding withdrawal of European-styled gardens, suggests that a process of legitimation is being acted out that mirrors positive changes in the Australians' relation with the landscape. Certainly the low-maintenance factor recommends the native garden to the house-proud, but that recovery of leisure – the delivery from the garden's tyrannical domination of the weekend – also signifies a growing sense of accommodation with the land, through which culture and nature have been made to co-exist more harmoniously. While creative and adaptive, the highly stylised character of the versions of 'nature' found in the native garden is nevertheless controlled by an edging of old railway sleepers and a covering of woodchips, the latter suggesting how ambiguous the putatively harmonious relationship can be.[18]

It is hard to know how to tackle assertions such as this, which are common enough in popular journalism. What is a European-styled garden? Is the 'style' of a garden necessarily dependent on the choice of plants? Are gardens using Australian plants necessarily low maintenance? Why should an increase in leisure signify a growing sense of accommodation with the land? (Its most obvious outcome has been increasing pressure on natural resources.) How many 'native' gardens are either creative or adaptive? As for the 'old railway sleepers', most are new – cut for the garden trade. Ancient red-gum forests along our inland rivers are steadily and relentlessly felled to supply them. Is this harmony with the land?

I would like to see more use of local plants, gardens that provide habitat for birds, gardens in which plants are chosen and sited with care so that they can thrive without excessive cosseting. Such gardens are rare, as they always have been. They are not generally a feature of popular culture today, except perhaps in the vegetable garden, and they were probably more common when manure was recovered in the wake of the milkman's horse, and water was too precious to be wasted.

So both back and front changed as the times changed. As Rob Ingram put it in 1989:

> With seven-and-a-half million square kilometres of playground available, Australians have already withdrawn to their own quarter acre. And why not? It's summertime and the livin' is easy … with the pool, the barbecue, and the old redwood setting. The suburban backyard has become the resort that we used to drag the caravan down the coast to.[19]

This retreat to the back yard – or 'patio' behind the inner city terraces – doubtless reflects attitudes to congestion on the roads and overcrowding and high prices at the resorts. Despite the transformations in function, the standard subdivisions persist, and thus the back yard space itself remains, or has done so until very recently. The free-standing house with space before and behind has been the Australian dream, but that too is now changing. Australia, for better or worse, or both, is becoming urban, and the generous old back yard may become a threatened species.[20]

NOTES

1   T.A.G. Hungerford, *Wong Chu and the Queen's Letterbox: The First Collection of Stories*, Fremantle Arts Centre Press, Fremantle, 1977.

2   Glen Tomasetti, *Thoroughly Decent People*, McPhee Gribble, Melbourne, 1976, pp. 4, 22, 24.

3   Max Neutze, *Urban Development in Australia*, Allen & Unwin, Sydney, 1977, p. 5.

4   Max Kelly (ed.), *Nineteenth-century Sydney: Essays in Urban History*. Sydney University Press, 1978, p. 74.

5   Quoted in Kelly, p. 76.

6   *Sydney Morning Herald*, 7 March 1851, p. 2, quoted in David Clark, "Worse than Physic": Sydney's Water Supply, 1788–1888' in Kelly, p. 57.

7   Bernard Barrett, 'From Cesspits to Cesspans', *The Inner Suburbs: The Evolution of an Industrial Area*, Melbourne University Press, Melbourne, 1971, p. 75.

8   C.T. Stannage, *The People of Perth*. Perth City Council, 1979, p. 278.

9   Barrett, p. 137.

10   Denis Winston, 'Nineteenth Century Sources of Twentieth Century Theories, 1800-1939', in George Seddon and Mari Davis (eds), *Man and Landscape in Australia*, Australian Government Publishing Service, Canberra, 1976, p. 188.

11   Stannage, p. 174.

12   Real Estate advertisements, *Sunday Times*, Perth, 18 December 1988.

13   Tomasetti, pp. 7–8.

14   Tomasetti, p. 4.

15   Tomasetti, pp. 130–131.

16   *Weekly Post*, Subiaco, WA, 10 January 1989, p. 6.

17   Tomasetti, pp. 10–11.

18   J. Fiske, B. Hodge and G. Turner, *Myths of Oz: Reading Australian Popular Culture*, Allen & Unwin, Sydney, 1987, p. 30.

19   *Sydney Sun-Herald*, 1 January 1989.

20   This essay was originally accompanied by the acknowledgement: "I am grateful to several friends and colleagues whose critical comments helped me, especially Mike Bosworth and Warwick Forge. Thank you also to Glen Tomasetti for her permission to quote from *Thoroughly Decent People*." [A.G.]

15

THE GARDEN
AS PARADISE

1997

ECISIONS AND CHOICES ABOUT GARDENS ARE not made in a vacuum. They are culturally mediated. A multitude of forces is at work, including, in our own day, the influence of fashion, travel, reading. At a deeper level there are also some concepts with a long history. One set of concepts is expressed in western cultures through a group of related words. The words are: Eden, Paradise, Arcadia, Utopia.

The relations between these words are complex and shifting. Most dictionaries, for example, give Eden and Paradise as synonymous, yet we all know that they are not interchangeable. They have a different etymology, different history, and a different range of application, even though the differences consist in subtle nuances. It seems appropriate to explore these differences a little, although necessarily in a super-ficial way, since they range across more than two thousand years of cultural history.

Utopia

Utopia is a good word to begin with because its origin is known with precision, and because it makes explicit a characteristic that in the others is usually implicit only. Utopia is a critique of the actual. The word was coined by Sir Thomas More in 1516 as the title for a book, conjoining two Greek words, où = not; topos = place. Utopia is an imaginary island, depicted as enjoying a perfect social, legal and political system. Sir Thomas More's England shared with Utopia the fact of being an island, but the resemblance stopped there. He does not present his imaginary island as a practicable alternative, but as a way of highlighting the imperfections of the world around him and of strengthening the will to improve them. This form of social critique is widespread, and pops up in some unexpected places. It is widely claimed today, for example, that Margaret Mead's well-known anthropological works on Samoa and the Trobriand Islanders are much more a criticism of the narrowly puritanical United States in which she was brought up than they are about the real life behaviour of the people she purported to be studying.

As noted above, the emphasis of Sir Thomas More's *Utopia* is on the social, legal and political system, as one might expect of the chancellor of the realm, but he nevertheless goes into some detail about the gardens (and makes them sound remarkably like Australian suburbia, a point that its critics might consider).

The stretes be twentie foote brode. On the backe side of the houses through the whole length of the streete, lye large gardens inclosed round aboute wyth the backe part of the streetes. Every house hathe two doores, one into the streete, and a posterne doore on the backsyde into the garden ... They set great

store by their gardeines. In them they have vineyardes, all maner
of fruite, herbes, and flowres, so pleasaunt, so well furnished,
and so fynely kepte, that I never sawe thynge more frutefull, nor
better trimmed in anye place. Their studie and deligence herin
commeth not onely of pleasure, but also of a certen strife and
contention that is between strete and strete, concerning the trim-
ming, husbanding, and furnishing of ther gardens: everye man
for his owne parte. And verilye you shall not lightelye finde in
all the citie anye thinge, that is more commodious, eyther for
the profite of the Citizens, or for pleasure. And therefore it maye
seme that the first founder of the citie mynded nothing so much
as these gardens.[1]

Sir Thomas More's word 'Utopia' has had shifts in meaning
since 1516: one that is used in the planning literature is to make it
the antonym of 'dystopia', the bad or dysfunctional place, compared
with 'the good place', although strict etymology would require that
to be spelt 'Eutopia' ('eu' meaning 'good' in Greek, of which More,
a good classicist, was well aware, his title intending the two possible
meanings). A much more familiar shift in meaning is that a 'Utopian
scheme' is now seen as impractical, the idle dream of the fanciful
who know nothing about the real world, and in this sense the term is
dismissive, even contemptuous. This shift, however, emphasises one
further characteristic of all of the words with which I began: Utopia
is *unattainable*. Attitudes to the unattainable then diverge. The
unattainable can be seen either as a delusory will-o'-the-wisp, leading us astray, making us long for something we can't have – we would
be better off without it, getting on with the realistically attainable.
Or it can be seen as the energising dream that leads us on creatively
to achieve far more than we could ever believe possible without it,
even though the perfection always remains just beyond our grasp.

This tension underlies a great deal of writing and thinking about the design and practice of gardening (and much else).

From Sir Thomas More's *Utopia*, I draw three points: that there can be no ideal world without gardens, and even, perhaps, Best Kept Street and Tidy Town competitions; that all Utopias are a critique of our mundane surroundings; that they set up unattainable goals – which can be seen either as inspiration or distracting folly (and I might add that every gardener I know is deeply ambivalent about these two attitudes, sharing now one, now the other).

Eden and Paradise

'Eden' and 'Paradise' have a longer history, and they are not so much imaginary as mythical, although they can be understood quite literally by fundamentalist Christians and Muslims. Eden shares with Utopia the characteristic of being unattainable: it is a lost world, from which we have forever been shut out by the original sin of Adam and Eve. Paradise, in one of its uses, is an attainable reward, to those who are literal in their faith, for living virtuously. Curiously, however, 'Eden' seems to have a much more concrete reality than 'Paradise'. It has been notionally located as an actual site somewhere on the Anatolian Plateau, for example, not without reason, given that most of our common fruits had their origin there. One recurring feature of imagined Edens is that there was always plenty to eat without much effort, and a range of fruit trees with an extended fruiting season covering much of the year seems to fill this need well. But it has also been used metaphorically of new-found lands by Europeans, if they were seen as being fertile, without climatic extremes, and, as a rule, inhabited by men and women perceived as living with noble simplicity.

Adam and Eve were naked, and Eden has always suggested an innocent sexuality – an element of Margaret Mead's Samoa of the Noble Savage, who was earlier identified in the European imagination with the American Indian – not, alas, in European behaviour, the identification being restricted to the literary imagination of the salons. This search for primitive nobility and innocent sexuality in the naked or semi-naked savage is not restricted to the Christian myth of Eden: it is fully developed in Tacitus, for example, expressed in his *Germania*, in which the forest dwellers to the north of the Alps were seen as having all the primitive virtues that had once supposedly characterised the Romans, but had been lost in a society that was urban, corrupt, autocratic, licentious, luxurious, effete.[2] This is another key theme, and it applies in varying degrees to all of my four words; the 'garden', however conceptualised, is antithetic to the vices of urban blight.

In Paradise, the sexuality was not always quite so innocent as it is portrayed in, for example, the almost puritanically innocent Adam and Eve of the sculptures and paintings of medieval Germany. Paradise might offer a more abundant sensuality, more like the guiltless but very active sexuality portrayed by Margaret Mead. The Muslim Paradise was (is?) conveniently furnished with houris, voluptuously beautiful nymphs with eyes like gazelles (that is the Arabic and Persian derivation of the word). This, it is apparent, is a male-oriented concept of the delights of Paradise: sexual equality would presumably require that there be a plentiful supply of graceful and virile young men at hand to pleasure the ladies who had made it to Paradise, but the Muslim concept is reticent on this point. The idea of a rich sensuality inevitably degenerates into license and sexual ambiguity in some versions of this theme. The Forest of Arden was the site of imagined indulgences of many kinds, including a loosening of the gender roles ('If you go down to the woods today, you're in for a Big Surprise').

The loosening of defined roles relates not only to gender, but to social hierarchy, another recurrent theme that has been expressed in a variety of ways through time. 'When Adam delved and Eve span, Who was then the gentleman?' is an assertion of the rights of man, but the democratic ideal was located by Tacitus in the Hercynian forests of Germany; Shakespeare inverts the social order – for a time – in the Forest of Arden, and Robin Hood in the greenwood, both part of a long tradition. The 'garden' in its various manifestations is usually (but not always) seen as a place in which distinctions of rank are laid aside. This carries through to the present in very minor but recognisable forms. There is, for example, a freemasonry of gardeners. 'Real gardeners' recognise each other and accept each other at once as equals, whether they be Dame Elisabeth Murdoch, Lady Law-Smith, or Jack's Jill. The Open Garden Scheme in Australia could not work without this recognition that gardens are for gardeners, and thus for sharing among equals.

Of course the dictionaries are correct in listing 'Eden' and 'Paradise' as synonyms, and the different nuances that attach to them are never used consistently. As well as differing in tense, however, they differ etymologically. 'Eden' has a Hebraic origin, associated with the word meaning 'delight' – hence the garden of earthly delights. Whether as part of the biblical story, Christian and Jewish, or as an ancestral memory of favoured valleys in Asia Minor, 'Eden' is earthly. The *OED* gives its primary and secondary meanings as '1. The first abode of Adam and Eve, Paradise, and 2. *transf.* and *fig.* A delightful abode, a paradise'. Both end up as 'Paradise', but Paradise has a much longer definition, and range of applications. Its origin is also Middle Eastern, but in this case, Avestic (Old Persian), with the original meaning of a large park. Its first recorded use in Greek is by the historian Xenophon, who used it to describe the parks of Persian kings and nobles. These were usually hunting parks, so they were extensive, and they contained wild animals, and this persisted as one of the later meanings as 'an oriental pleasure ground, *esp.* one enclosing wild beasts for the chase. *b.* Hence an English park in which foreign animals are kept. 1613'. When it is used synonymously with 'Eden' it refers to the *earthly* Paradise, whereas the *heavenly* Paradise is the abode of the blessed, either Christian, Jewish or Muslim.

The difference in origins is reflected in the metaphorical application to gardens: the walled garden, full of flowers, fragrance and sweet ease is an Eden derivative, whereas the English estates improved by Capability Brown and Humphry Repton in the eighteenth century are paradisiac, offspring of the Persian hunting park, although the wild animals were usually restricted to deer, which were self-propelled lawnmowers. These estates in England were the product of a pastoral economy: they are based on grazing rather than digging and delving – agriculture – and thus can also be seen as reflecting through the ages to our own day as two approaches to 'the garden' (using the word in the broad sense). One is actively interventionist, turning the sod, pruning, weeding, maintaining; a branch of agriculture. The garden space is enclosed, and animals, other than a dog or cat, are excluded. Animals are inimical to intensive agriculture. The other is more extensive and more expansive, less obviously bounded, relying for its pleasures on mature trees, groves of them where possible, grassy clearings (which we now call 'lawns') with an understorey of shrubs in the woods and at their margins, but no defined planting beds: in short, a pastoral system rather than an agricultural one, in which it grades imperceptibly into the 'Arcadian', my fourth word, and still to come. The persistence of lawns into contemporary suburban gardens in Australia is a very clear indication of the extent to which garden design is mediated through cultural history. Australia was settled at a time when the dominant social group in Britain was nurtured by a pastoral economy. The lawn is an Arcadian remnant.

This distinction between Eden and Paradise is neither clear-cut nor consistent. The nuances shift and change. The Eden of the Book of Genesis was not agricultural (the delving followed the Fall), but it was certainly not a hunting economy, and graphic representations show the lion lying down with the lamb. The dietary regime at the Hotel Eden is not specified in detail: Eve certainly did not spend the day over a hot stove, so elaborate food preparation is out. One gets the impression that wild honey, milk (possibly) and lots of fruit, apples excepted, were the staples. In other words, close to the diet of the frugivorous primates of the Great Apes to this day. Is Eden a memory? It is possible to see the Fall as the beginning of agriculture, with its life of backbreaking toil, not so much a milestone of evolutionary progress but a consequence of increasing density of population. Anthropologists have used the phrase 'primitive affluence' of hunter-gatherer societies, and it has been argued that the Aborigines in Australia in the eighteenth century had a more nutritious and more varied diet, acquired with substantially less expenditure of effort, than their European counterparts. Perhaps we can see the gatherers in Eden and the hunters and herders in the Paradise myth, representing two strains of a pre-agrarian society.

Nevertheless, the Eden derivatives among our gardens do require intensive labour, and this is precisely because of the Fall. We can re-create imagined Edens, gardens of earthly delights, but their cost is unending hard work – pleasurable, perhaps, but work.

Arcadia

Arcadia or Arcady overlaps considerably in meaning with 'Paradise', but it is a product of the Greek and Roman cultures, not the Middle Eastern. It was supposedly drawn from a real place in the

Peloponnesus, one favoured by nature. In both cultures, it was imagined as a wooded rocky place, the haunt of satyrs, the realm of Pan with his sweetly haunting pipes. It is the myth of a pastoral economy, idealised by city dwellers, and to that extent, it can be read as escapist fantasy. The Theocritean poetry of shepherds, shepherdesses and their innocently amorous pursuits was in part a product of urban overcrowding, first in Greek Alexandria, later in Rome. It had a febrile revival at the French court, where there were eager swains aplenty ready and willing to pursue their reluctant loves through the woods. In England, an Arcadian-Paradisiac ideal became the basis of landscape design, as we have seen. Because of the Enclosures and the switch from agriculture to a pastoral economy on the large estates in the eighteenth century, a productive grazing estate could also be conceived as a *landscape* of shady groves and open meadows, and the 'garden' or park was a semi-natural, productive world of Nature refined of its coarser attributes. An apparently natural harmony between people and their setting is central to the Arcadian ideal, and it can be illustrated well in many of the older rural estates in the better-watered and more fertile parts of Australia, which were receptive to the Arcadian imagination, since they are all part of the pastoral economy. The influence of the Arcadian dream is strikingly apparent in Australia from the self-image that so many graziers evince through the names they gave their land: the key word is 'Park'; Sefton Park, Camberley Park, Alton Park, Camden Park. How many 'Parks' do you know in your neighbourhood? They are not, of course, parks – they are sheep farms or cattle farms. A park is devoted to leisure pursuits, not to earning a living. It is only by invoking the Arcadian dream that the two can be yoked satisfactorily.

A good example of an Arcadian landscape 'on the ground' is the driveway and broad setting of Dame Elisabeth Murdoch's Cruden Farm at Langwarrin, on the outskirts of Melbourne, and one could use three of the words we have been discussing to name its parts. There is a walled garden that is a 'garden of earthly delights', which is to say, 'Eden', sheltered, bound, fragrant, full of flowers – but because of that apple-eating, requiring a great deal of hard work. Around the house there is a more open garden with grassy walks, shrubberies and many fine trees, more Paradise than Eden; this runs out to a working farm, with a gentle transition. But the 'farm', which is pasture and shade trees, is carefully groomed. The curving driveway itself is of gravel, not bitumen, which maintains the rustic feeling, but increases the maintenance. Beside the avenue of trees, there is a split-rail fence, and beyond that, the blond pastures of summer. Intensely Australian, naturalistic, but the effects are highly contrived, without any appearance of contrivance.

The Critical Use of Terms

If we define each of my four terms carefully, and use them precisely and consistently, can they then have a more rigorous employment in the analysis of garden history? The answer is, alas, no. They will always shift and change. 'Eden', 'Paradise' and 'Arcadia' will continue to be used interchangeably on many occasions, and all are used with a Utopian context, in the sense of being ideals. The point of considering them at all is to gain insight into the complexities of cultural history.

Paradise Translated

The European imagination has often located Paradise in the New World. The French have been specially fertile – Jean-Jacques Rousseau and the Noble Savage, Gauguin and his languorous Paradise in the South Seas, the 'Paysages Exotiques' series of the Parisian painter Henri Rousseau, the customs officer who had never travelled, but worked from the Jardin des Plantes, the Botanic Gardens in Paris. His paintings pick up several of the themes noted already. It seems always to be spring. The colours are bright and clear. Apes play happily with golden fruits. Another French fantasy is the account of the voyage to La Terre Australe by Jacques Sadeur (1693).[3] Remember that there are only four large animals, and none of them dangerous, there are no venomous serpents, there are no troublesome insects and, happily, there are no flies. We live on fruit that ripens the year round – and so on.

The English were more pragmatic: to describe a new land as 'like a garden' or 'a second Eden' was generally a prelude to occupation. 'The country was a Paradise', said Thomas Arnold, of New Zealand. One early 1800s English traveller to Australia was impressed enough by what he saw being achieved here in New South Wales 'even under the worst auspices, and in a country filled with the dregs of our own … How much more then, must New Zealand flourish, which is itself a beautiful garden and capable of being rendered the most delightful spot on earth.'[4]

The sting is in the tail. If the place is already a beautiful garden, where the soil is so fertile that it provides readily for all the necessities of life, then what further 'rendering' is required? The answer is that part of taking possession is to put your own stamp on the land. Very often this has meant wiping out the qualities that made the place so attractive in the first place, and trying to reproduce the landscapes and gardens you left behind. Thus the garden in the New Worlds, the Americas, Australia, New Zealand, can be seen as one of the tools of imperial power; it remains one of its symbols and the slowest to loosen its hold.

Future Directions

John of Gaunt called his England 'this other Eden, demi-Paradise', a sentiment of the kind most often heard in times of war, when patriotic fervour runs strong. But it also expresses a mood of acceptance and celebration. Eden is here. Embrace the actual – or, in language less elegant than Shakespeare's, but still pungent: 'This is as good as it gets', says Paul Keating.

This mood is strong in Australia today: we should abandon the delusive dreams – and there is more than one. The Utopian dream of Gabriel de Foigny and his imagined voyager Jacques Sadeur gives way to the reality: there are flies, venomous serpents, destructive insects of all kinds. The English imperial dream is also dispensable, the dream of conquest and transformation. We do not need to achieve social standing by recreating Knole or Bodnant in hot and dry Australia. Macedon, Bowral, the Adelaide Hills and Toowoomba are not the only places in Australia where it is possible to have fine gardens, although the gardening literature would lead us to think so. They are regularly described as having climates 'favourable to gardening', which means, of course, slightly more amenable to pursuing generally inappropriate goals than the rest of the country.

Nevertheless, the ambiguities remain. No matter how much we dedicate ourselves to ecologically responsible gardening, gardens do not look after themselves, and we cannot leave it to nature. The better introduced plants are adapted to local conditions the more likely they are to become dangerous garden escapes. The Australian environment everywhere is already a disturbed environment. Weed invasion is unending. If we aim for a garden that is productive as well as decorative, problems multiply. Where I live, in Fremantle, the olive and the mulberry look after themselves, and fruit generously. Lemons need some fertiliser and summer water, but are pretty tough. Figs, however, need constant baiting. They fruit prolifically, but are full of fruit fly. And so it goes. Moreover we demand a higher level of comfort and design in our immediate environment than the natural environment generally offers.

If the European imagination has often idealised the lands of the sunny south as a place of warmth and leisure where the flowers always bloom and the ripe fruits drop effortlessly into your lap, those who live and garden there know a different world – one where plants grow rapidly, but also senesce and decay rapidly, where weeds also grow rapidly, rampantly, where there are no winters cold enough to kill off predatory insects, where air that is both humid and warm encourages the growth of fungus, mould, scale, virus, black spot … where the organic content of the soil oxidises rapidly and where heavy rain leaches the soil of nutrients, yet also where the heat of the sun is such that even a few days without rain can constitute a drought, and four or five months without it, a significant challenge.

We can and should redefine our concept of Eden, Paradise, Arcadia, using local idioms and in ways that reflect more of the actual. But there are dreams that are enabling as well as dreams that are disabling. The latter feed on hope of some celestial bonanza, unearned, and they are escapist. We can have a better world, but it will be here, not over the hill or beyond the blue horizon, and we have to make it with our own two hands. This is the sustaining dream.

Postscript

It is not usual for a book on understanding and conserving landscape to devote a whole section to gardens. Yet Voltaire thought it necessary to cultivate one's garden. My reasons are his, and others that were not his. One is that gardeners are, in fact, one of the most important groups of land managers in this country, since between us we manage more than 50 per cent of all urban land in Australia, that is, the land that carries 80 per cent of the population: land that is not vast in area compared with that managed by farmers, pastoralists, miners and state agencies, but greater in value and in resource consumption than all of them. *Gardeners are key land managers.* Our choices therefore lie not in whether but in how we manage the land. We would all agree that we must do it in an ecologically responsible way.

But most Australians are *not* gardening in an ecologically responsible way at present, although some of us are trying. If we take the sum of gardening in Australia, it is undeniable that the resource input is gross. As with the rest of the world, we are an extreme reflection of the consumer society. The consumption of land alone is impressive. Perth, for example, stretches north-south for 120 kilometres and east-west for 70 kilometres, and this huge area houses 1.2 million people, at a density lower than that even of Los Angeles, and the reason is that nearly everyone has their own garden. Moreover, this is not just any land – although the soils are of low fertility, it lies in the only corner of the state that has a temperate climate and a substantial and reliable rainfall. The other state capitals, which house most of our population, are also favourably situated.

Next, the water consumption is heavy: it averages 515 kilolitres per household, and it is estimated that 40 per cent of this goes on parks and gardens. Lawn grass is a major irrigated crop in Western

Australia. There are now concerns about both the quality of the water and the rate of replenishment.

Moreover, water moves nutrients in solution. Since our parks and gardens are heavily fertilised with chemical fertilisers brought in from distant sources, there is an oversupply of nutrients to the coastal lakes and rivers, and this is causing eutrophication and algal blooms. There is a long list of resources consumed: topsoil is brought in and peat is quarried, along with other soil-amending agents. Nearly all of them are in quite short supply in the natural environment. Oil and petrol are consumed by garden machinery, especially by lawnmowers. Large quantities of garden waste are generated, through weeding and pruning. This may be chipped and composted, but much of it is carted off to sanitary landfill sites. Waste disposal is an increasingly expensive component of our urban economy. Finally, a whole range of insecticides and fungicides is sold and used, and some of these toxic chemicals find their way into the food chain, especially for birds. It is difficult to get good statistics for these inputs. The Australian Bureau of Statistics reports that Australians spent $910 million in 1991 on nursery and horticultural products. This equals $172 per household, but the ABS statistics cover sales from nurseries only. Supermarkets and chain stores would double that figure comfortably, and for Perth the figure is likely to be much higher than the national average given the more demanding gardening environment. Clearly we need to lift our game. How?

The *appropriate* goals, it seems to me, are fairly easy to spell out. To reach them is harder, and requires commitment. We could return to the gardening practices of our parents, although in their case they followed from necessity, while in ours we have been undone by availability. No more bags of peat moss, nor loads of pirated topsoil, nor chemical fertilisers, nor toxic insecticides. Stick to pyrethrum, garlic sprays, hose off the aphids, make your own compost and mulch, keep seeds, swap cuttings and go easy on the water. Above all, learn what works in your neighbourhood. There has been a great and healthy interest in garden design over the last few years, and this is both desirable and overdue, but the search for an Australian *style* is a chimera. John Brookes, the English garden designer, urged recently that we should be incorporating motifs from Aboriginal culture to make our gardens more distinctively Australian. My response is that we have taken enough from the Aborigines already without trying also to appropriate their culture, and that, in any case, the goal is wrong. Good design is good design. We do not need an Australian garden design style. What we do need is better design, and to evolve sound Australian gardening practices, which must be frugal, and, of necessity, regional, even local.

Notes

1   Sir Thomas More, *Utopia* (1516), trans. Ralph Robinson, 1551, 1556, George Sampson (ed.), G. Bell and Sons, London, 1910, p. 90.

2   Simon Schama, *Landscape and Memory*, Harper Collins, London, 1995.

3   Jacques Sadeur (Gabriel de Foigny), *A New Discovery of Terra Incognita Australis, or the Southern World, by James Sadeur a Frenchman*, Charles Hern, London, 1693.

4   Geoff Park, *Nga Uruora: The Groves of Life*, Victoria University Press, Wellington, 1995, pp. 323–324.

16

THE OLD COUNTRY

2005

I THINK I HAVE HAD AN EPIPHANY RECENTLY, BUT I AM still thinking about it. It was about birds. The word 'epiphany' is not much used at the breakfast table, but assorted writers have had them, or claimed to have had them. James Joyce had them. William Blake had them, but – unpretentiously – called them 'fancies'. Keats, Wordsworth, Coleridge, Gerard Manley Hopkins and Yeats had them, or something akin to them. An epiphany is more than an insight or an inspiration, which are positive. It is more like a revelation. The Bible has a whole book of them, and some of them are pretty scary, as was mine. When the veils are ripped off the mundane, what you see may well be confronting. Think of the Anglican dean Swift writing in Catholic, conquered Ireland: 'The other day I saw a woman flayed, and I have never seen anyone whose appearance was so improved for the worse'. The bite of this spare observation comes from the way in which several implied value systems come into violent collision: concepts of humanity, male respect for the gentler sex, his Christian role, the need to maintain public order in a repressive and fragile colonial society always on the boil and in constant danger of eruption, and the power of social institutions of which he was a part and a beneficiary.

My epiphany was modest, but still confronting. As I said, it was about birds, which have often been instruments of epiphany, from

Greek tragedy (*The Birds*) to Edgar Allan Poe's raven, Coleridge's albatross, even Blake's Fancy: 'How do you know that every bird that cuts the aery way is a whole world of delight, Closed off by our senses five?' Well, we *don't* know. I find it attractive to think that birds may experience a world inaccessible to us, but it is still confronting. Our 'senses five' are still limiting, only one possible window on reality. What Blake does, what I think that all epiphanies do, is to question the relation between the observed and the observer and his assumed position of privilege.

My birds were kookaburras, a family of them, four in all. I was writing about a part of the campus of the University of Western Australia known as the Great Court, a large rectangle defined by handsome buildings. In the early days, there was a gardening shed in one part of it, and the gardener of the day planted trees around it. The shed has long gone, but the trees have thrived prodigiously in a sheltered location with a high watertable and fertile soils (old swamp soils of humus-rich silt and clay). The trees have grown so luxuriously and created such a dense canopy that they are now known as the Tropical Grove. None of the species is specifically tropical, but *en masse* they give that effect. A colleague suggested that I might mention the amiable family of four kookaburras in the Tropical Grove:

> they are very tame, living off offerings of sandwiches and pilfered pies. And they also seem more equitable in their pecking order than those terrorists of the bird-world, seagulls. They should really be cult figures as cultural custodians of the campus – they may even be metamorphosed spirits of old professors.

Almost a Blakean 'Fancy', more endearing than confronting at first sight, but I rejected it with all the force an 'old professor' could muster. The idea of metamorphosis is not unattractive in itself, and the implication that professors of any age tend to live off the casual bounty of students has a certain propriety, but kookaburras on campus, forsooth! Kookaburras anywhere in Western Australia are an ecological disaster. May Gibbs was a sharp-eyed naturalist in top gear while she was based here, but she left Western Australia and went into neutral in Sydney. Snugglepot and Cuddlepie are true sandgropers, based on marri and the red-flowering gum (*Corymbia calophylla* and *C. ficifolia*), very distinctive of the West. In Sydney she made a hero of the jackass by presenting it as a snake-killer. In the popular psyche from the Garden of Eden on, the serpent is bad news, evil and loathsome, so the kookaburra becomes a knight in shining armour.

Kookaburras may indeed occasionally kill a snake, but snakes are shy and few on the ground, so a kookaburra-induced mortality must be a rare event. The bird is, however, a fierce predator, eating frogs, worms, caterpillars – and eggs and baby birds. It is not indigenous to Western Australia. It was introduced to Yanchep National Park one hundred years ago, and has since spread. The indigenous avian fauna did not evolve with the kookaburra and there is no close equivalent in the south-west. The small and largely defenceless birds that belong here are a delight; the singing honeyeaters, the little brown honeyeaters, the New Holland honeyeaters, the striated pardalotes, rainbow bee-eaters and more. They are a source of immense pleasure to many people in Perth, they serve a range of ecological functions including insect predation – and they are at risk.

Sydney and Melbourne have lost most of their small birds: in Melbourne, mostly because of their replacement with introduced birds that have taken over their habitat, especially the sparrow, blackbird and mynah. In Sydney, there has also been a big increase in the number of the large predatory birds, especially ravens and currawongs. When there are few small birds there is little bird-song.

The harsh cries of the ravens, currawongs and kookaburras are no substitute for our 'dawn chorus' – which persists well beyond the dawn as a succession of choristers take up the melody through most of the day.

If I had to go back to Melbourne, there are things about Perth that I would not miss at all, but I would miss the small birds intensely. Their enemy is my enemy; hence the kookaburra is an unwelcome intruder from 'the Eastern States'. This is a good and loyal sandgroper point of view. But I came from Melbourne myself, so I am an intruder here too, doubly so since my family came from Britain. Moreover, this is a university, a Universitas; opposed in its very nature to the parochial. The Great Court, home to the Four Kooks of the Apocalypse, is a grove of trees almost all of which come from somewhere other than the Swan Coastal Plain. I have travelled a great deal, to the four corners of the earth, and am, so far as I am able to be, a citizen of the world. But ecology is implacably particularist, and the richness of our global environment depends on this particularity, not on the citizens of the world, the rats and seagulls and the sparrows. Kookaburras don't belong here.

The Nazis thought that Jews did not belong in Germany, and did their worst to return to racial purity. Notions of 'ecological integrity' apply not only to people and birds, but to plants and gardens. Some recent German historians have seen the 'wild garden', using only the plants local to the area, and favoured by ecologically minded opponents of French or Italian formal gardens, as complicitous with the 'blood-and-soil' ideology of Nazism.

It is beyond argument that the gardening impulse of western culture, especially in the last three hundred years, has become a part of imperial domination, bringing back trophies from the ends of the earth. Zygmunt Bauman, the distinguished Polish sociologist, has linked this will to global domination of nature with the nightmare politics of twentieth-century totalitarianism: Baumann's reflections are prompted by Ernest Gellner's wild/garden distinction in *Nations and Nationalism* (1983).[1] Gardens are not the scene of primal innocence. They are, rather, a battleground of conflicting values and ideologies. Too often for comfort, moreover, the battle rages within, as incompatible value systems struggle for supremacy, as they do in me.

But I still think kookaburras are alien intruders in the West. They don't belong here; I am for the honeyeaters. To counterclaim that the kookaburra is an 'Australian icon' carries no weight with me. Indeed, to write or speak of 'Australian animals and plants' is to use a convenient fiction that can also lead to serious confusions. The term has its uses, but its use always requires caution.

The caution is needed because plants know nothing of nationality. Consider the following, from Patrick Fairbairn:

A nation's animals and plants are among its finest works of art. Each species is as individual as any creation of the artist. Destruction of any species or its life support system is vandalism indeed.[2]

These are fine sentiments, and with a few reservations I share them, but it is easier to make such pronouncements based on cultural conditioning than it is to find rational support for them. My first hesitation is that they are a luxury; they were not held by many of the convicts and early settlers of Port Jackson, whose central preoccupation was survival in a strange environment. They were and are held, we are told, by the Aborigines of the area, who could afford such luxuries because of their low density of population and, therefore, the limited demands on what for them was not a hostile environment but a known and sustaining one. They were held also by an enlightened few of the elite who could afford such fine feelings, maintained directly from Britain rather than dependent on the local scene.

Affluent middle-class Australia can afford them too – and should.

'Vandalism' is a key word. If its meaning is restricted to '*wanton destruction*', well and good. The difficulty is that 'destruction' can also be unwitting, or the by-product of other activities generally considered necessary or acceptable by society – in Australia, by clearing for agriculture, by the introduction of hooved mammals, by the spread of pathogens like *Phytophthora cinnamomi*, and by introduced plants that can out-compete the indigenous flora. These have all been more significant than wanton destruction.

The Case Against?

Fairbairn's first sentence, 'A nation's animals and plants are among its finest works of art' seems unarguable. Yet even allowing all the above qualifications, there is still a view in partial opposition to his full statement, put forcibly in a recent issue of *Greenplaces* by the Landscape Regeneration Manage for the Peabody Trust in Britain:

Wildlife xenophobia

I get a buzz from seeing ring-necked parakeets (India) skeeting overhead, red admirals (yup, European visitors) feeding on buddleia (eastern China) and Californian poppies bursting forth out of nearby wastelands. They are as much a part of my cultural landscapes as bluebells, hornbeams and green woodpeckers.

I therefore take issue with some of the sweeping xenophobic statements made by John Lovell in respect of 'foreign invaders'. Our biodiversity and landscapes are the result of the impact we have made over countless generations, a consequence of the influences of very many peoples arriving on these islands over the past 7000 years or so. Hundreds of species of animals, plants and fungi have been brought here with us, some purposefully and others incidentally.

The three species Lovell mentions – giant hogweed, Japanese knotweed and Himalayan balsam – were intentionally introduced. Indeed, Japanese knotweed was introduced by the Royal Botanic Gardens, Kew some 150 years ago, and in the following years horticulturalists took great delight in extolling its ornamental credentials. The same happened with giant hogweed, where seeds were sold for their proliferation throughout the countryside. I accept that in many places they are causing problems and need effort to control them, but they did not 'invade'.

The term 'invasive' is problematical: in ecological circles it is too commonly attached to 'alien', ignoring the fact that native species are perfectly good at being invasive themselves. Oak, bracken, silver birch, common reed and stinging nettle all act brilliantly at out-competing other species if circumstances permit.

At root, I suggest that too many of us are wedded to a romantic pre-urban idyll, where good, honest British species once innocently frolicked unthreatened by nasty foreigners. However, we are one of the mostly densely populated nations on earth, and our cultural heritage reflects this. The hundreds of introduced species are with us to stay. Some of them are a problem (such as the aquatics azolla and parrot's feather), most are benign and many brighten up our landscapes.

Sweeping statements about foreign invasives bringing 'detrimental consequences' to people's 'quality of life' are not supported by evidence, and can lead to confusion of a public already perplexed about what wildlife is 'good' or 'bad'. If we deem non-natives per se as bad and requiring 'zero tolerance', what message does that send to the multicultural society of which I am proud to be a member?[3]

Mathew Frith's views may well be appropriate for his small island, but not for our big one. Is it too late, is it even possible, to 'shut the door' on 'invasive' plants and animals? This is a misleading metaphor. Even for Britain, the case for maintaining remnants of the indigenous flora is not incompatible with accepting most of Frith's points, and that case is far stronger in Australia.

Another difficulty with purist attitudes is that they are static. The clock ticks on, and there is always change. The London Basin was tropically luxuriant in the Eocene, not so long ago in geologic terms, full of Nipa palms and an exotic fauna – including our early ancestors, who looked, according to the reconstructions, not unlike today's straphangers on the Underground. This interval was followed by others and, in time, the Ice Age wiped out just about everything growing, from which there has been a slow recovery, not yet carried very far. At least some of the introductions have probably done little more than speed up natural recolonisation.

As for our island, the time element is inescapable. Australia is a cruise ship that has been heading north – majestically – from the Antarctic to the tropics for sixty million years, and is still doing so. Together with climate change, the consequences for the flora are noteworthy, particularly in Western Australia:

Western Australian ecosystems are in a dynamic state on a trajectory determined by biological responses to environmental changes set in train as the continent moved from high latitude, moist, equable climates to warmer, drier, more seasonal ones … In this process, the cool-climate, moisture-dependent elements have been restricted to refugia …[4]

'Refugia' is an interesting word, as are 'alien', 'invasive' and 'multi-cultural'. Their connotations appear to change according to context. From the above, we might conclude that invasive plants are undesirable in Australia, and so are invasive people, but some parts of Australia can provide refuge for some Australian plants under stress elsewhere, but not for some people, while it is desirable that our population policy (for people) be multicultural, but not our conservation attitudes.

Weighted words distort discussion. I believe that Australians should be growing more local plants, but it is important to scan the arguments. It is not unusual today to be told that Australians should be growing more plants from their own country in their gardens, but why should they? The case has been argued in the past from pseudo-nationalistic grounds, and even at the home-gardening level, from a mixture of good reasons and bad. The result has been some good gardens and some very bad ones: lemon-scented gums pushing into the foundations of valuable nineteenth-century terraces in their minute front yards in the inner suburbs of Sydney and Melbourne, for example.

The bad arguments led twenty years ago to a belief that the 'bush garden' was self-maintaining: you bought the plants, put them in the ground, and your task was over. Neither gardening nor plants are like that, nor ever have been, but the failures may have set back by a decade or more the campaign to persuade Australians to grow more plants from their own country. So before we begin planting, let us first turn to a little weeding: weeding is as important in clarifying ideas as it is in gardening. Some of the arguments for growing Australian plants are overstated, need qualification, are incomplete, or in conflict with other beliefs, and some of the terminology is imprecise or misleading. Then we can turn to the good arguments.

'Australian' Plants

Nations and nationality are the outcome of political history, of conquest, invasion, change, chance, all of which might, in our own case, have led to quite different boundaries. The western third of the continent might well have been claimed by the French to the north and the Dutch in the south-west, with the Dutch again in Van Diemen's Land, and the Germans and the Dutch or the Indonesians or the Japanese in the northern third of the continent other than the Kimberley. So the words 'Australia' and 'Australian plants' might have applied only to the land and flora of the south-eastern mainland.

The nation of Australia, however, now comprises a continent, *the only nation state to do so*. Thus the political boundary coincides with a natural boundary, with the exception of a few bits and pieces that we will come to presently. This colours our thinking in many odd ways, usually unconscious. North America has eight nation states plus Greenland (Danish) and another five Caribbean island countries, just counting the larger ones, while all the other continents have many more. Yet our continental unity is also misleading; it encompasses many highly diverse environments and the plants from one often fail to survive in another, although there are also many interesting exceptions.

Europe is called a continent, even *the* Continent (although strictly a mere subcontinent of Asia, like India). Now that the political boundaries grow close to the natural ones by courtesy of the European Union, we could be tempted to speak of 'European plants' and urge that these should dominate European gardens. Of course we do not, for two very good reasons. One is environmental and one cultural. The cultural reason is that gardens are human constructs, and Europeans have ransacked the world for 'garden-worthy' plants, and then bred and refined them. They are not likely to repatriate them. The second is ecological. *Quercus suber*, the cork oak, is indigenous in Portugal and southern Spain, but there would be little point in planting it in Finland, nor in planting birches in Portugal, although both are European plants and European countries.

Plant affinities often ignore national boundaries. They may also ignore natural boundaries. For our region, the most significant natural boundary is Wallace's Line, the dramatic gap in the Indonesian Archipelago between Lombok and Flores, dividing the biotic realm of South-East Asia and Australasia. It works well for the fauna (tigers and monkeys to the west of it, kangaroos and their kin to the east) but less well for the plants. The flora of Australia has many shared characteristics at the continental scale, but there are also many plant species and genera that look outwards rather than inwards to the centre.

Popular speech reflects this sense of a continent and a people looking out from the coastal fringe rather than inwards. It makes sense to speak of the 'American heartland', a powerful political and cultural force, but here the heart is dead. We call non-coastal Australia 'the outback', and if it is well out, 'beyond the black stump'. What it is not is 'in'. We even define ourselves by the oceans we face. Sydney fronts the Pacific, Perth the Indian Ocean. North America and Europe have transcontinental railroads. Until recently we had just one, which we call the 'Indian Pacific', ocean to ocean – as if there were little of significance in between.

Many plants look out across these seas. Kangaroo grass (*Themeda*), which we think of as quintessentially Australian, is common in southern Africa, as I once discovered to my surprise. The distinctive boabs (*Adansonia gregorii*) of the Kimberley have close relatives in Madagascar and southern Africa, but none in eastern Australia, while some of the evergreen figs of tropical and subtropical Australia have their nearest relatives in India. Tasmania has a suite of gymnosperms that are almost unknown in south-western Australia (*Podocarpus drouynianus* in the high rainfall area of the extreme south-coastal area is the sole exception); but there are related species up the east coast, across the Tasman to New Zealand and even further to Chile. The greatest concentration is in New Caledonia. To give a few more examples, we have one species of kauri (*Agathis robusta*) on the east coast of Queensland, and New Zealand has one (*A. australis*) We have three Araucaria – *A. heterophylla* from Norfolk Island, *A. bidwillii* and *A. cunninghamiana* – while New Caledonia has many species of these two genera, especially Araucaria. The western four-fifths of the continent has none. Tasmania has the Huon pine (*Lagarostrobos franklinii*), the celery-top pine (*Phyllocladus aspleniifolius*) and *Microcachrys tetragona*, all members of the Podocarpaceae; most of the related species are in New Zealand.

All of this is the outcome of the geological past, of Gondwanan links, including linkages through a more temperate Antarctica, of chance seed dispersal by birds or waves, and so on. The point is that the current geographical location of plants in Australia may provide only limited significant information. To talk of 'Australian' plants is therefore accurate and tolerably precise only if it is intended to mean no more than those plants now growing naturally in Australia. Even then we have to exclude recent introductions that have naturalised. We also have to exclude from the concept of Australia some of the outlying islands, while including others such as Norfolk Island, Tasmania, Rottnest, Kangaroo Island and so on, by criteria that are obviously quite arbitrary, since if we restricted ourselves to the Australian continent, they would all be out too. Beyond that imperfect geographical sense, the word 'Australian' applied to plants is a joker, sometimes rich in meaning, sometimes poor and misleading.

The danger of confusing political with natural boundaries has already been illustrated by the kookaburra which, like the plants, knows nothing of nationality or state boundaries. Birds know nothing of the nationality of plants, either. My wife and I treasure the singing and New Holland honeyeaters in our garden. Their preferred winter food is the abundant red pea flower of the big old coral tree, *Erythrina sykesii*. That it is exotic to Fremantle is of no concern to the honeyeaters. A prolific supply of nectar is their consuming passion.

Local Plants

There is, however, a strong case for using plants from your immediate locality, literally indigenous plants. Such plants are likely to need no or little supplementary watering, immensely important as water becomes an increasingly scarce resource. They are adapted to local soils and should rarely need the mineral fertilisers responsible for the nutrient build-up in our waterways (the nutrients lead to algal blooms, which deplete the water of oxygen, the fish die, and so on down).

Local plants are usually resistant to local pests and are therefore less demanding of toxic pesticides, although this, alas, is not always the case. There are few general statements in either horticulture or ecology that do not admit of exceptions. Where plant breeders are able to cross two related species, the F1 hybrids often show hybrid vigour and are tougher than either parent. More often, however, the nurseries even of 'native' plants practise selective breeding within a given species, aiming for showy flowers or a longer flowering season. The resultant cultivars may need more care in the garden than in nature, more nutrients, more water, and of course they are not necessarily resistant to all the plant pathogens and predators we have introduced into the garden environment, especially in the towns and cities where most of us live.

A second and powerful reason for using the plants of your own locale is that they cannot become 'garden escapes', by definition. In one sense, that of the last paragraph, it is wise to use plants, whatever their source, adapted to your immediate environment (soil, rainfall, hours of sunshine, temperature range). Thus plants from comparable Mediterranean zones in the other continents are generally well suited to southern Australia, but these are also the plants most likely to become invasive (feral, if you like). Bulbs and corms from southern Africa are among the worst, but there is a long list, rapidly getting longer, of introduced plants that are invading the bushland of south-western Australia, and many are now out of control. This problem can also occur with 'native' plants used in a new setting. One well-known case is *Pittosporum undulatum* from Gippsland, now regarded as a serious invasive weed in the Dandenongs, where it is not indigenous. If you live on the coastal limestone in Fremantle, as my wife Marli and I do, our garden cockie's tongue (*Templetonia retusa*) might yield seeds that are spread by birds, and if they grow they will be indistinguishable from the survivors still to be found in adjoining pockets of bushland.

They will, at least, be indistinguishable to the naked eye, but even here, a caveat is needed. They should also be indistinguishable genetically. If the seed collection was from another area, or if there has been some genetic modification through nursery practices, then the effect could well be to reduce the genetic diversity of the species and potentially, therefore, its capacity to adapt to environmental change:

> Gathering seed from anywhere in a species' range and broadcasting it across the landscape is little more than gardening, and may well lead to reproductive failure ...[5]

'Little more than gardening' may seem an odd phrase to come from the (then) Director of Kings Park and Botanic Garden. It is certainly a purist view, as should be the case with a dedicated conservationist, but its practical application is not difficult: seed should be collected only from the provenance in which it is to be used, and not from just anywhere in the range of the species.

Happily, this is almost certainly the case with our *Spyridium* and *Templetonia*; both occur naturally and abundantly within the western third of the metropolitan area of Perth, and both germinate so easily from seed, especially the latter, that there could be no temptation to seek seed further afield.

Love 'Em or Lose 'Em

The genetic argument may seem to undermine the whole case for gardening with Australian plants, but there is a counter-argument: the 'love 'em or lose 'em' proposition, of which the Wollemi pine is a spectacular example. It has been found in two small and almost inaccessible natural habitats in the Blue Mountains, but is now being busily propagated in a Queensland nursery, for release to the gardening public. This is an interesting case, in that the 'conserve biological diversity' argument runs head-on into the purist approach to environmental conservation. For instance, the anti-*Pittosporum* case in the Dandenongs is essentially an argument against the increasing homogenisation of the natural world and the blurring of the distinctive character of specific habitats. The outcome, however, is beyond doubt: the Wollemi pine will sell like hot cakes, and will be tried all over the place (if I were younger I would be tempted to try one myself). The Araucaria species are an extreme example; all three have a limited natural distribution, and all three are widely planted beyond it. The extreme example is the Norfolk Island pine.

There are similar examples from the western side of the continent. Some of the mountain bells such as *Darwinia collina, D. leiostyla* and *D. macrostegia* occur only on one or two peaks in the Stirling Range. Another example of valuable and beautiful plants with a very limited natural distribution are the Qualup bell (*Pimelea physodes*) and *Banksia coccinea*. All of these are vulnerable. They are not yet common in cultivation, but *Corymbia ficifolia*, the red-flowering gum, does so well in southern Victoria that it is sometimes called the Melbourne gum. It is restricted naturally to a small area in the extreme south-west of Western Australia that gets some summer rain. Its distribution has been pushed steadily southwards as the climate has become drier over the last ten thousand years and it will be pushed right off the south-western edge of the continent if this trend continues, as is generally predicted. The western half of the continent runs out of south too soon for further migration, whereas southern Victoria offers ideal habitat for this and other vulnerable species from the extreme south of Western Australia. If they had properly understood that they are 'Australian' species, they might have moved to Victoria of their own accord!

Many plants are increasingly vulnerable in the natural environment, for a whole raft of reasons, of which limited natural habitat is only the beginning. Increased fire frequency and intensity and clearing for agriculture have had a massive impact. In areas of pastoral leasehold, which take up a third of the continent – stretching from the Pilbara and the Kimberley across to north-west Queensland and western New South Wales – selective grazing and trampling by sheep, cattle, goats, donkeys and camels have eliminated or threaten many species. In southern Australia, garden escapes often out-compete the indigenous flora, and there are also introduced insect predators and pathogens, of which the worst is *Phytophthora cinnamomi*. Dieback has done immense damage in some of the floristic treasure houses of Western Australia such as the Stirling Range and the Fitzgerald River national parks. The Proteaceae are especially at risk ('jarrah dieback' is a misnomer), so if you live on the Mornington Peninsula and can grow *Banksia coccinea* you might be rendering a service to posterity. The 'love 'em or lose 'em' argument can be compelling.

The Pleasures of Experiment

A fourth reason for growing 'Australian' plants is that it is fun. Gardening is rewarding when it is experimental: there is not much challenge in growing petunias, but there is in growing *Leschenaultia formosa*. I have seen some strikingly successful experiments in Melbourne gardens; in one garden the owners grow and flower several species of the prostrate banksias from the south coast of Western Australia. They are not ecologically appropriate, so they have recreated a suitable environment by importing a mound of free-draining sand. This is exactly what traditional gardeners do – artificially recreate the conditions that are natural for the plant, be it a rhododendron or a cattleya orchid. Success has come through skilled gardening. So the lovely little banksia cones enrich their manufactured environment thousands of kilometres from their natural home, but nonetheless both a delight and a triumph.

Sometimes Australian plants are surprisingly versatile and can be grown in a wide range of environments, even though their natural habitat may be severely restricted. An extreme case is the Norfolk Island pine (*Araucaria heterophylla*), which has been grown almost right around the coast of temperate Australia from Brisbane to Geraldton and beyond. The silky oak (*Grevillea robusta*) and the Geraldton wax (*Chamelaucium uncinatum*) are other examples, and there are more. The silky oak comes from well-watered subtropical Queensland, but it can tolerate environments that have cold winters and hot, dry summers: it lines the main street of Heathcote in central Victoria, for example. We have in our garden three plum pines (*Podocarpus elatus*). This species also comes from a humid climate with summer rainfall in coastal Queensland, and it has no right to grow in Fremantle, with its searingly dry summers, in 'soil' with a pH that approaches 11, a thin layer of grey, water-repellent sand that overlies dense lime stone caprock. Yet they flourish, and show that they are quite 'at home' by reproducing prolifically, with unwanted seedlings requiring constant removal.

So there is great scope for experimenting with Australian plants from environments remote front our own, so long as we remember that this is not different in kind from trying to grow roses or Chilean bell-flowers. Strictly speaking, the *Podocarpus* in our garden and the prostrate banksias in the Melbourne garden are exotics. Indigenous gardens use local plants only. All gardens that include non-indigenous plants are eclectic gardens, even those that are restricted to Australian plants.

Soil Constraints; Design Constraints

Apart from the pleasure of successful experiment, there are other reasons for wanting to grow *Podocarpus* in Fremantle, so far from its natural habitat. Were we to grow only the plants indigenous to the limestone hill on which we live, we would be restricted to heathland plants. We do have them, too, abundantly: cockie's tongue (*Templetonia retusa*); *Melaleuca acerosa* with its generous yellow flower heads; and native dusty miller (*Spyridium globulosum*), a plant that should be used much more widely, in my view, since it is both attractive and very undemanding. But for trees, our only indigenes are *Callitris preissii*, of which we have about twenty, and *Melaleuca lanceolata*, which prefers more shelter than we can provide in a very exposed site. We needed more trees, some for shade and privacy and others chosen for design or functional considerations; some deciduous to allow winter sun and summer shade, like the old mulberry and several coral trees (*Erythrina sykesii*) with its red pea flowers bright against the winter-blue sky.

In any case the mulberry and the coral trees were here when we bought the house and are part of its history. We have introduced other exotics ourselves, for example some evergreen oaks (*Quercus suber* from the Iberian Peninsula, *Q. ilex* from Italy, and *Q. agrifolia* from California). Why? In part for horticultural reasons and in part for design reasons. The practical problem is that very few Australian trees can tolerate our hyperalkaline soil; although plants from alkaline soils can often adapt to soils that are neutral or weakly acid, the reverse does not hold. Most eucalypts, for example, like a neutral or slightly acid soil, whereas these oaks from Mediterranean climes are familiar with limestone.

The design reasons are the usual ones: for contrast, form, colour. In our strong light, a green so dark as to be almost black helps to give solidity and substance to the design in summer, but there is also a wonderful flush of new foliage in spring, especially with the *Podocarpus*, a burst of lime green against the sombre black-green of the mature foliage.

Strong light intensities prevail in much of Australia, and especially in the southern sweep from south-western Western Australia across all of South Australia, through most of Victoria, and then north through New South Wales and southern Queensland west of the Divide. This, along with the need to conserve water, has led to adaptive consequences in the natural environment, and they are significant for garden design. Foliage is often fine, sometimes very fine, as in nearly all the plants of the heathlands (*Micromyrtus*, for example).

The colour range is highly distinctive: grey, grey-green, blue-green, black-green, and then translucent copper reds in the new flush of growth (because in nutrient-poor soils, the production of anthocyanin outstrips that of the more nutrient-demanding chlorophyll). Foliage is often pendant and tough (sclerophyllous) as a protection against insolation; prickly or harsh as a protection against grazing and browsing animals. Foliage is often resinous, too, a fresh fragrance to our Australian noses, but a deterrent to many insect predators. Flowers may be exquisite but small: even banksia cones are made up of a multitude of small individual flowers. Flowers are often rich in stamens, like tiny pincushions, but poor in petals. In less brilliantly lit climes, large petals guide the fertilising bees and moths to the functional core of the flower, stamens and stigma, but such crude traffic signals are rarely needed here. Our flowers are often rich in honey, too, easy to manufacture in a sun-rich world.

What we do not commonly find in this world of the sun are plants with large mid-green leaves, wilting as soon as their water-filled cells are thirsty; nor large flowers like those of, say, the rhododendrons, and prolific to the point of covering the bush or tree, going all out to get fertilised in their native gloom. I have seen groves of rhododendrons growing under sheltering deciduous trees in Bodnant, one of the great gardens of the British Isles. The flowers glow like jewels in the low light. If you were able to grow them in Bendigo you would need to keep them under a humidifying spray through the summer and they would look gross, lacking all decent restraint.

The point I am making is that such foliage, such flowers, look out of place in much of this country, not just horticulturally and ecologically, but visually. Of course there are exceptions, like Mount Macedon and Mount Wilson, but they are indeed exceptions. By contrast, designing with a palette of indigenous plants can allow a subtle harmony of all the foliage colours listed above, and more; some are very pale grey, almost white, like *Leucophyta brownii* and some of the emu-bushes (*Eremophila* spp.), which are good for accent or contrast, just as the black-greens are so good for giving solidity, anchoring a composition that might otherwise etherealise in the heat-haze and float away.

Design Lessons; Design Models

There are design lessons to be learned from the local flora. The common kangaroo paw in Kings Park was named for Captain Mangles. His kangaroo paw, *Anigozanthos manglesii*, is a splendid creation in vivid green and red velvet, clearly designed by Jacques Cartier for display as a single stem against a black backdrop in a window of the Faubourg St Honoré. It looks even better in the bush. What a poor thing, by comparison, is the King Alfred daffodil, whose bulbs, as I write, are in prominent tubs near the entrances of all the nurseries. In the bare sands of the Swan Coastal Plain, they are like the forsaken mermaid, out of their element, grieving for Wordsworth's Windermere. There, they bloom in their multitudes, springing up in the thick grass, holding their pale gold cups against the green, lifting them to the grey skies, and at home. They are at their best in Australia in a few areas of Tasmania and around Mount Macedon where they are allowed to 'naturalise', a most revealing word.

Gardens must serve all kinds of people, with differing needs in different places, so it is unwise to be too prescriptive about design. A common design model in suburban Australia, which is most of it, is what I call the 'clearing in the forest', a lawn opening out from the rear of the house, backed by a half-circle or irregular u-shape of shrubs and trees. When much of Europe was densely forested, a clearing gave some security; approaching predators could be seen in advance. The study of human behaviour in such settings has led to the 'prospect and refuge' hypothesis:[6] that people going for a picnic in a park, for example, will generally choose to sit neither in the middle of the open space nor in the encircling trees, but at the edge, exhibiting a behaviour pattern that has a long ancestry. We have inherited this design model, along with much else, from Britain, and it survives perhaps for primeval reasons (it still offers a comfort zone), but also for more practical ones: the surrounding trees give privacy, while the open space, usually under grass, is well suited to the needs of children, dogs, family life.

Natural clearings in the forests of Western Europe were usually the outcome of lightning strikes and local fire, but such clearings are almost unknown in the Australian bush, where fire is rarely local. Away from the coast, moreover, forest soon gives way to grassy woodland, heath, grassland or shrub steppe. If you are intending a naturalistic use of indigenous plants, therefore, the 'clearing in the forest' is not an appropriate model (although that does not mean that you cannot follow that model and yet include indigenous plants). A naturalistic design will not be that of a static composition seen through a picture window. Such gardens are to be enjoyed from a preferred viewing point, with all those formal elements so deeply embedded in our culture: foreground, middle ground, background, asymmetric framing elements on each side, a 'picture' more or less conforming to the golden mean of the Greeks – which is roughly the proportion of most paintings, most photographs of landscapes, even of the viewfinder of the camera.

Fred Williams, the landscape painter par excellence, broke with this painterly convention by painting strip pictures, his contention being that the Australian landscape is often a seamless continuity rather than a series of set views. It is hardly practicable for a suburban garden to present a seamless continuity. Naturalistic gardens using Australian plant material may also break with this convention, but in a different way; they will be intricate and dynamic, not static. Such gardens have been called 'walkabout gardens', a good term. They can be quite small. You move around them, apparently at will, discovering hidden treasures, and the scale of attention is often minute. You are constantly tempted around the next corner, all apparently artlessly, although of course the artistry lies in concealing the art.

This is not new: Guilfoyle designed the Royal Botanic Gardens Melbourne on just such principles, although on the grand scale and not in the naturalistic mode. The English poet Robert Herrick once wrote of a young woman that 'there is a sweet disorder in her dress', and this might apply to such a garden, which can accept and be enhanced by, fallen twigs and leaves, although once again with hidden management in the background to ensure that treasured plants are not smothered. 'Leaf litter is not litter' might be a new slogan in such a context. We are all on a steep learning curve about a country of which we still know so little, and of which we have destroyed so much.

Notes

1   P. Beilharz (ed.), *The Baumann Reader*, Blackwell, Oxford, 2001, pp. 103–112.

2   Patrick Fairbairn in Roger F. Pasquier (ed.), *Conservation of New World Parrots: Proceedings of the ICBP Parrot Working Group Meeting, St Lucia, 1981*, Smithsonian Institution Press / International Council for Bird Preservation, Washington DC, 1981, p. 12.

3   Mathew Frith, letter in *Greenplaces*, no.2, February 2004, p. 18.

4   Stephen Hopper et al., *Gondwanan Heritage: Past, Present and Future of the Western Australian Biota*, Beatty and Sons, Sydney, 1996, p. 35.

5   Hopper et al., p. 36.

6   Jay Appleton, *The Experience of Landscape*, New York, Wiley, 1975.

THE ART OF ADVISING

17

—

A LANDSCAPE ASSESSMENT OF THE SOUTHERN MORNINGTON PENINSULA, VICTORIA

1974

This is an extract from a report to the Western Port Regional Planning Authority, undertaken by Seddon as Director of the Centre for Environmental Studies at the University of Melbourne. It was prepared with the assistance of W.B. Calder and M. Davis.

THE MORNINGTON PENINSULA IS AN ADJUNCT OF the city of Melbourne. Its special values and special dangers both stem from this fact. Much of the money earned and spent in the region comes either directly or indirectly from Melbourne – directly from holiday visitors, weekend cottagers, weekend farmers, and the retirement contingent from the city; indirectly from those farm ventures such as market gardens and chicken brooders whose economic success depends on proximity to urban consumers, and indirectly also from those large, well-managed and economically viable agricultural holdings that are nevertheless not the main or sole source of income for those who own them.

Planning Policy No. 2 requires the Regional Planning Author-ity to prepare a conservation plan for the Peninsula, essentially to maintain it as Melbourne's favoured playground. In short, it is to be a green belt. However, we find in the preamble to the policy that: 'few of the attempts' (to establish and maintain a green belt) 'have enjoyed marked success'. This is an under-statement. The green belts around London and Sydney have simply not worked. This one must work. Can it?

It escapes one of the major problems that destroyed London's and Sydney's green belts, both of which were continuous around the land-perimeter of inexorably expanding cities. Urban expan-sion therefore leap-frogged the green belts, which were left as a no-man's-land in mid-suburbia. Melbourne will not easily leap-frog the Mornington Peninsula into Bass Strait, and it plans for a linear rather than a radial expansion.

The second major problem, especially for London's green belt, was that it was taken for granted that the farmer would do our landscap-ing for us, for nothing. Why should he? He declined, around London. The land was zoned rural, but its effectiveness as working farmland declined, and although it could not be subdivided, much of it began a drift to dereliction, awaiting a rational function. It might be possible, and is surely desirable, to maintain the rural character of the Pen-insula, but it is not enough to zone it so. It is of critical importance to find incentives that work; these need not only be financial, but there may be some cases where negative rating is necessary, especially among orchardists; to put it bluntly, we may have to pay orchardists to grow apple trees to look at on our Sunday drives.

A third problem with green belts was the undoing of Sydney's: the Cumberland County Council did not have the power to enforce its policies effectively. Australian communities outside Canberra have not been used to extensive planning regulation in this century (it was otherwise in the first half of the last century – for example, the citizens of Perth and Fremantle had to submit their proposed street facades for approval in the 1840s). The Western Port Regional Planning Authority will need great regulatory powers to achieve its policies. The powers should not be arbitrary: they already provide for consultation, representation and appeal. But they should be great enough to override sectional interests, including those who are lucky enough already to own land on the Peninsula, and the local and public authorities that impinge upon it, notably the State Electricity Commission, the Country Roads Board and the Shire Councils.

It is devoutly to be hoped that the local communities of the Peninsula will see the need for such powers, and willingly accept them. They have much to lose by fighting them. The alternative is clear; without strict controls, the Peninsula is doomed to suburban invasion. By supporting strict control, presently entrenched residents stand to gain, as near as may be, a guarantee against deterioration in their environment (an extraordinary and rare privilege); and properties that will greatly increase in value. But they will have to pay quite heavily for the privilege, both in high rates to pay for a high standard of public amenity, and in restrictions on doing as they please with 'their property' (that is, the land of which they are custodians for a brief spell). If they are not prepared to pay the price, they will have to realise their capital gains and get out. *Land is a scarce resource in the Peninsula, and it must be used rationally; that is, it must be rationed.*

Standards of Value

Aesthetic awareness is the opposite of anaesthesia, a numbness of the senses. It includes all the senses, including taste, hearing and the consciousness of muscular well-being. Much of our pleasure in country landscapes and the bush comes from their sounds and smells, but there is not much to say about them. A healthy landscape looks right, sounds right and smells right. Its appearance can usually be taken as an index of its other qualities. But how do we judge it to be right? Because judgements of value are subjective, some of the basic assumptions underlying this report are discussed below.

Decorative, Cosmetic and Functional Aesthetics

There is nothing wrong with decoration. All societies, from the most primitive to the most sophisticated, spend a great deal of their time and energy in decorating their bodies, their dwellings, their environment. Australians in general, and Victorians in particular, devote a quite remarkably large part of their leisure to a purely aesthetic pursuit – gardening. Our problem is not a lack of interest in aesthetics, although this is often said (quite wrongly) of Australians, but an inappropriately formed taste, in which there are three major elements. The first is that the taste was formed in the British Isles, and it still has a large element of nostalgia in it. Most Australians will say that they 'love the bush', but this love is rarely reflected in the way they build, site and landscape their homes. The light, texture, forms, materials and mood of the Australian environment are rarely reflected in the Australian house and garden, which is, as a rule, discordant with its larger environment.

The second element is that the tastes we brought with us were largely formed in nineteenth-century industrial Britain, and they reflect an aesthetic of retreat, a defensive response to an industrialised landscape. The Englishman's home was not always his castle; it became so when he was forced to withdraw from effective participation in the larger landscape, a withdrawal that is beautifully parodied by Dickens in describing the domestic fortress of Wemmick, the underpaid lawyer's clerk in *Great Expectations*.

Dickens' account is affectionate, and Wemmick is not to blame, but he signals a society in retreat from its environmental problems. Australian cities and towns are Wemmick writ large. Portsea is Wemmick triumphant. It is nothing less than disgraceful that the Portsea community should tolerate a town centre like this, among private homes that generally evince a high level of taste and cultivation born of privilege, wealth and education. A high proportion of the members of this community are architects and professionals, with an abundance of the skills necessary to look after the public estate. Flinders presents a similar picture of private elegance and public squalor, a combination that spells out 'selfish retreat' in large letters. It is at best a partial excuse that the more privileged members of the community are mostly long-weekenders. However, much can be forgiven Portsea for the Lord Mayor's Camp, generously conceived and executed with style.

Wemmick never quite dominated the scene in England, or even in North America. The English had other, older traditions to draw on, and although retreat from the larger environment into the security of the home was marked in Victorian England, there were still many men and women who took a custodial view of the public as well as the private landscape, and who worked to maintain it in health. There were also men of outstanding vision in the early days of Victoria. La Trobe's legacy to Melbourne, its public gardens, are the city's major assets, but his taste and his vision of the common estate were not established as a tradition among the native-born, and the boundary between nineteenth- and twentieth-century Melbourne is one between a generously and a meanly conceived city (admittedly, one in very different economic circumstances). 'The Melbourne Establishment' has among it many highly civilised and cultivated men of impeccable private taste, but this has rarely extended to effective concern for the public domain.

The third major element directing our aesthetic behaviour is world-wide: our inability to design for, and to contain, the motor car. Its dominance has been so sudden and its convenience so great that very few western countries have been able to civilise it; Germany has perhaps been most nearly successful, while Australia is one of the least. It is ironic that we are just beginning to learn how to design for it in this country as its future begins to seem limited. Nevertheless, it could still wreak untold damage in the Peninsula in the next few years, and its use must be controlled. The private motor car is an incomparably flexible means of individual transport, but loses its point if its mass use destroys the charm of our journey and destination. Road design is so important that it comes up in almost every section of this report, as well as in a special section.

These three elements, and other lesser ones, go into the making of the Great Australian Ugliness, and they should properly be put right by public education. This should be the goal, but education is slow, and in the meantime there is no alternative to regulation by an authority with highly trained, professional staff. *The authority needs to look with special care at local proposals for 'beautification'*, not, as we began by saying, that decoration is wrong in itself, but because in this country, for the reasons outlined above, the decoration is so likely to be inappropriate. A country town in north-eastern Victoria runs a large-scale, efficient sewage disposal unit, using a system of large lagoons; behind them is a river with a fringing forest of river gums. The entrance to the sewerage works has been beautified with beds of marigolds and zinnias. The instinct to enhance the environment is admirable, but the choice is inappropriate: the garden flowers are grotesque in that setting, and an avenue of red-gums would have been fine.

The Peninsula has avoided the worst excesses of 'beautification', and it has some examples of quiet understatement in design, such as the wooden picnic table off Callanans Road in the Railway Reserve at

Red Hill South; or the Settlers' Graves reserve at Sorrento, pathetically cramped, but sensitive and appropriate within those inappropriate limits; or the small, shingled kiosk at Arthurs Seat. It also has many minor failures, for example, the 'beautification' of the main street at Hastings with shrubs and small trees, no two of which are the same, and none of them big enough to make an effect. The interest of this example is that it shows what is so often wrong with 'beautification', which turns out not to be decoration for its own sake, but cosmetic in intent – an attempt to hide basic defects. There are too many things wrong with the main street at Hastings for such a puny cosmetic attempt to have any force, and the shrubs merely add to the clutter. Nothing less than a double avenue of tall trees – as at Bacchus Marsh, for example – would serve to powder Hastings' red and shiny nose, but a 'green tunnel' is difficult to achieve in a street suffering from basic, functional disorders, the prime ones being badly located power lines and a confusion of roles as a traffic artery and a busy pedestrian precinct (that is, the usual ribbon development problems).

Some things are better hidden. Clear plastic sewage pipes would not appeal to most of us. A coat of paint is cosmetic. Nevertheless, *a cosmetic approach to landscape is dangerous*. It is indicated by the use of words like 'screen', 'tucked away', 'almost invisible', 'well-hidden'. When they are used extensively, it suggests that we are trying to hide the real landscape behind a sham one. There will be a great temptation to attempt this on the Peninsula in the next few years. The real landscape will be, in its functional economy, that of suburban Melbourne on 10-acre blocks – hidden behind a purely cosmetic rural facade. The more horse-shoes on the walls of the saloon bar, the fewer the farmers. Ranch-style is not ranch, and cows are not decor.

Landscape Quality

There can be no objective definition of landscape quality, and the awarding of points for quality is in general a futile exercise, although it can have value within a narrow and sharply defined frame of reference.[1] It must be related to the mode of experience, as well as to the cultural background, purposes, knowledge and mood of the observer, or participant – the latter word is appropriate because the degree of engagement with the landscape profoundly affects a man's experience of it. Even if one considers only the pleasure of the casual visitor, the density of incident needed to give variety and richness to a landscape is quite different for a hiker and a motorist.

There are, however, some general principles. Aesthetic pleasure is derived from a perceived balance between order and disorder, the fulfilling of expectations according to a discerned pattern, that nevertheless maintains surprise, an omnipresent threat to order. An excessively ordered landscape – whether the order is natural or man-made – soon loses its interest. An excessively disordered one leads to weariness and confusion. Thus variety or contrast, and harmony, are both essential components of the experience. One kind of landscape that meets these requirements is the landscape that shows a pleasing balance between human occupation and natural forces – in extreme form, Swiss villages and meadows in the foreground with the Jungfrau rearing up behind them, or a patchwork of intensively cultivated fields up the slopes of a volcano in Indonesia; or in less extreme form, the big skies and cloudscapes over the prairies of North America and the paddocks of inland Australia.

Our landscape preferences tend to choose the interface between two systems – the meeting of land and water, and of land and sky are primary boundaries. The interface between two systems is almost always an area of high biological productivity, as ecologists well know, so there may be a deep-rooted psychological basis to our aesthetic preferences.

The dominance of natural forces is apparent in the Peninsula along the Port Phillip, Bass Strait and Western Port coastline, and in lesser degree in the remnants of natural bushland, swamps, streamlines and high hills, especially along Main Ridge, Bald Hill, Red Hill, Mount Martha and Arthurs Seat. *The significant boundaries and contrasts are those between these elements and the agricultural landscapes.* Country landscapes in Australia are generally functional, and a welcome relief from the big cities, but they often come in large units, without much local variation. The landscapes of the Mornington Peninsula are unusually varied, changing quite dramatically within a few miles, for example from the enclosed, high, well-watered gullies of Red Hill South, to the rolling, open pasture-land of the basalt slopes, with almost no trace of indigenous vegetation, and sombre pines and cypresses the only tree, to the bare cliffs from Flinders to Cape Schanck, fronting Bass Strait – all within a ten-mile drive. People with no scientific training or special knowledge of the area respond to and enjoy this variety in the landscape. Those who know the area better can see its complexity as the product of a complex geological history, yielding a variety of soils, a varied topography, rainfall distribution and land use.

The physical diversity of the region is complemented by a cultural landscape of some richness. The farms bear the mark of long occupation. The landscape has an air of permanence, stability and quiet well-being. Much of it bears the imprint of loving care over many years. Thus although the Peninsula is unmistakeably Australian in character, it is sometimes said to be 'English', because it has two characteristics of the English landscape, both fairly rare in Australia: that of rapid variation and changes in scale from the open to the intimate;

and an air of considerate human occupancy. Both these qualities are threatened by a homogenising technology. The function of this report is to analyse the character of the landscapes, and ways of maintaining their essential qualities through change.

Notes

1   For example G. McK. Wright, 'Landscape Quality: A Method of Appraisal', *Royal Australian Planners Institute Journal*, vol. 11, no. 4, 1973, pp. 122–130.

18

A LANDSCAPE OF POWER

1975

This is an edited extract from a landscape assessment of the proposed Loy Yang coal field development in the Latrobe Valley, Victoria. The report was prepared for the State Electricity Commission of Victoria by Seddon and John Turner.

'A good landscape is part of the nation's standard of living. The cheap production of consumer goods does not, desirable as it is, in itself ensure a good life, and the maintenance of a countryside worth looking at is even more important than the unlimited production of cars in which the countryside may be reached.'[1]

LANDSCAPES ARE ASSESSED BY WHAT THEY MEAN TO us. Industrial landscapes can be – or can be felt to be – oppressive, inhuman, bleak. This is in part a matter of what is now known as 'image'; and Victorians will feel about the landscape at Loy Yang much as they feel about the SEC in general; on the whole, rightly, because the Commission will express its values through its preconceptions of environmental design. Its operations *should* symbolise power, warmth, vitality, and they should invite the sense of participation, sharing, public pride in a public enterprise for the common weal. But they may symbolise paternal authoritarianism (Daddy knows best), exclusivism and a cold technological expertise with little humanity.

[...]

We are among the many Victorians who greatly admire the efficiency and superb technical competence of the Commission, and in this section we take the liberty of offering some comments on the role that it might take in the general field of the environment. Clearly, the Commission's primary role is in the supply of energy for a highly industrialised state – but we emphatically disagree with the view (expressed by at least a few of its senior engineers) that this should be its only role. Like the Country Roads Board, the Commission necessarily makes a massive impact on the environment, and it has the duty (whatever is stated in its Act) to assist in all ways possible in ensuring that this impact is not destructive of amenity. Further, we argue that the Commission could do more to demonstrate quite openly that a landscape created by industrial processes can have a beauty and attraction of its own. This has sometimes happened by accident (as in the canals of England and in the old Cornish and Derbyshire lead-mining areas), and by design over the last few decades in much of Europe and North America. In the past, unplanned industries have led to unplanned and blighted landscapes. Today in Australia there can be no excuse for establishing major industries without concomitant planning for amenity.

Of course the Commission has already demonstrated its interest in the environmental field. One of us was closely concerned with the SEC in the early days of the Kiewa project and the engineer-in-charge, Mr H.H. Williams, collaborated fully in the work on soil erosion, conservation of alpine vegetation and the rehabilitation of the Rocky Valley dam site. The townships of Bogong, Mount Beauty and Yallourn are outstanding examples of the Commission's interest in civic planning. But the Commission has also been criticised – notably where power lines and high-tension transmission lines are concerned, and the recent controversy over Newport (on which we express no opinion) has undoubtedly overshadowed the good image that was created in the earlier days of the Commission.

There is also – at least among those sensitive to landscape and townscape – an unpublished, but nevertheless real, aversion to some aspects of the Latrobe Valley landscape, which probably becomes unconsciously transferred to the Commission. The Melbourne road from Berwick to Drouin is of fine landscape quality, with excellent rural, forest and hilly country, especially to the north. The Latrobe Valley proper does not begin until Moe is reached but we believe that most people driving from Melbourne to Lakes Entrance and beyond associate the Brown Coal developments and the SEC with the main road and its townships between Warragul and Traralgon. These townships – Yarragon, Trafalgar and Morwell – grew from small agricultural settlements at a time when the future of the region must have seemed very different from our own view of it. Whatever their social and other virtues, they are – at least when viewed from the main road – an aesthetic disaster. The road itself is also open to criticism – it carries a great deal of mixed traffic for which it is ill-designed and surfaced; the surviving roadside trees and planted exotics are rarely of fine landscape quality; the hideous power poles of the electrified railway and the general poor state of the railway reserve – all add to the depression. The average traveller rarely sees the excellently designed township of Yallourn, which is doomed. There is, of course, superbly unspoiled bushland in the ranges to the north of this road and the fine natural and man-made landscapes of the Strzeleckis to the south. But generally speaking, the motorist travelling eastwards from Drouin is glad when he has passed Traralgon, or when he can turn off in to the hills. The generally low standard of the landscape as seen from the main road is one reason – the other is the constant unpleasantness of the sulphurous fumes from Maryvale and the somewhat oppressive climate of The Valley.

None of these adverse features is directly connected with the Commission, but we cannot help feeling that the Commission's image is affected by them. What we wish to propose is that there is an urgent need for a consortium (say of the SEC, CRB, APM[2] and Town and Country Planning Authority) whose task would be to create in the whole valley a landscape (partly rural, partly industrial) of real distinction. In this we believe the SEC, the major employer in The Valley, should take the lead. The first requirement is a new main road (not necessarily a freeway). The siting of a major road is subject to many considerations, most of them economic and functional. Nevertheless, the Princes Highway is also one of Australia's major tourist roads, and one consideration in relocating it should be to exhibit to the travelling public, not only a handsome rural landscape, but a landscape of power. The siting of the road and its side branches should be such as to encourage the public to appreciate the magnitude of the energy installations, the beauty of well-designed power stations, the sheer magnificence of the enormous open cuts – which incidentally were an inspiration to our Canadian landscape architect, Robert Parkin. One site for the Princes Highway worth consideration is the line of roads north of the Latrobe River, through Yallourn North and Tyers. This could then become a scenic highway or parkway, leaving the present highway to serve commuter traffic between The Valley towns. The road to the north of the river is generally higher than the valley, and it therefore presents the opportunity for some good viewing points of Yallourn; Loy Yang would be reached by a detour through Traralgon. The only section of road that currently does justice to the

SEC is the visually exciting approach to Yallourn West along John Field Drive from Moe.

There is a precedent for the unashamed demonstration of what the engineer can accomplish when his interest in the environment is aroused in the work of the Snowy Mountains Authority, and we believe that the Commission could accomplish a great deal to benefit Victoria in attracting tourists from interstate and overseas – and at the same time in taking the pressure off other tourist attractions (such as national parks) which are more sensitive to the pressures of over-population. *At present in the Latrobe Valley the wrong wares are in the window* – the unplanned townships without individuality, shape or distinction; the weedy railway line with its gallows posts; the undistinguished roadside planting; the ribbon building along the roadside. There should be far easier access to good viewing points and a series of small museums which tell the story of the geological history of the coal seams. The road to Gippsland should display the fine farms, the hill landscapes, well-designed uncluttered power stations and the immense open cuts.

Notes

1   Sylvia Crowe, *The Landscape of Power*, The Architectural Press, London, 1958, p. 26.

2   APM is Australian Paper Manufacturers Ltd., who own pulp and paper mills at Maryvale in the Latrobe Valley.

19

—

PASSING WATER: WAYS OF HANDLING STREAMS

1975

This article was written for Memo, *the official magazine of the Local Government Engineers' Association of Victoria.*

IT IS CURRENT FASHION TO DESCRIBE TOWNS AND CITIES as organisms. This is no more than a metaphor and it is often misused and misleading. Cities are not organisms, but constructs. Nevertheless, they have been made to function in some ways like organisms and one of them is that they discharge wastes from time to time, including liquid wastes. We have constructed our cities in such a way that we use a centralised disposal system. The higher organisms, including our own species, have a similar system; and for them it is a natural system, but it is not 'natural' for cities and the organic metaphor may blind us to alternatives.

The disposal problem I wish to consider is that of storm-water and I choose this topic because it is a recurrent cause of conflict between 'conservationists' and engineers. What I aim to do is not to take sides, but to analyse the conflict and to look for possible resolutions and their costs.

The relevant engineer is very often a local government engineer. He has a clear brief, limited funds and a training that predisposes him to solve problems in certain ways (this is true of all professional training). The brief is, simply, to get rid of storm-water. The citizenry do not want puddles and ponds at their doorstep. Nor do they want muddy or flooded roads. So rain-water is drained from the house-block to the street; the street is paved, kerbed and guttered, and the water is carried off to the streams: where such services are not provided the engineer and his council are under constant pressure to provide them. In short, he is responding to a community demand.

The sequence I have outlined above does not apply throughout Australia; and where it does apply, it does not always present problems. For instance, it does not apply in Perth, where the householder may not discharge storm-water from his roof into the street gutters and the street gutters themselves do not, as a rule, empty into streams (although some do). The householder is supposed to construct soak-wells, which allow the water to soak into the ground and, incidentally, to recharge the ground water, which is used extensively to water lawns and gardens. Many street gutters also are carried into large soak-wells and this is one – although only one – reason why the Swan River is so clear so much of the time. But Perth is built on highly porous sand. Soak-wells would not work in most towns in Victoria.

Nor would they work in Sydney, which discharges large volumes of storm-water. Paddington, where I used to live, is in some parts in excess of 80 per cent paved – even the back 'gardens' are impermeable, consisting of quarry tiles and plants in tubs. Yet this rarely creates a problem, despite the high rainfall – the gutters race into the storm drains, which roar down the steep hills to the harbour, which is flushed daily by the tides. There are, of course, parts of Sydney where the storm-water pours into basements and shops and the Wakehurst Parkway regularly takes on a quite Venetian character.

The point is elementary: cities are easy to drain if they are built on a porous substrate, or on steep hills. Melbourne – like Brisbane – is neither. It is built, for the most part, on clays of low permeability, and on gently undulating or flat land, drained by two modest rivers and a network of minor creeks and tributaries, many of them arising within the metropolitan area itself. In this respect at least, Melbourne is a fairly typical Victorian town and Bright, in the mountainous north-east, is not.

So Melbourne is drained by running its storm-water into the natural drainage system. But this no longer operates naturally. Every house is a 20-foot waterfall. Sealed gutters and concrete drains deliver the water rapidly to the trunk streams. Before clearing of the natural vegetation, rain-water had its force broken by trees and shrubs, was held by leaf litter, soaked into the soil, in part transpired and evaporated: the rest was released slowly over a period of weeks. In an urbanised catchment, much of the water during a rain-storm is delivered to the trunk streams in a few hours and at high velocities. During dry periods there is little flow and the streams are reduced to a foul-smelling trickle.

The Board of Works, Melbourne's main drainage authority, then has no choice but to get rid of the storm-water delivered to it. It has done this by 'improving' stream flow – bed obstructions are removed, streams are desnagged, banks are straightened. In the end, streams go into barrel drains or two-level concrete trenches like Moonee Ponds Creek or Gardiners Creek below the South-Eastern Freeway. A great deal of urban debris is swept into these drains so maintenance requirements are exacting and the banks are generally graded, grassed and kept clear of trees and shrubs. Thus natural streams are converted to frankly functional drains. This system has served Melbourne fairly well from the strictly functional point of view, but it is not indefinitely expansible and steadily increasing urbanisation will put the whole system at risk. The 1934 floods in Melbourne would be a great deal more destructive today. The system may need re-thinking.

Now let us turn to the other side of the coin. Streams are precious to the conservationist for a number of very good reasons. One is that they are a major landscape resource. By their nature as erosive agents they create contour. Overlapping spurs, spits, bars, high banks and water meadows, all make streams and valleys into areas that are of high topographic variety and interest. Running water is itself a source of perennial fascination. There are few natural or 'wild' rivers left anywhere in Victoria and those few, mainly in the north-east part of the state, such as the Big River from Bogong Saddle to the Omeo Highway, are among our most rewarding landscapes. A second closely related reason is that they are a major recreation resource. Swimming or fishing in a natural stream is one of the supreme delights. But even tamed rivers, like the Yarra at Alexandra Parade, have major recreational value; so did the small tributary streams a few decades ago. They are especially valuable in cities built on the rectangular grid, which ignores contour and deadens all sense of natural landforms. Streams are an irregular thread weaving their way across our urban graph paper and offer great opportunities for bicycle paths, footpaths and jogging tracks (and let me note in passing that joggers pounding along city streets, even down the median strip of the Mulgrave Freeway, are a clear indication that a demand is not being met).

Next, streams have high biological value. Together with the road reserves, they are among the last refuges of the indigenous vegetation in many outer-suburban areas, although often choked with blackberries and watsonia in the east, thistles and boxthorn and other noxious weeds in the west. They still play a major role as biological corridors for birds. Not however, for indigenous fish, or mammals other than the possum. 'Conservationists' sometimes know, and engineers generally do not know, that most Australians live in surroundings that are biologically impoverished compared with their urban counterparts in North America and Europe. Even Los Angeles, not renowned among conservationists, has quite large populations of coyotes within the city limits, breeding and sheltering in the canyons and arroyos of that city. It also has many other small indigenous mammals such as chipmunks and generous remnants of indigenous vegetation in good health. London has no less than fifteen indigenous (native) mammals flourishing within the city limits and some of them are common – for example, the hedgehog. In Melbourne, however, the native animals have gone, all but the possum; and the natural vegetation is going. Such remnants as we have are in general severely degraded. It is a consciousness of these problems that raises concern to near-hysteria among some conservationists. There is great urgency if we are to recreate an urban environment in Melbourne as biologically rich as that of London or Amsterdam. Finally, natural streams are a resource in environmental education. No environmental policies can be effective without an environmentally educated public. Where are our children to learn?

The engineer has not created these problems. They are especially acute in urban Australia because our flora and fauna are that of an island, especially vulnerable to invasion by introduced weeds and pests. Feral cats, the rabbit, blackberry, gorse and so on are all far harder to handle in Australia than they are in the northern hemisphere where they are part of the natural scene. All the above reasons, however, make the remnants of our natural stream systems of high value.

This is not, of course, a simple conflict between the barbarian engineer and the noble conservationist. It represents two conflicting community demands. The community demands that its cities be drained. The community demands that respect be paid to conservation values. The demands are in conflict and the conflict cannot be fully resolved – it is basic. The built environment is not, cannot be, a 'natural' environment. There are, however, some partial solutions. They are of two kinds.

The first is to raise design standards using existing methods. In many ways, our grandfathers did better than we did with the same methods. One area in Melbourne worth attention is the Warringal Parklands in Heidelberg, which are drained by two small streams. The stream beds have been reformed for functional efficiency, but they are elegantly contoured and beautifully paved with bluestone, which has the additional virtue of allowing some water infiltration, to the benefit of the nearby trees. The nearby bird sanctuary on the river flats at Heidelberg is also worth a visit. Sullivans Creek at the Australian National University in Canberra is another example of good design and the small lake also serves as a settling pond and water-bird refuge. The treatment in this case was doubtless more expensive than a concrete channel, but natural materials are not necessarily prohibitively expensive, as examples from Perth can show, where the local limestone has generally been used for river embankments in preference to concrete. The alternative costs should at least be explored, including those of long-term maintenance. Carpet tiles are cheaper to replace than wall-to-wall carpet. Concrete is a maintenance-free material for some years, but concrete failure through cracking or undercutting can lead to very expensive repairs.

Note also that good design needs good designers and local government might make much more extensive use of professional design skills than it generally does. This adds to costs, at least initially, which of course brings us back to the will and capacity of the community to pay for high standards. Other examples of good hard-edge urban stream design are the small stream at Suva, in Fiji, with a colonnade of shops on one side and a tree-shaded path on the other, fenced off from the stream bank with a Lantana hedge. The San Antonio River at San Antonio, in Texas, is worth the attention of Australians. Here the river is lined with shops, cafes and promenades at two levels, all paved, but closed to cars and shaded with trees, making a major pedestrian thoroughfare, promenade and recreation area in the heart of the city. Compare this with the Yarra below Princes Bridge.

The second partial solution is to treat the cause rather than the symptom. The cause is the urbanised catchment. The entire catchment of streams such as Gardiners Creek, Ruffey Creek and Koonung Creek in eastern Melbourne are becoming urbanised. The effects of accelerated run-off in newly subdivided areas could be greatly reduced and thus reduce the need to turn the streams into concrete storm-sewers. There has been a good deal of experiment along these lines over the last few years overseas, especially in the US. Pervious paving materials have been developed (and let me point out again here that Melbourne's old bluestone gutters and lane-ways allow some water infiltration. Replacing them with concrete is not desirable and has in some cases led to the death of street trees). Gravel driveways and minor roads allow some infiltration – at, of course, some inconvenience, especially to cyclists. Natural bushland has an infiltration rate of 0.6 inches per minute as against 0.1 inches per minute for lawn (average figures for eastern US). Bushland reduces water yield in its area because it enables much of the rain that falls on it to be evaporated or transpired and hence unavailable as run-off. This is especially pertinent in Melbourne and most of Victoria, because the high-intensity storms that are a major source of run-off occur in summer, when evaporation rates are high.

The extent of impervious area can be reduced in various ways. Collector road width can be reduced. Two-storey housing can reduce by up to 50 per cent the nett roof area for a similar floor area. A return to the old domestic water tank is highly desirable and it is incredible that we ever let it go out of fashion as it functions both as an additional water supply and in reducing run-off. Holding ponds also have their uses – the hillsides of suburban Doncaster-Templestowe were covered with small earth dams fifty years ago and now they are gone.

This is not the occasion for detailed exposition or for technicalities – there are many good papers on this subject. My main point is this: that engineers are predisposed by their training to look to centralised disposal systems. We have neglected the possibilities of site disposal. We cannot continue to do so, because centralised disposal is not indefinitely expansible and has a high cost. Present practices are unsatisfactory. The developer, the local council and the Board of Works work at their own part of the problem without any comprehensive attempt at watershed management, which should be planned before subdivision. Suitable techniques for watershed analysis and the management of urbanised catchments are well known and laid out in detail in publications such as the US Soil Conservation Service's *Engineering Field Manual*.

The first step in any area ripe for subdivision should be a catchment analysis, to determine natural levels of run-off and peak discharge. The next is to determine the carrying capacity of the natural stream system. It will, as a general rule, be adapted to that discharge and an increase will initiate a cycle of erosion and siltation. Using the devices indicated above, controls can then be set to maintain the appropriate discharge levels. The Wissahickon Watershed Study in the US offers a good case-history.

I said earlier that the built environment cannot be the natural environment. It can, however, emulate it. It is possible, with appropriate controls, to maintain an artificial system that simulates all the significant features of the natural hydrologic cycle. One might call such work 'ecological engineering'. It will require most of the traditional skills of the engineer, together with some new ones. It is time they were put into practice in Australia.

20

———

AN OPEN SPACE SYSTEM
FOR CANBERRA

1977

This is extracted from a policy review prepared by Seddon for the National Capital Development Commission.

THIS IS A GOOD MOMENT FOR CANBERRA TO REVIEW its open space provisions and to frame a policy for the future. Canberra has always had a generous provision of parkland, and it has been in the forefront in some areas of urban design, especially in the provision of schools and playgrounds that can be reached by footpaths, and cycle ways insulated from motorised traffic. Until recently, however, there has not been much formal provision for recreation outside the city area, except for a few picnic spots. This is changing rapidly, at a time of rapid growth – with new centres at Tuggeranong, Belconnen and Gungahlin – and also of rapid changes in recreational behaviour. Nude beaches were scarcely thought of five years ago, but Canberra now has one. Hang gliding had not been heard of. Trail bikes have become common. New forms appear, such as orienteering, and old ones like horse-riding expand dramatically. Despite the speed of change, most of these new recreation patterns have one thing in common – they take

278

up a good deal of space. Many of them require substantial capital investment in equipment – water-skiing is a good example – and make quite heavy demands on fossil fuels. This makes planning especially difficult, because the high growth rates are probably not sustainable in their present form. Nevertheless, people who have had these new experiences of outdoor recreation are not ever likely to go back to watching football on Saturday afternoons; especially when they can watch the television replay at home on Saturday night. New demands are also being made on urban open space. Finally, broad-acres alone do not provide recreation. Recreation is an experience, not an activity – a recurring theme of this report.

The object of the report is to see what Canberra has by way of open space and opportunities for recreation, what it lacks, what it could have, what it should have. The structure of the report is to consider the functions of an open space system in Canberra; the accessibility, distribution and capacity of elements in the system; the quantity of open space – how much, and what it would cost – and the quality of open space, including a discussion of diversity and of design and maintenance standards; recommendations and conclusions.

Historical Development of Open Space Systems

Three great waves have broken across the face of Britain since 1800. First, the sudden growth of dark industrial towns. Second, the thrusting movement along far-flung railways. Third, the sprawl of car-based suburbs. Now we see, under the guise of a modest word, the surge of a fourth wave which could be more powerful than all the others. The modest word is *leisure*.

Leisure is a compound of six decisive factors – population, income, mobility, education, retirement and the free time of adults. Each of these has grown dramatically in the last decade and will continue to grow apace in years ahead.

We cannot tell exactly how these changes will affect our leisure. The Americans have taken the trouble to find out. The conclusions in the report Outdoor Recreation for America, published in early 1962, could well be true for us – that active use of leisure goes up with income; that growing mobility is putting heavy pressure on recreation resources never used before; that widespread education not only releases more youngsters on holiday but changes their attitudes towards leisure, the better educated being more active; that older people are remarkably keen on the less vigorous leisure activities, such as walking, driving, sight-seeing, fishing.

The broad conclusion of the American report was that their population would double, but the demand for outdoor recreation would *treble*, by the year 2000.[1]

Thus begins an influential article with the title: 'Fourth Wave – The Challenge of Leisure'. Data from the USA show steep growth rates in use of some outdoor recreation areas in the 1960s; nearly 9 per cent increase in the annual use of the National Park System, nearly 12 per cent increase in use of national forests, and a massive 23 per cent increase in use of water supply reservoirs; although these rates of growth have eased recently, they are still high.[2] Good data are lacking for Australia as a whole, but it is easy to see similar broad patterns.[3] These changes have been quite rapid, and they make very heavy demands on the outdoors environment, requiring new policies.

Public open space as we know it is a phenomenon of the modern industrial city. Most of the compact pre-industrial cities had little need for urban open space because the countryside was readily accessible. The medieval paved market square provided a central area for community activities. Gardens were the private domain of royalty and the well-to-do.

The French monarchy first began to open their pleasure gardens to the public in the eighteenth century, and originated the idea of the 'cours', a form of planted promenade. Baron Georges Haussmann, Prefect of the Seine under Napoleon III, introduced circulatory and ventilation systems into the congested urban agglomeration of Paris in the mid-nineteenth century. Within the network of streets created by large-scale demolition, he introduced a hierarchy of planted areas: promenades such as the Champs Elysées, squares similar to London's private residential squares, public gardens in romantic style and suburban parks at the eastern and western edges of Paris (Bois de Boulogne, Bois de Vincennes). The primary function of Haussmann's open space system was to ventilate the city, although its recreational uses became very important.

In England the rapid, uncontrolled growth of the nineteenth-century industrial cities brought overcrowding, squalor and disease. As the houses and factories spread outwards, there was almost no pro-vision for community uses. Social reformers such as Edwin Chadwick and Charles Dickens awakened public opinion to the need for green recreational areas for urban dwellers. A number of private and Royal gardens, especially in London, were opened to the public. The Public Health Act in 1848 empowered Local Boards of Health to provide and maintain public walks and pleasure grounds, and over the next fifty years, many parks were established in British cities. The physical form and function of the Victorian public park derived from both the botanical garden and the popular pleasure ground, with the design basis provided by the great eighteenth-century landscape designers such as Repton and Capability Brown. Areas for organised games and children's play were not generally provided until late in the century;

on the other hand, village greens and commons had been tradition-ally used for games for centuries.

The English concept of the public park tended to remain that of an isolated garden oasis in the urban fabric, but the Americans, notably Frederick Law Olmsted, extended the park to become a linked open space system and structural element in the shaping of a city. Olmsted designed Central Park, New York, as a refreshing, natural contrast to its rectilinear urban surroundings, yet the park was closely linked to the city by its four separate circulatory systems – for carriages, horses, pedestrians and through traffic. The parkway, or tree-lined boulevard linking parks and city focal points, was first suggested by Olmsted in 1869 to join his planned suburb of Riverside with Chicago. At the same time, he was developing the idea of a series of parks linked into a working complex; this was first applied in Boston in 1891, and sub-sequently in many other world cities.

✳

The comprehensive plan published in 1909 by Burnham and Bennett for the future development of Chicago was a pioneering work in city planning in America. Burnham's earlier design for an 8-mile lake-front park was one part of the structural frame formed by the major parks, which were connected via continuous strips of greenery to secondary parks. In contrast to Britain, where the impetus for town planning arose from the sanitary and housing reform movements, the idea of comprehensive planning of cities and their environs in America came about largely through the earlier experience in plan-ning complete open space systems.

In the early twentieth century, large municipal park systems were established in many American cities. In New York, for exam-ple, the city and state park systems were co-ordinated on a regional basis, and considerable areas of land were acquired in outlying parts.

Eighty thousand men and a professional planning staff of 1800 were employed on the development and expansion of New York's recreational areas through work relief programs during the 1930s Depression.

The national park movement has been influential both in providing open space and in creating a demand for it. Yellowstone National Park was established in 1872. Australia was in the vanguard of this movement for a time, with Royal National Park in New South Wales, dedicated in 1886, Ku-ring-gai Chase in 1891 and Tower Hill National Park in Victoria in 1892; but this early start was not maintained. The national parks in the US helped to foster the taste for recreation in the natural environment, and their interpretative centres have played a significant role in environmental education. Powerful conservation bodies like the Sierra Club have been a part of this movement, which has found more recent expression in the setting aside of wilderness areas, and the dedication of wild rivers. The American concept of the national park as a tract of little disturbed land in public ownership has generally been followed in the New World, but in countries with a long history of settlement, little such land is available. National parks in countries such as Japan and England, for example, include cultural landscapes within their boundaries, and the land generally remains in private ownership. The national park is therefore a *management* concept, to maintain compatibility between recreation and a range of pre-existing land uses, such as agriculture, forestry and quarrying (which is a major land use in the Peak National Park in Derbyshire).

Another significant trend in open space planning in the twentieth century has been the breaking down of the previous distinction between public park and urban, or living area. Stein and Wright's plan for the community of Radburn, New Jersey in the late 1920s became a model for suburban layout. Its two principal elements are the 'superblock' with entrant culs-de-sac for automobiles, and continuous parkland as the backbone of the layout and setting for pedestrian routes. The houses face onto the open space instead of the streets; and Stein and Wright insisted on including open space and generous plantings as part of the first costs of housing.

The English Garden City movement, begun by Ebenezer Howard towards the end of the nineteenth century, strongly influenced the Radburn plan. The Garden City, to have the advantages of both town and country, was to be encircled and limited in size by a permanent agricultural green belt. Such a green belt was established around London by legislation in 1938, and green belts have since been established around most larger English cities. Functions of green belts now include the separation of different urban areas or incompatible land uses, the provision of a wide range of recreational facilities and attractive nearby countryside for a city. Recent sub-regional study proposals for Nottinghamshire and Derbyshire provide for recreation facilities in 'greenways', or extended green belts which link regional parks to one another and to the towns.

This represents one of many modifications that the earlier green belt concept has undergone. The difficulties with a rural belt around the perimeter of an expanding city have been that development leap-frogs the green belt, and rural uses become increasingly difficult in what has become an urban zone. In an attempt to minimise these difficulties, plans for urban expansion generally now propose a finger or urban corridor pattern, with green wedges of rural land between the fingers. Copenhagen has followed such a plan with fair success, and it is at least a paper plan for Perth and Melbourne – but when the rural land of the green wedges remains in private ownership and land values increase, it is unusual for farming to remain an economically viable land use. The linear city offers, inter alia, a third attempt at managing the urban/rural boundary; this concept was proposed in the 1890s for Madrid by Soria Y Mata, but the theory has rarely been put into practice, because few cities have been able to control their form so precisely. (Tuggeranong will give Canberra a linear extension to the south, but the Y-plan north of the Molonglo ignores the reality of Queanbeyan, which is an eastern component of the ACT conurbation. Maintaining effective open space between Canberra and Queanbeyan will require very determined planning.)

Because of its simplicity, the 'standards approach' to determining public open space requirements in an urban area has been a durable prescription in this century. The Playground Association of America proposed in 1910 a standard of 1 acre (0.4 hectares) of open space for every 100 people. In 1925 the English National Playing Fields Association formulated a standard of 6 acres (2.4 hectares) of playing space per 1000 of the population. With some modifications these gross standards have since been recommended by numerous agencies, including Australian authorities, with little or no attempt to test their validity for different areas and conditions.

A more refined approach to the planning of recreational open space utilises the concept of a functional hierarchy of parks, ranging from small local parks to large regional or national ones, thus bringing together the two streams discussed above. In part, this approach may have grown out of the standards for different categories of open space such as playgrounds and community playing fields suggested by the National Recreation and Park Association of America in the 1920s–1940s. Playgrounds and neighbourhood parks must be readily accessible to mothers and children on foot, whereas the more specialised parks are visited less often and do not have to be close to every home. As suggested by the Californian Committee on Planning for Recreation, Park Areas and Facilities in 1956, the hierarchy can be closely related to the neighbourhood concept centred on the primary school, with a larger district served by a secondary school.

In 1969 the Greater London Development Plan rejected the previously crude standards (expressed in acres/1000 population) introduced in 1943, and proposed a hierarchy to 'satisfy the main open space needs of all the population'. This attempted to relate park function, size and distance from home. The origins of this functional hierarchy with the larger, more specialised parks having catchment areas superimposed on a number of areas served by equidistant smaller parks can be readily traced to classical Central Place theory.

The Panel of Inquiry into the Development Plan rejected the hierarchy proposal because it did not take account of varying densities of population or accessibility by public or private transport. Nevertheless it was admitted that a better means of assessing or prescribing open space requirements was yet to be developed, and the concept of an open space hierarchy has now been generally accepted around the world by planners and park administrators – although it has rarely been put into practice.

Closely linked to the concept of an open space hierarchy is the concept of a park *system*, which is also generally accepted as a goal, but is one that few regions have put into practice. To operate the open spaces as a system requires either a single management team or a strong co-ordinating body. The potential advantages are very great. In a co-ordinated system, use can be regulated by design. Some areas can be rested, some protected, some specially designed for very heavy use. Actual use can be monitored, which allows feedback to management. Costs can be monitored, and economic balancing becomes feasible. Most Australian cities and their recreation hinterland are administered by so many local government units and statutory authorities that unified management of the open spaces will be hard to bring about, but Canberra already has the necessary administrative structures.

The major trend in recreation over the last two decades has been an increase in mobility. The one-day trip and the weekend trip (by car) now play a basic part in our recreation. The effects of the new mobility, and the responses to it, have been diverse. The designating of 'scenic rivers', scenic roads and parkways in the US is largely a response to the needs of the pleasure motorist. Because the rural landscape now plays such a significant part in recreation, much thought has been given in some countries to its protection, and to the resolution of conflicts in land use. Many European countries have a long experience in this field: Denmark and Holland are in the forefront. The Countryside Commission in England was established to plan for the diverse demands now being made on rural landscapes. [...] In Australia, the problem of reconciliation of rural land use with recreation, which includes the hobby farm and weekend cottage, is acute around all the major cities, and a current source of conflict. The Western Port Regional Planning Authority in Victoria has attempted to resolve such problems in its Conservation Plan for the Southern Mornington Peninsula,[4] but the competing demands of landowners, developers, farmers, conservationists and the recreating general public have not yet been fully reconciled.

A recent trend in recreation runs counter to the heavy dependence on the motor car. Bush walking, horse-riding, bicycling, canoeing, orienteering, are all increasing in popularity. They may still begin with a car trip to get out of the city, but congested roads at the weekend are making even the purely functional car journey less attractive, and there is a new demand for open-air recreation within the city that is quite different from the organised sports of earlier years. Some examples in Melbourne are the opening of large metropolitan parks within the city limits (Brimbank Park on the Maribyrnong is an example), the provision of bicycle trails, and phenomena such as 'creek walks': up to 500 people now will turn up for a planned walk and barbecue beside Gardiners Creek, a very minor and wholly urban tributary of the Yarra River.

All of these trends can be exemplified in Canberra and the ACT, often in an exaggerated form because of the high growth rate of the city and of the comparatively high level of education and affluence of her citizens.

Open Space and Canberra

'As far as possible, the environment planned for working, trading, circulating, and dwelling should be recreational as well as utilitarian. To be effective, recreation has to be found casually in the factory at the hour of rest, on the way home, and at home.'[5]

Canberra has much under-utilised land and much dead ground – despite which, it lacks an open space system adequate to present and future demands. It is therefore right that it should be planning for such a system now. The city of tomorrow can have only the open spaces that are reserved for it today.

This may seem paradoxical. To many people, the problem in Canberra is not so much to find the open space as to find the City. For this there are at least three reasons. The first is that from many of the viewpoints commonly encountered in daily travel, the garden city is hidden in the garden. One can look at the well-settled suburb of Yarralumla from the lower slopes of Black Mountain, and see nothing but trees. The second is that the topography functions in isolating the urban system as a whole. Neither Belconnen nor the Woden Valley can be seen from Central Canberra, nor from each other. The third is that much land has been necessarily reserved for future use, especially in the National Area. It was not possible or desirable to build the city all at once – as Walter Burley Griffin recognised – but it was possible to create the garden setting, and then fill it up as needs and resources allowed. Hence the National Gallery and High Court building now under construction are on sites long reserved for such buildings. The apparent emptiness of Canberra is misleading. Moreover, it has special problems and special responsibilities: the problems arise from its being an artificial and an inland city sitting in a fragile landscape; and the responsibilities from its being a national capital, 'a show place to provide, as it were, the essence of Australia to both nationals and visitors'.[6] The Burley Griffin plan, to which Canberra has long been inescapably committed, also presents some unique problems and responsibilities.

Certain key themes dominate this report, surfacing under many individual headings or sections, and it may be worth listing them at the beginning.

(a) Canberra is the largest inland city in Australia. Most Australians living in large urban centres relate to the sea and well-watered coastal landscapes for their recreation; in Canberra the problem is to find a satisfactory comparable relationship with a highly sensitive system of inland rivers and hills. A very real danger following Canberra's development would be a deterioration in water quality. Thus the open space system must be designed to protect the river system. It can do this in part by creating recreation facilities away from the rivers that are literally attractive, and by making much better recreational use of urban Canberra.

(b) The customers for the open space system are not only the local residents, but also the tourists, and the tourists are unusual, because they are not looking for a holiday in the ordinary sense. They come for many reasons, but the primary one is to experience the National Capital, as Americans go to Washington. It is, in a sense, a pilgrimage, intended as an act of piety – although in practice, the experience is meagre, and the intention realised perhaps only at the War Memorial. Nevertheless, a visit to Canberra should ideally confirm and renew for every Australian his sense of national identity, and give him a deeper understanding of what it is to be an Australian. In practice, many – perhaps most – Australians feel strongly alienated from Canberra, for a complex of reasons and prejudices, many of which have nothing to do with the physical planning of the actual city. Some relate to the initial choice of site, remote from the industrial cities in which most Australians live. This is indeed a consequence of physical planning, but one to which there was no practicable alternative at the time, and which is in any case irremediable. Some relate to the Australian dislike for the bureaucracy, for politicians, for the present archaic Constitution, and for federal–state relations in their current form. Some spring from the healthy Australian talent for irreverence; others from the unhealthy Australian penchant for the cheap jibe. Canberra is often attacked for shortcomings that turn out to be the common and very nearly inevitable characteristics of new communities – the unbalanced age structure, the lack of accessible grandparents, a high incidence of mental ill-health and so on. Nevertheless, the image of Canberra is also partly a creation of physical planning, and it can be modified by physical planning.

(c) For the above reasons, there is also much discussion of urban Canberra. Many articles on open space systems are concerned exclusively with playing fields, parks and access to the countryside. This report concerns the need for an integrated open space *system*. Such a system will have both rural and urban components. The way people use their city partly determines the way they use the countryside. Indeed, the distinction between the two is in part artificial. The country is sometimes seen through sentimental eyes by city people as if it belonged to a different century, but in fact all land in the ACT is dominated by urban needs, by urban economics and by urban technology. Canberra has an exceptionally sharp urban/rural boundary, but this admirable characteristic is the outcome of conscious planning and management policies, and not of untutored economic forces.

Notes

1   Michael Dower, 'Fourth Wave: The Challenge of Leisure', *The Architects Journal*, 20 January 1965, p. 123.

2   Marion Clawson and Jack L. Knetsch, *The Economics of Outdoor Recreation*, Johns Hopkins Press for Resources for the Future, Inc., Baltimore, 1966, p. 122.

3   David Mercer, *Leisure and Recreation in Australia*, Sorrett Publishing, Melbourne, 1977.

4   George Seddon, *A Landscape Assessment of the Southern Mornington Peninsula*, Centre for Environmental Studies, University of Melbourne, 1974; *Phillip Island: Capability, Conflict and Compromise*, Centre for Environmental Studies, University of Melbourne, 1975.

5   Artur Glikson, *The Ecological Basis of Planning*, Martinus Nijhoff, The Hague, 1971, pp. 28–29.

6   R. Johnson, *Design in Balance: Designing the National Area of Canberra 1968–72*, University of Queensland Press, Brisbane, 1974, p. 29.

21

WHITHER THE WEST

1977/1995

This piece began life as a short editorial for Habitat, *the journal of the Australian Conservation Foundation. Seddon later prepared reflective comments on the editorial, for a 1991 conference on water-sensitive urban design. The editorial and subsequent comments were published together in* Swan Song *(1995).*

ZIMBABWE, MACHU PICCHU, ANGKOR WAT ARE GHOST towns renowned as works of art: Herculaneum and Pompeii for their pornography. Scattered over the face of the earth, there are remnants of abandoned settlements and cities. The Vikings were driven out of Greenland by climatic change. Coolgardie and Walhalla emptied when the gold ran out. Hall's Creek in the East Kimberley is another town that shrank with a shrinking economic base, and the old town in its narrow valley was finally abandoned completely with a change in communications, requiring an airport. Venice is drowning, and Tallangatta, drowned. Cities have been deserted because of plague, war, natural catastrophe, changes in the economy and environmental mismanagement. The last is hardest to demonstrate, but it is clear that the combined effects of the goat, excessive clearing, over-grazing and soil erosion – together with the collapse of elaborate hydraulic systems and the effects of endless wars, and probably also of climate change – were the death warrant of many great cities in the Mediterranean basin. It is hard now to visualise Mediterranean North Africa as a major granary, as it was for centuries.

For what would Perth be remembered, if it were abandoned? Would it make a good ruin? It has always seemed to me an exceptionally vulnerable city, for two reasons – one, its almost total dependence on stored water; and two, that it has no visible means of support. Let me elaborate these two statements.

First, water. Every large city, and most small ones, depend on stored water, but Perth's dependence is peculiar. There are now about 800,000 people in the Perth area. Water consumption is growing rapidly, with a predicted trebling of demand over the next twenty years. Ninety per cent of this water comes from the Darling Range. Unlike the cities of eastern Australia, or Los Angeles, its nearest physical counterpart, Perth has no mountain catchments; the Darling Range is merely the western rim of the vast and generally arid plateau that makes up much of the western third of the continent. There is an adequate and fairly reliable winter rainfall along this western rim, but streams generally get less rain in their headwaters than they do in their middle reaches. The jarrah forest of the Darling Range protects this catchment, and it is subject to four hazards: salination consequent on clearing, which has made the waters of the three major rivers, the Swan, Murray and Blackwood, unfit for drinking; *Phytophthora cinnamomi* or dieback, a fungus which kills trees by attacking their roots; bauxite mining; and wood chipping. Although there is no need at all to assume disaster, it is prudent to recognise the role of the Darling Range in supplying the water needs of more than 90 per cent of the population of Western Australia, and the dangers to which it is subject. If dieback were to prove as efficient as Dutch elm disease, for instance, the consequences could be extreme.

It may seem odd to say that Perth has no visible means of support, yet almost any traveller who has come upon Perth for the first time from the east will know what I mean. Nothing prepares one for it, by air or road or rail. Miles of Nullarbor plain are followed by miles of a semi-arid plateau, a relatively narrow belt of wheat farms, efficiently farmed, but with very low yields per hectare – then further miles of harsh, grey-green jarrah forest, until without warning, one drops down to a coastal plain spanned from scarp to sea for 30 kilometres by a large modern city. Perth bears no obvious relation with its hinterland.

This may seem equally true of Sydney, but despite its amphitheatre of barren Hawkesbury Sandstone, one soon meets the rich pastures of the Illawarra, or the Hunter Valley, and the coal of Wollongong and Newcastle, as well as the industrial and managerial wealth of Sydney itself. Perth is largely a service city. It is true that beyond a certain critical point, cities seem to be self-maintaining, but despite this appearance, there must be an economic base. Mining, government and agriculture have been the base for Perth. The subsidies to Perth as a seat of government have been very substantial: it had cost the British taxpayer some two million pounds by 1868; the last party of convicts arrived in that year, but the system – and the subsidy it represented – was not disbanded until 1886. After Federation, the Australian taxpayer (in effect, Victorians and New South Welsh) took over the privilege of part-subsidising Perth.

The major surges of prosperity have been due to mineral booms, beginning with gold and on to nickel and iron. The reserves of iron ore are vast, but not literally inexhaustible. It seems sensible to me to sell these resources to those who can make use of them, but foolish to describe a mammoth quarrying operation as 'developing the north-west'. A worked-out quarry is only that.

Dry farming in Australia, yielding wheat, wool, mutton and beef, is one of our most efficient and relatively un-subsidised economic activities. But it is an exporting activity and thus vulnerable to over-seas fluctuations in demand and price (as are mineral exports); and there is a fairly high energy input, in the form of fossil fuels. In Western Australia, most of the energy is used in transport, especially from producer to consumer, and increases in energy costs would give the competitive edge to high-yield, labour intensive, low energy farming as against the low-yield, low labour, energy intensive farming to which so much of Western Australia is suited and only suited.

It is as easy to write disaster scenarios for most cities today as it was to take a rosy view of their future progress a hundred years ago, and both may prove to be largely fashions of the day. But it is easier to write such scenarios for Perth than it is for most other cities. Our experience of a high-technology city in such a fragile environment is brief, and there are so many things that could go wrong in Western Australia that a high degree of vigilance is called for. It would not be disastrous if a change in the terms of trade led to a decline in population, but a tempting response to a decline in prosperity is to squeeze the environment harder. Human ecosystems in older lands are generally buffered by a more tolerant environment. It may therefore be prudent to insist on more than usually generous safety-margins in planning for Perth and Western Australia.

Notes, 1995

So what has changed in the last fifteen years?

First, Perth has grown substantially, now to 1.2 million and still with a high percentage increase (3.2 per cent), and a current increase of around 30,000 a year. It is no longer a 'claimant state', and contributes substantially to the national economy. Water consumption has increased both absolutely and relatively, i.e. the per capita consumption continues to increase as water guzzlers like dishwashers become more widely used, along with reticulated garden watering systems – theoretically more efficient in delivering the desired result, but in practice often consuming more water simply because they require less effort to operate. (There was a total sprinkler ban from the end of July 1977 to the end of September 1978, a period of severe drought, so there was a forced drop in consumption, but consumption soon passed its pre-drought peak.)

Secondly, Perth has gone 'palm', my shorthand way of saying that the popular image moves more and more towards the image of a lush tropical paradise. Fifteen years ago, most people were prepared to have a tough old buffalo lawn and hardy shrubs which have tough leathery leaves and will survive the summer without supplementary watering. There is now a strong group of enthusiasts for native plants, but even those plants usually get over-watered, and the preferred image is for tropical luxuriance. In short, we are still moving away from water-sensitive design. Gardens are described as 'lush' in the real estate promotions, which dominate image-formation. When I was young, a lush was someone who consumed too much liquid, a drunk, and I like this sense of the word.

Since 1976 the problems of dieback, clearing in the catchment areas and salinity are well recognised and are being tackled, but they are far from resolution.

Since 1976, the ratio between mining and agriculture has changed, so that Perth now essentially has only one sugar-daddy where once she had two. Long term, the decline in agriculture may be a good thing. I would like to see us farm less land, better – but the transition is acutely painful, and it is heartbreaking that the farmers should be so hard pressed financially at the very point where recognition of the need for better land care has become general.

A big change is that we are no longer largely dependent on the hills catchments. In 1976, there was one public bore into the Leederville Formation, and a number of private bores tapping the ground water. Today it is estimated that between 50–60 per cent of all water used in the metropolitan area comes from these sources, and of course this has bred a new set of concerns about aquifer recharge and water quality; these have become planning issues.

This dependence on ground water and bore water presumably increases our vulnerability, because it becomes increasingly difficult to safeguard water quality. But are we vulnerable? This is a key question. It is easy to pose extreme scenarios. For instance, the Darling Scarp is one of the earth's great lines of weakness, comparable with the San Andreas Fault, and although it is believed stable, the magnitude of the Meckering earthquake and more recently of the Newcastle earthquake took even the seismologists napping, to a certain extent. One good quake along the scarp could spill all our dams in one hit.

But one can take the other tack, point out that we live in a market economy which is also an import-export economy, and that you can buy almost anything if you can pay for it. Singapore imports most of its water from adjoining Malaysia, and the island of Mykonos in the Aegean supports its huge influx of summer tourists by bringing in nearly all its water by tanker. Denmark even imports gravel for construction and road building (from Sweden, because its own land is so good agriculturally and so closely settled, that it is too valuable to dig up). So, if we can pay for it, we can tow icebergs from the Pole, or bring a pipeline down from the Ord, or set up nuclear desalination plants, or re-use water, as many European cities do.

There is no immediate need to do any of these things, given that the South-West has an estimated resource of 1840 million kilolitres, while Perth has a current consumption of 230 million kilolitres per year. Perth actually exports 28 million kilolitres per year from its region to the Goldfields and the Wheatbelt. Water supply is not an absolute constraint on metropolitan growth. We are in fact less vulnerable, not only than Adelaide, the extreme case, but even than Melbourne, which is much bigger, has a significantly lower rainfall, and a significantly more variable rainfall, and is currently bringing water from the Thomson catchment in central Gippsland.

But there is always an opportunity cost. I would argue that water is both under-priced and that it costs too much, and that this is not inconsistent as it may seem. Water is still under-priced in that there is still no great incentive to be frugal, at least among the relatively affluent middle classes, who tend to establish the standards of what we should all aspire to, and the ground water is still a free good, which of course benefits the minority who can afford to sink wells, install pumps and pay for reticulation. At the same time, however, too much of our development costs in servicing new land go into infrastructure costs; even so some infrastructure is substandard – we have the lowest percentage of sewered sites of the capital cities, for example, although this is at last being tackled.

A further consequence of high infrastructure costs is that there are far too few resources available for social support. In fact by far the biggest change that I see in the Perth that I once knew and the Perth to which I returned two years ago is that it has changed from being a (relatively) cohesive and equitable community, where most people had reasonable access to the good things the city had to offer, to a city that is markedly inequitable and no longer cohesive, with very poor access to its urban goods for many people. There are many reasons for this, but one of them is our pattern of urban growth, which includes the way we waste water.

Finally, I would argue that we remain a society that is fundamentally alienated from our physical environment, and that this has all sorts of consequences, including psychological ones. We do not accept that we live in a winter-wet, summer-dry environment. We want it to be something else, indeed the tropical paradise of which I spoke earlier. I have been conscious of this for years, and I think that the degree of alienation is increasing rather than decreasing. The explanation may of course lie, in part, in the fact that this is a city of newcomers, and this is particularly evident among the professional classes. Many of the planners I know are fairly recent arrivals, and in the department of which I am a member at the University of Western Australia, only two out of thirty are native born. And nearly all of these newcomers come from more humid environments. In *Swan River Landscapes*, I offered the one-line piece of advice for Perth: 'Fear the hose', meaning that once you start watering, you are hooked on it. Now I suggest a new catch-cry: 'Down with the palms' – not of course the rough old date palms and fan palms from the desert, but the ones from the wet tropics that have invaded all the 'nice' suburbs. I see them as a botanical version of our chronic balance of payments problem.

22

PROBLEMS IN ENVIRONMENTAL EDUCATION: THE AUSTRALIAN CASE

1985

This article was first published in UNESCO Review *in 1981, with the title 'Consider the Eskimo'.*

DOES A TRADITIONAL ESKIMO GROUP OR DESERT tribe of Australian Aborigines have a problem with environmental education? It would seem not. Such a phrase would be inappropriate because traditional societies have evolved a way of life that is well adjusted to their environment, difficult though it may be. Environmental rapport is achieved in three ways: first, a young Eskimo or Aborigine must learn the skills of survival, reading his surroundings accurately for minute clues which promise food or warn of danger. These are the short-term day-to-day skills. Secondly, the society as a whole has evolved patterns of behaviour – including population controls – which keep it in a stable relation with the resources that sustain it. Finally, both Eskimo and Aborigine are able to derive spiritual sustenance from their environment. Gaiety and a sense of fun are as much in evidence in Eskimo craftwork depicting their life in its surroundings as are the accuracy and minuteness of their observation. Thus the natural environment is an object of reverence, a source of interest, and of food and fun.

Problems in environmental education arise only with maladaptive societies. Technological man shows a number of maladaptive traits and these are the subject of our present concern. Some of them are well illustrated by the way we use words, and I shall begin with examples. One of my favourites is *reclamation*, as in 'reclamation of Botany Bay'. When we reclaim stolen goods, or an umbrella that has been left on a tram or train and is picked up – reclaimed – at the lost and found depot, we are re-establishing our claim to property that was ours in the first place, but has somehow got into the wrong hands. Thus the implication in the phrase *'reclaiming part of a bay or estuary'* is that it was really ours all along, and that all those interdependent marine organisms, including the fish that breed there, were somehow usurpers. The extreme conservationist view that man is the usurper is, we may note, equally defective in grasping the ecological reality, which is that we are part of a natural system in which both our species and the flora and fauna of estuaries play a part.

Another barbarous word in common use is *improvement*. This word is a survivor from the eighteenth century, a confident and vigorous time for England. Capability Brown, the great landscape designer was an *'improver'*, and many of his creations are among the glories of England today. Nevertheless, the notion that Nature unaided can't quite do the job is inimical to conservation goals, as was brought out neatly by one of Capability Brown's contemporaries, reported as saying to Brown: 'I hope I may die before you, Sir, so that I shall see Heaven before you have improved it.' One may note in passing that the notion of Paradise as a place that offers what we now tend to call 'wilderness values' is a very ancient and enduring one.

Much of the constructive energy in Australian society has come from the eighteenth-century spirit of 'improvement', but it has always had a destructive element as well. This limitation is preserved in phrases such as *river improvement,* and *River Improvement Trust.* Such usage is both arrogant and ignorant – a bad combination. It reflects the inadequate view that natural systems are defective and simple, and also that the supposed economic benefit of a small group can be equated with the community interest. The same set of assumptions appears more subtly in phrases such as: 'It is essential to improve the hydraulic properties of the river'. A little analysis shows that 'hydraulic properties' are defined in terms of 'river improvement' and that river improvement is defined in terms of 'reduction in flooding' and that all three definitions are circular. That rivers have significant hydraulic properties other than rapid disposal of waste water, and that flooding may have beneficent biological, recreational and aesthetic functions is ignored, and such phrases generally indicate a monocular program of desnagging, bank straightening and sometimes tree removal, without regard for other objectives. Note again that the extreme conservationists view that 'Nature knows best', and that we meddle with her at our peril is equally one-eyed. I am not arguing that flood control is unnecessary, rather, that we should reject a vocabulary that suggests that work on rivers should have only one legitimate objective.

These two examples are relatively trivial. They reflect a view of 'nature as the enemy' common among pioneer societies, especially in a difficult environment, as ours has been and still is. Nevertheless, such examples have serious consequences for conservation of the natural environment. My next example is of a different kind, the word *consumption.* This is a grossly self-deluding word, and we should abandon it. We do not in fact consume the objects we use, and would have to break the law of conservation of matter to do so. Would that we could. Technological man would not then be faced with the massive problem of disposal – the disposal of goods that have *not* been consumed. We use them, and discard them. Until very recently, all of our design skills and most of our product legislation has ignored the residual use of goods. Clearly, we must design products with regard both to their initial use and their afterlife, but to do so requires major re-education.

To speak of *renewable resources* is also self-deluding. The concept of a non-renewable resource is useful: when we use up the reserves of fossil fuels, that cupboard will be bare. This is different from forestry; for example, when we cut down a forest, we can grow another in its place. But this is not like the never-emptying purse of the fairytale. To grow a new forest takes time and an input of energy and nutrients. Evidence is mounting that in large areas of Australia forests are in a finely balanced equilibrium, with tree and leaf fall returning just enough nutrients to maintain subsequent growth, but any small disturbance is enough to tip the balance and lead to a decline in production. It is worth noting that nutrients, if replaced in the form of a fertiliser, must come from localised and finite deposits, and also that a part of the energy input in forest harvesting and management is in the form of fossil fuels, and that both are essentially non-renewable resources. My objection to the phrase *renewable resources* is basically that it encourages a something-for-nothing view of nature, and diverts attention from the ecologically significant truth that we inhabit a planet that is in most respects a closed system, except for the input of solar energy. The word *recycle* has similar limitations, in that it tends to suggest an effortless natural process and thus encourages the view that there can be no long-term resources shortages, once we have learned to recycle all the materials we use. In practice, recycling of most materials requires a substantial energy input and heat loss to the atmosphere.

My second group of words thus tend to mislead us about pollution and resources use. My third example seems at first sight to be quite unrelated to the first two; it concerns Eurocentrism, which I shall explain by example. Consider the phrase *the Continent*. There are six, or more strictly, five continents; Europe is in fact not a continent, let alone *the* continent, but a subcontinent of Eurasia, as is India. The phrase is harmless enough in itself but it carries with it the whole weight of the cultural arrogance of western man. *The Third World* has similar overtones – the Old World, the New World, the Third World (most of it older than the Old World as a seat of civilisation). There is only one world, not three, and we all share it.

These three groups of examples will serve to introduce three main concerns to which environmental education must address itself: concern for conservation of the natural environment; concern for regulation of resource use and of pollution; and concern for all of the people who inhabit the earth, if for no other reason than because their destinies are inextricably intertwined. How successful are we in this country in re-educating ourselves in these three ways?

First, let us look at concern for conservation of the natural environment. This is an area in which Australia used to be very backward, but has made great progress in the last few years. Until very recently, the average Australian, who is a suburbanite, knew almost nothing about the natural history of his own continent and had very little opportunity of finding out about it if by some chance his interest was aroused. There were few books, few films, few teachers.

I remember vividly my first experience over twenty years ago of the interpretive centres of the US National Parks Service, with their clear models and diagrams, film shows and slide sequences, maps and booklets, that explained just about everything in the Park, starting from the geology and physiography through to soils, the ecology, flora and fauna. There was nothing like them in Australia then and we are still far short of that standard, although the NSW Parks Service now has some good centres. However, in other respects we have caught up; there is a profusion of books and booklets on natural history in Australia, and although they vary in quality that is probably appropriate for a diverse public. Our natural history films are now as good as any in the world; programs such as *In the Wild with Harry Butler* and similar series of the Australian Broadcasting Commission are of very high quality. The attitude in schools has changed and city children are now likely to know far more than their parents about natural history. The intending visitor to an area of natural interest can now usually inform himself adequately about the resources of the area, a situation that was rarely achieved ten years ago.

How far this marked improvement in educational resources has led to a change in attitude towards the natural environment is another matter. Melbourne remains one of the great alienated cities of the world (in this respect it is like Los Angeles), in that the city is an almost wholly artificial environment, bearing little relation to the natural environment it has replaced. Its cultural preoccupations – football, racing, and gardening with exotics of the northern hemisphere – owe almost nothing to its physical location as the southern city of a southern continent, and everything to its British and Irish forebears. There is nothing wrong with this in itself; the danger is that such transplanted cultures rarely have an adequate grasp of the physical realities of their new environment, and this has been true of the Melbourne establishment in the past. However, education is a slow process, and I think that the fruits of current programs will be apparent in years to come.

If we now turn to the second of my three topics, the regulation of resource and pollution, the picture is much less rosy. Our pollution control programs are, in general, competent and on a par with those of other industrial nations. Apart from some localised problems our performance is fairly good compared with similar countries in that our air and water are generally a little below the levels of pollution in Europe, North America and Japan. However, this is largely attributable to our lower densities of population, in short, to good luck rather than good management. In resource use, we are again on a par with other industrial nations; in use of energy 'per person', for example, we are fifth, exceeded only by the US, Canada, Sweden and the UK. Where Australia differs from her peers is not so much in performance as in low levels of awareness, and this must be attributed to a failure in education.

We are a wasteful consumer society with little general awareness that our way of life is not sustainable and with no discernible political will to move towards a sustainable society. Experience is without a doubt the best teacher and Australia was very unlucky to miss out on the recent energy crisis which has had such an impact on our peers. It is true that this is an energy-rich country, with huge coal reserves, but energy sources are not simply interchangeable. Different sources have quite different characteristics. Petroleum accounts for 50 per cent of the energy used here; we currently produce about 60 per cent of our crude oil consumption, but our oil is deficient in the heavier distillation fractions, which are imported. The full implications of this do not seem to be recognised, even in obvious ways. Oil is, for instance, our cheapest fuel, although it is also our scarcest. Rationing a scarce resource by price control is the least equitable and least rational of controls but it is better than no control at all. Australia is in general extraordinarily well endowed with what are called 'non-renewable resources'. This tends to obscure from us the global depletion of minerals such as copper, lead, zinc, mercury and platinum, of which known high-grade reserves will be exhausted by the end of the century. Thus the urgency of the need to move towards a sustainable society is not generally accepted, and certainly not by those politicians who have been urging us to consume more in order to stimulate the economy.

Finally, the third of my three topics with which environmental education must concern itself – the ecological view of the world and all its people as a single, interdependent system. How far have Australians achieved such a vision? The answer is, hardly at all. Our contribution of GNP to international aid is about 0.4 per cent which compares with a global average of 0.34 per cent (although several Nordic countries contribute over 0.9 per cent). To this can be added our subsidy to the 1000 or so Asian students who arrive annually to attend our schools and universities, as well as the even greater number who come for short courses.

Nevertheless our performance falls short of the needs of the situation, which without exaggeration is one of impending catastrophe on a scale new to human history, with the Black Death as the nearest likely parallel. The major problems are in the cities of the developing countries; twenty-five years ago, there were sixteen such cities with a population of over one million people. Today, there are over sixty, with a growth rate of over 5 per cent. In other words: at current trends, the urban areas of the world will have to absorb over 1000 million people in the next twenty-five years, almost all of them desperately poor, in addition to their present population of 700 million. We have just one quarter of a century in which to build more cities – with houses, jobs, water and all their other complex supply systems – than mankind has built in the whole of his history to date. The magnitude of this task is breathtaking, and hideously urgent. Yet the Habitat Conference in Vancouver, which I attended several years ago, had almost no significant media coverage in Australia, while the Olympic Games, an event of almost total triviality by comparison, dominated the media for three weeks. Lavish circus displays are said to have characterised the declining days of the Roman Empire, to distract the attention of the populace from critical problems. The parallel is not perfect, but it is adequate to indicate the magnitude of the task in environmental education.

ACKNOWLEDGEMENTS

I WOULD LIKE TO THANK LA TROBE UNIVERSITY PRESS and Chris Feik of Black Inc. for supporting this project to recover and promote the work of an important Australian public intellectual. I am indebted to Dion Kagan at Black Inc. for his cheerful, sympathetic and tireless editorial work. The sharp eyes of copyeditor Nat Book and indexer Kerry Anderson have also made this a better book.

Discussions with Tom Griffiths and Libby Robin about George Seddon, his writing and his legacy, materially assisted my thinking. Both scholars also generously loaned me invaluable collections of documents by and about George. Jack Seddon graciously answered my questions about George and his writing, and the National Library of Australia facilitated access to George's papers and published works.

My family have provided space and encouragement for my work. I sincerely thank all of these people and institutions: the book would not have been possible without you.

SOURCES

CLASSICS

1. *Sense of Place: A Response to an Environment, the Swan Coastal Plain Western Australia*, Nedlands, WA, University of Western Australia Press, 1972.

2. 'The Rhetoric and Ethics of the Environmental Protest Movement', *Meanjin*, vol. 4, December 1972, pp. 427–38.

3. 'The Evolution of Perceptual Attitudes', in *Man and Landscape in Australia: Towards an Ecological Vision: Papers from a Symposium Held at the Australian Academy of Science, Canberra, 30 May–2 June 1974*, Australian Government Publishing Service, Canberra, 1976, pp. 9–17.

4. 'The Genius Loci and Australian Landscape', *Landscape Australia*, vol. 2, 1979, pp. 66–73.

5. 'Managing a Resources Boom, or In Praise of Country Boys', in Stephen Murray-Smith (ed.), *Melbourne Studies in Education 1982*, pp. 35–48.

6. 'A Snowy River Reader', *Meanjin*, vol. 45, no. 3, 1986, pp. 309–30.

7. 'Cuddlepie and Other Surrogates', *Westerly*, vol. 33, no. 2, June 1988, pp. 143–55.

8. 'The Nature of Nature', *Westerly*, no. 4, December 1991, pp. 7–14.

9. 'Two Centres of Excellence in the Mediterranean', *Westerly*, vol. 39, no. 4, Summer 1994, pp. 81–92.

10. 'Farewell to Arcady, or Getting off the Sheep's Back', *Thesis Eleven*, No. 74, August 2003, pp. 35–53.

GARDENS IN CONTEXT

11. *Swan River Landscapes*, University of Western Australia Press, Perth, 1970.

12. 'A Captive Jungle, or Rainforest in South Yarra", *Landscape Australia*, vol. 6, no. 3, 1984, pp. 189–197.

13. 'The Suburban Garden in Australia, *Westerly*, vol. 35, no. 4, 1990, pp. 5–13.

14. 'The Australian Back Yard', *Australian Garden History: Journal of the Australian Garden History Society*, vol. 3, no. 2, 1991, pp. 2–9.

15. 'The Garden as Paradise', in *Landprints: Reflections on Place and Landscape*, Cambridge, Cambridge University Press, 1997, pp. 176–187.

16. 'The Old Country', in *Australian Landscapes, Plants and People*, Cambridge, Cambridge University Press, 2005, pp. 2–25.

THE ART OF ADVISING

17. With the assistance of W.B. Calder and M. Davis. 'A Landscape Assessment of the Southern Mornington Peninsula, Victoria: A Report to the Western Port Regional Planning Authority', Centre for Environment Studies, University of Melbourne, 1974.

18. With John Turner, 'Loy Yang Project Landscape Assessment: A Report Prepared for the State Electricity Commission of Victoria', Centre for Environmental Studies, University of Melbourne, Melbourne, 1975.

19. 'Passing Water: Ways of Handling Streams', *Memo*, no. 18, May 1975, pp. 29–31.

20. 'An Open Space System for Canberra', NCDC Technical Paper no. 23, Canberra, October 1977.

21. 'Whither the West', in *Swan Song: Reflections on Perth and Western Australia, 1956–1995*, Centre for Studies in Australian Literature, University of Western Australia, Perth, 1995, pp. 53–58. (First part originally published in the Australian Conservation Foundation's *Habitat*, vol. 4, no. 6, 1977, pp. 4–5.)

22. 'Problems in Environmental Education: The Australian case', *Environmental Education and Information*, vol. 4, no. 1, 1985, pp. 2–5.

SELECT BIBLIOGRAPHY

Principal books

Swan River Landscapes, University of Western Australia Press, Nedlands, 1970.

Sense of Place: A Response to an Environment, the Swan Coastal Plain Western Australia, University of Western Australia Press, Nedlands 1972.

A City and Its Setting: Images of Perth, Western Australia, Fremantle Arts Centre Press, Fremantle, 1978. (George Seddon and David Ravine).

Somewhere to go on Sunday: A Guide to Outdoor Melbourne, Centre for Environmental Studies, Melbourne, 1978. (Ann McGregor and George Seddon).

A House, a Cottage and a Shop: 186 High Street, Fremantle, Bookmark Publishing House, Guildford, 1993.

Searching for the Snowy: An Environmental History, Allen & Unwin, Sydney, 1994.

Swansong: Reflections on Perth and Western Australia, 1956–1995, Centre for Studies in Australian Literature, The University of Western Australia, Perth, 1995.

Landprints: Reflections on Place and Landscape, Cambridge University Press, Melbourne, 1997.

The Old Country: Australian Landscapes, Plants and People, Cambridge University Press, Melbourne, 2005.

Essays

'The academic as science student', *Gazette of the University of Western Australia*, vol. 16, no. 4, December 1966.

'Jet-set and parish pump', *Quadrant*, vol. 17, no. 3, 1973, pp. 46–52.

'Abraham Gottlob Werner: History and Folk-history', *Journal of the Geological Society of Australia*, vol. 20, part 4, December 1973, pp. 381–395.

'Xerophytes, Xeromorphs and Sclerophylls: The History of Some Concepts in Ecology', *Biological Journal of the Linnean Society*, no. 6, March 1974, pp. 65–87.

'Western Australia: Some Changing Perceptions', in *European Impact on the West Australian Environment 1828–1979*, Octagon Lectures 1979, The University of Western Australia, Perth, 1979, pp. 154–186.

'Landscape Studies in Australia', *Landscape Planning*, no. 6, 1979, pp. 225–269.

'Eurocentrism and Australian Science: Some Examples', *Search*, vol. 12, 1981, pp. 446–450.

'The Rottnest Experience', *Journal of the Royal Society of Western Australia*, vol. 66, parts 1–2, 1983, pp. 34–40.

'A Rice Culture: Lessons from Flatland China', *Landscape Architecture*, vol. 73, no. 3, 1983, pp. 59–63.

'Landscape and Human Ecosystems: Reflections on a Journey Through Natal' *Landscape Australia*, no. 3, August 1983, pp. 184–191.

'The Conservation of Rainforest', *Landscape Australia*, vol. 7, no. 1, 1985, pp. 20–31.

'Landscape Planning: A Conceptual Perspective', *Landscape and Urban Planning*, vol. 13, 1986, pp. 335–347.

'Figures in a Landscape', *Landscape Australia*, vol. 9, no. 2, 1987, pp. 107–114.

'Some Men from Snowy River', *Overland*, vol. 144, 1989, pp. 72–79.

'About Rainforest', *Meanjin* vol. 49, no. 4, 1990, pp. 700–722.

'Imaging the Mind', *Meanjin*, vol. 52, no. 1, 1993, pp. 183–194.

'Words and Weeds: Some Notes on Language and Landscape', *Landscape Review*, no. 2, 1995, pp. 3–15.

'The Evolution of a Gardener: Part 1', *Landscape Australia*, vol. 17, no. 4, 1995, pp. 279–82.

'The Evolution of a Gardener: Part 2', *Landscape Australia*, vol. 18, no. 2, 1996, pp. 43–49.

'Thinking Like a Geologist: The Culture of Geology Mawson Lecture 1996', *Australian Journal of Earth Sciences*, vol. 43, no. 5, 1996, pp. 487–495.

'Return to Portugal', *Meanjin*, vol. 56, no. 3–4, 1997, pp. 545–555.

'Land and Language', *Meanjin*, vol. 58, no. 2, 1999, pp. 140–152.

'Perceiving the Pilbara: Finding the Key to the Country', *Thesis Eleven*, no. 65, May 2001, pp. 69–92.

'Letter from the Galapagos', in Peter Craven (ed.), *The Best Australian Essays 2001*, Melbourne, Black Inc, 2001, pp. 562–583.

'Time, Gentlemen, Please', *Griffith Review*, no. 12, Winter 2006, pp. 89–96.

INDEX